Poetics of Cognition

CONTEMPORARY NORTH AMERICAN POETRY SERIES

Alan Golding, Lynn Keller, and Adalaide Morris, series editors

POETICS OF
COGNITION

Thinking through Experimental Poems

JESSICA LEWIS LUCK

UNIVERSITY OF IOWA PRESS, IOWA CITY

University of Iowa Press, Iowa City 52242
Copyright © 2023 by the University of Iowa Press
uipress.uiowa.edu
Printed in the United States of America
Design by Nola Burger

Printed on acid-free paper

Library of Congress Cataloging-in-Publication Data
Names: Luck, Jessica Lewis, author.
Title: Poetics of Cognition: Thinking through Experimental Poems / Jessica
     Lewis Luck.
Description: Iowa City: University of Iowa Press, [2023] | Series: Contemporary
     North American Poetry Series | Includes bibliographical references and index.
Identifiers: LCCN 2022044964 (print) | LCCN 2022044965 (ebook) | ISBN
     9781609389055 (paperback; acid-free paper) | ISBN 9781609389062 (ebook)
Subjects: LCSH: Experimental poetry—History and criticism. | Poetics—
     Psychological aspects. | LCGFT: Literary criticism.
Classification: LCC PN1483.L83 2023 (print) | LCC PN1483 (ebook) | DDC
     808.1—dc23/eng/20230119
LC record available at https://lccn.loc.gov/2022044964
LC ebook record available at https://lccn.loc.gov/2022044965

A previous version of chapter 2 appeared as "Entries on a Post-Language Poetics
in Harryette Mullen's Dictionary," *Contemporary Literature*, vol. 49, no. 3, 2008,
pp. 357–82, doi:10.1353/cli.0.0033. A previous version of chapter 3 appeared
as "Larry Eigner and the Phenomenology of Projected Verse," *Contemporary
Literature*, vol. 53, no. 3, 2012, pp. 461–92, doi:10.1353/cli.2012.0026. A portion
of the epilogue appeared as "Isn't the Pedagogical Always Avant-Garde?" in
"Teaching Modern Poetry," edited by Emily Setina, *Modernism/Modernity*, vol. 1,
cycle 1, doi:10.26597/mod.0012.

For Chad and Fletcher

Contents

Acknowledgments

Extended cognition, the idea that thinking is not just confined to the brain but relies on and extends into other structures and minds in its environment, is not only a central premise of this book; it is also an essential part of its creation. The thinking through experimental poems that I practice here was enabled by the scaffolding of many other minds, which I would like to acknowledge here. I am grateful to James S. Hans, who first got me thinking about the intersections of cognitive science and literature, and to Paul John Eakin, whose scholarship offered me a model for how to use neuroscience in literary analysis and whose mentorship nurtured my early efforts. Many thanks to Michael Davidson, Alan Golding, Lynn Keller, and Dee Morris, who have encouraged and supported this work as it emerged over the years. I first met them at the Louisville Conference on Literature and Culture Since 1900, which became an essential part of my education in experimental poetry and poetics, as well as a site for trying out many of the ideas in this book. I am grateful for panelists and interlocutors there and at the Modern Language Association conference, the Modernist Studies Association conference, and the Pacific Ancient and Modern Languages Association conference, where I also shared and developed some of the ideas here.

I am also deeply appreciative of the warm and supportive community of creative scholars and talented teachers I have in the English department at Cal State San Bernardino (CSUSB). My colleagues have supported me through writing support groups, writing retreats, and forums where they gave me feedback and encouragement. Thanks to David Carlson, Alexandra Cavallaro, Miriam Fernandez, Jasmine Lee, Chad Luck, David Marshall, Vanessa Ovalle Perez, Yumi Pak, Martín Premoli, Karen Rowan, Kate Simonian, Caroline Vickers, and Chad and Jennifer Sweeney. I extend my gratitude to department chairs Juan Delgado, Sunny Hyon, and David Carlson for their unwavering belief in and support of my work. I also thank poet Julie Sophia Paegle, who first showed me how to be a mom and still get writing done. We lost her far too soon.

I'm grateful for the material support the book received over several years from CSUSB, including research minigrants from the Office of Academic Research for course reassigned time and a sabbatical. Many thanks to Dean Rueyling Chuang and the College of Arts and Letters for a grant that paid for this book's indexing. I am much obliged to my amazing students at CSUSB, who have gamely played with all the strange and difficult poems I throw at them and who have enthusiastically participated in my avant-garde pedagogy experiments. Experimental poetics can create a much more democratic classroom, and I learn as much from them as they do from me when we encounter this work together. Extra thanks to the students in my two special topics courses in Experimental Poetry and Poetics who allowed me to use excerpts from their writing in the epilogue.

Thank you to Peter Middleton for extensive, thoughtful feedback. I am grateful to Betsy Phillips for her advice and encouragement during the proposal and submission process. Thanks also to editor Meredith Stabel and editorial assistant Margaret Yapp, who were quick to answer my many questions as I put the book together for the press. Any errors that remain are my own. Gathering permissions for all of the images in this book was an adventure that sometimes made me question my interest in visual poetics. I appreciate all the archives, poets, and artists who allowed me to use their work here. Thanks in particular to Nancy Perloff, Jesse Glass, Mayako Glass, Paul Stephens, and Rui Torres for helping me track down rightsholders for some of the concrete poets.

Finally, this book would never have been completed without the profound love and support of my family: my kind and steadfast parents, Greg and Jennifer Lewis, who nurtured my embodied mind from the beginning, and my sisters, Becca A. Lewis and Elizabeth Lewis, who keep me grounded in our weekly Sister Zoom. Thanks to Becca for taking the author photo and for enthusiastically reading chapter drafts. Warm thanks as well to my generous and fun family-in-law, John and Carlah Luck, Nicole Luck, and Jake MacDonald.

I extend eternal gratitude and love to Chad and Fletcher, to whom this book is dedicated. Chad is always my first and toughest reader, and this book is immeasurably better because of our games of "thinkball" and his feedback on drafts. Fletcher was born while I was writing this book, and I am sustained every day by watching his own mind develop and flourish, as well as by his joyful and curious spirit. Thank you both for giving me the time and space to read, think, and write. Here's to our next adventure together.

Introduction

> The poem is not "expression," but a cognitive process that, to some extent, changes me.
>
> —ROSMARIE WALDROP, "THINKING OF FOLLOWS"

> This whole genre of poetry deforms its audience's minds.
>
> —PLATO, *REPUBLIC*

At the top of the 11:30 PM newscast on February 13, 2011, the KCBS news desk in Los Angeles cut to Serene Branson, reporting live from the Grammy Awards. What should have been just a routine synopsis of the night's events, however, came out of her mouth something like this: "Well a very very heavay, ah, heavy dih burtation tonight. We had a very darris, darrison by ... let's go ahead tarris tasin' lesh pavette da head pavette" (CBS, "Serene Branson"). Branson, in perfect news reporter cadences, tried out two sentences, realized something was wrong, and, still babbling, threw the broadcast back to the anchors. Over the next few days, those ten seconds of gibberish became a YouTube sensation, generating millions of hits and eventually making national news. Viewers were alternately amused and disturbed by the incident. Some commenters claimed she must have been drunk or high; others worried she had suffered a stroke.

As her brief Internet celebrity status began to wane, the actual cause emerged: a migraine aura had given her temporary aphasia. Branson was back at work soon afterward and has experienced no more on-air aphasic incidents since.

What interests me about this event is not so much the etiology of migraine auras and aphasia but rather the audience's fascination with its effects. Certainly some of the appeal was the schadenfreude from seeing an attractive public figure look foolish, but many commenters on YouTube were also drawn to the gibberish itself:

"I memorized what she said. It's so interesting to try to decode it."

"That's what you would sound like if you delay looped the sound."

"I like when she says vertasion."

"I like the part where she goes 'deres do taiounm here leste has the pet' lol."

Many commenters playfully attempted to translate what she said in different ways. One even read the message as political: "this was a bench-mark sign for all mass media professionals to watch their tactics and mouths so not to further promote ignorance and nonsense trash-info to people."[1] With all the "trash-info" that is served up daily by the media, though, Serene Branson's "nonsense" really cut through the clutter. What is so mesmerizing about nonsense?

Part of the attraction of this particular eruption of nonsense is that so much of the scene was banal: the medium of the live report, the outdoor scene, her tone, her facial expressions, and the idiomatic tics of the reporter, "Well a very … tonight … We had a very … let's go ahead." Even the syntax of the sentences sounds vaguely grammatical. The adjective "heavy" seems to modify "burtation," which ends in a familiar noun suffix. It's as if someone switched off the semantic function in her brain, leaving her listeners with pure syntax. The normal is transformed not into the abnormal but what might be termed the ultranormal.

Bear with me as I make a quick leap across species to define this term. Neuroscientist V. S. Ramachandran defines ultranormal stimulus by describing an experiment with baby herring gulls. When the chicks are first born, they let their mothers know they want more regurgitated food by pecking on the bright red dot on the mother's long yellow beak. Nobel

Prize–winning biologist Nikolaas Tinbergen found, perhaps not surprisingly, that the chicks exhibit the exact same behavior when presented with a long yellow stick with a bright red dot on it. For the chick's brain, "long thing with red spot = mom" (Ramachandran 210). Then things get ultranormal. Tinbergen substituted a different stick with three red stripes on it rather than a dot, and the chicks went berserk, "pecking at it much more intensely than at a real beak" (210). The chicks actually seemed to prefer this strange pattern to the normal image, a pattern Ramachandran calls an ultranormal stimulus, explaining that the excited response to them is unpredictable without knowing the exact logic and circuitry of the bird brain's processing of beak images. He then makes his own big leap across species to speculate that this ultranormal stimulus might actually reveal why human beings are drawn to avant-garde works of art: "By trial and error, intuition or genius, human artists like Picasso or Henry Moore have discovered the human brain's equivalent of the seagull brain's stick with three stripes. They are tapping into the figural primitives of our perceptual grammar and creating ultra-normal stimuli that more powerfully excite certain visual neurons in our brains as opposed to realistic-looking images" (212). Perhaps Serene Branson's nonsensical news report functioned as the verbal equivalent of those three red stripes, exciting certain language-processing neurons in our brains that are accustomed to clear semantic meaning. Such ultranormal linguistic stimuli may make us peckish for more.

Which brings us to some of the most ultranormal linguistic stimuli out there: poetry that is known variously as avant-garde, innovative, or experimental. Take, for example, the bizarre word clusters of Clark Coolidge—"hum over glow trout" and "cog world sigh blimp" ("Calypso" 36)—or Harryette Mullen's aphasic similes—"as horses as for / as purple as we go" (*Sleeping* 80)—or Lisa Jarnot's experimental sonnet "Zero Onset":

> an eagle added attaboy ongoing outboard oak
> of after agile april airs in inner age awoke
> apparent oaten apple arcs, amazing amish ax
> and undulating ache of air in archival attacks

o agitation angrily, o okra ocracoke
and after orange onset ilk upon update approach
all-knowing error out of earth, o undulate aardvark
applicable of oft aft oars, androgynal embark
antagonistic afterburn, appalling anvil adze
adversity, ambivalence, ashore ashore advance
astrology all edible, of aging update om
and opening and opening, unpacked allowed aroam
authentic arching anarchist, allowance all awry
an afternoon, albanian, unurgent and espied. (*Night Scenes* 18)

Like Serene Branson's aphasic report, this poem retains the vestiges of
grammatical structures: subject–verb–object in "an eagle added attaboy,"
preposition–adjective–object "in archival attacks," even a seemingly
exclamatory imperative in "ashore ashore advance," while other construc-
tions explode traditional syntax, as the stacked prepositions in "of after
agile" and past participles of "unpacked allowed aroam." Yet there's still
something stimulating about this nonsense. Like many poems in this
section of the book *Night Scenes*, "Zero Onset" contains traditional lyric
meter, form, and rhyme. Not only is it a sonnet in rhymed couplets; it's
also a perfect fourteener, with seven iambic feet per line, though the
content is certainly nothing like its Philip Sidney counterparts in the
sixteenth century. Most significant is experimentalism's notorious absence
of the lyric "I"; this poem is generated by constraint rather than the voice
of the poet. "Zero onset" is a linguistic term; the "onset" is the first of three
sounds comprising a syllable. (In the word "ball," /b/ is the onset and /
all/ is the rhyme.) A zero onset occurs when syllables begin with vowel
sounds, as with all the words in this poem. (In the word "all," there is only
the rhyme, with no onset sound.) The poem highlights the absence of the
lyric "I" in the constraint itself—only four words out of ninety-six begin
with "I." If the Branson incident revealed the pure form of a newscast
without semantics, then Jarnot's poem similarly offers the scaffolding
of a fourteener with its sense and voice function switched off—an ultranormal sonnet.

There is also evidence that disorienting but stimulating encounters
with nonsense can have some benevolent effects on cognition—*nonsense*

enabling *new*sense, as Joan Retallack writes (12). Cultural psychologists Travis Proulx and Steven J. Heine have studied the ways that reading nonsense can prime the brain to sense patterns it would otherwise miss—in mathematical equations, in language, and in the world at large. They speculate, "We're so motivated to get rid of that [nonsense] feeling that we look for meaning and coherence elsewhere" (qtd. in Carey). In a recent study, they had twenty college students read an absurd short story based on "The Country Doctor" by Franz Kafka. After the story, the students studied a series of letter strings of six to nine letters, like "XMXRTV." They then took a test on the letter strings, choosing those they thought they had seen before. In fact, the letters were arranged in subtle patterns, with some more likely to appear before and after others. The test is a standard measure of what researchers call implicit learning, or knowledge gained without awareness. The students had no idea what patterns their brains were sensing or how well they were performing. However, they performed well, choosing about 30 percent more of the correct letter strings than a control group of students who had read a coherent story. Interestingly, the researchers found a highly similar effect when, instead of reading a nonsense story, students were asked to argue against their own self-unity before they studied the letter strings and took the test. Reading nonsense, experiencing a loss of self-unity—these scientific studies mirror the experiments that experimental poetry conducts on its readers. Might we speculate, then, about a similar transformative effect from hearing or reading the seeming nonsense of experimental poetry?

Questioning the existence and effects of any "experiments" in experimental poetics has lately become a critical commonplace. Natalia Cecire argues that beginning in the nineteenth century and across the twentieth, "*experimentalism* came to be disarticulated from specific *experiments* (situated, material, and historical)," instead manifesting as more of an oppositional disposition or attitude (16, 15). Jonathan Monroe asserts, "While textual effects can be prepared for, they cannot be predicted or assured" (760). Rita Felski agrees that "political function cannot be deduced or derived from literary structure" (9). And Alan Gilbert complains that the "active reader" theory in experimental poetics has "never presented a single piece of empirical evidence that what it proposes is true in reality" (111).[2] Yet critical theorists have also longed for the radical materialism that this sort of empirical evidence might provide. Even a staunch historicist like Raymond Williams intuits that "there is a very deep material bond between language and the body, which communication theories that concentrate on the passing of messages and information typically miss: many poems, many kinds of writing, indeed a lot of everyday speech communicate what is in effect a life rhythm and the interaction of these life rhythms is probably a very important part of the material process of writing and reading" (340). He goes on to propose, "Indeed, if I had one single ambition in literary studies it would be to rejoin them with experimental science, because of work that is now being done which would make it possible to do so" (341).[3] *Poetics of Cognition* offers a modest effort to respond to Williams's materialist ambition of joining literary study with experimental science in order to explore "the physical effects of writing" (341), as well as to critics who question the material force of experimental poetic forms. The book seeks to put the experiment back in experimentalism, so to speak, investigating the material effects of experimental poetics using new evidence emerging from cognitive science. It asks, how do experimental poems "think," and how do we think through them?

Theories of embodied cognition over the past three decades have radically transformed midcentury models of the mind as a modular, computerlike computational device. Contemporary cognitive psychologists and neuroscientists are now exploring ways that cognition is deeply integrated into the body's sensorimotor systems, revealing that the brain is not a computer and not the isolated seat of cognition (see Damasio, Ledoux, and Varela, for example). This shift has had wide-ranging effects, inspiring disciplinary transformations and exciting new research in psychology, neuroscience, philosophy, robotics, and linguistics, among other fields. These transformations also have important consequences in the field of poetics. While Chomskian linguistics sees language as an innate mental phenomenon expressed by abstract symbols, for example, cognitive linguists Lakoff and Johnson have shown that our abstract concepts are mostly metaphorical, with the metaphors derived from our bodily experience in the world. In the realm of neuroscience, brain imaging studies in the last decade have found that simply reading action words such as "kick" or "pick" activates portions of the motor cortices in the brain associated with those actions (Hauk et al.). González et al. found a similar effect when subjects read odor-related words such as "cinnamon," which lit up olfactory centers in the brain. While words can stimulate embodied cognition in this way, the body also affects mental processes. For example, studies of second-language learning and mathematics pedagogy found that students acquire new vocabulary and new mathematical concepts when they and their teachers perform relevant gestures when learning them (see Macedonia). Bodily states and affects can also influence a positive or negative evaluation of a piece of writing or a person—whether your posture is slumped or upright, whether you are smiling or frowning, or whether you are holding a glass of cold water or a warm drink (Niedenthal et al.; Bargh and Shalev). As Lawrence W. Barsalou asserts, we have to study cognition as it is grounded within all these different systems, including perception, action, memory, affect, sensorimotor, language comprehension, conceptual processing, and social cognition.[4]

Thinking is embedded not only in the body but also in the body's environment and context; the embodied mind learns and solves problems by interfacing with external tools. Andy Clark, perhaps one of the most significant theorists of this idea of extended cognition, explains that "certain forms of human cognizing include inextricable tangles of feedback, feed-forward, and feed-around loops: loops that promiscuously crisscross the boundaries of brain, body, and world" (xxviii). Simple examples of this interface, or what Clark calls scaffolding, include a baby taking its first steps hanging onto a parent's hands, a writer taking notes in a notebook or computer, or elementary students manipulating pie pieces in order to calculate one fourth of eight. (Martin and Schwartz found that this use of external scaffolding was much more effective for solving the problem than viewing the pieces or using abstract numbers alone.) Theories of extended cognition state that thinking also takes place outside our heads, spilling into objects and structures in the world around us.

Experimental poems can also function as a powerful scaffolding for extended cognition for both writer and reader, materializing not so much the content as the activity of the embodied mind. One of my important lines of inquiry here considers how the experimental poem manifests and emerges from the particular embodied, embedded consciousness of the poet: Lyn Hejinian's improvisations with myopia, Harryette Mullen's procedural practices of *Sleeping with the Dictionary,* and Larry Eigner's critical engagement with his disability as a creative constraint. This focus on the writer's experimental poetics of cognition leads to my second line of inquiry: exploring how these forms work to rematerialize and reshape the activity of the reader's mind, creating new forms of attention, perception, and cognition. A remarkable result of this interdisciplinary approach is the emergence of experimentalism as perhaps the most "organic" of all poetics. From Aristotle to Emerson and from John Dewey to Cleanth Brooks, many theorists have noted that poems have a structure analogous to living things as well as a privileged connection to the rhythms of the body, such as breath and heartbeat. The traditional organic analogy, of course, implies notions of unity, essentiality, and closure that experimental poets resist in favor of openness and indeterminacy. However, current cognitive theories of embodied cognition suggest that indeterminacy is not antithetical to organicism but actually constitutive of it. Human brains are not hardwired, unified, and closed, but rather autopoietic, plastic, self-making, and self-organizing, emerging and evolving within the constraints of a bodily and genetic code as well as the structures of the environment.

A cognitive materialist approach also allows us to expand the experimental canon. As many critics have pointed out, experimentalism's resistance to ideas of identity and expression has often resulted in the exclusion of innovative minority writers (see Mackey; Wang; Mullen, "Poetry and Identity"; Yu; Moten; Shockley; Cecire; and Gladman and singleton). Dorothy Wang diagnoses the problem: "To be experimental in the 'best and broadest sense of the term' is, implicitly, not to discuss race or ethnic identity" (31–32). As Harryette Mullen explains it, the assumption is that "writing that was oppositional in a politically, socially, or racially conscious way was somehow incompatible with writing that might be described as experimental, avant-garde, [or] innovative" ("Untitled" 11). The (coded white) avant-garde deploys abstract, formal, literary techniques while minority writers are understood in terms of their content, emerging from their bodily, material, sociocultural situatedness (Wang 22).[5] However, the work of experimental Black women poets such as Harryette

Mullen and Tracie Morris, which I analyze in the chapters ahead, reveals the ways that experimental method is not essentially abstracted (as Cecire insists) but rather performative and physical, emerging from a writer's material situatedness in a particular body-mind in a particular context. Their poetics insists that engaging identity or politics *in* a poem doesn't somehow preclude the rich possibilities of the formal politics *of* the poem. Indeed, the most powerful transformative effects of experimental poetics might occur when content and form are wielded simultaneously. My approach ultimately works to uncover the embodied cognitive scaffolding that connects form and content, poetics and identity, and technique and expression in experimental forms.[6]

Literary critics have recently attempted a material exploration of experimentalism and its effects on readers via a turn to affect. Affect theory focuses on nonlinguistic forces, including the bodily experiences that happen before thought, cognition, and representation.[7] Not surprisingly, in this approach, critics have emphasized the particularly paralyzing affects that the avant-garde generates.[8] Rita Felski in her taxonomy of the *Uses of Literature* considers it in her chapter on shock. She is skeptical of the avant-garde's utopian linking of aesthetics and politics, of the notion that shocking works of art could somehow "topple banks and bureaucracies, museums and markets" (109). In another phenomenological taxonomy, affect theorist Sianne Ngai in *Ugly Feelings* treats the avant-garde in her chapter on "stuplimity," which she defines as a paradoxical synthesis of shock and boredom (271). While Ngai is more hopeful than Felski about the subtle subversive potential of this avant-garde-induced affect, her book finds that these ugly feelings are ultimately more "diagnostic" of our own sense of "limited agency" and art's limited agency to effectively intervene in a market society (5, 36); they offer no "therapeutic solutions" to its problems (3).

Yet contemporary experimental poems activate more than just powerful, paralyzing emotions in readers. Shifting from the feeling to the thinking that such forms prompt reveals an expanded agency of the experimental poem, and of its reader. Indeed, like affects, most of human cognition is actually nonconscious and nonreflective; it happens underneath our conscious control. Katherine Hayles in *Unthought* believes that the new materialisms of the affective turn and phenomenological criticism have limited themselves by not considering consciousness and cognition, fearing that their introduction would risk a return to received ideas and shift focus too far away from materiality (65–66). However, as Hayles points out, "Separating materiality from cognition does not, however, strengthen the case for materiality. On the contrary, it weakens it, for it erases the critical role played by materiality in creating the structures and organizations from which consciousness and cognition emerge" (66). By considering the force of the material structures of cognition as well as affect, my approach expands the potential blast radius of experimental poetic effects into areas of linguistic, sonic, and visual processing, revealing a transformational potency that strictly affective approaches miss. The cognitive research I draw on suggests that the strangeness of experimental poetry can disrupt the linguistic and perceptual habits of the reader, working not as a mirror or a lamp but as a virus, subtly reshaping the embodied mind from the inside out.

Hayles notes "an enthusiasm for all concepts Deleuzian" in the new materialism that may also be observed in studies of poetics (67). Jon Clay's book on the "transformative intensities" of contemporary poetry, for example, uses a Deleuzian framework to argue that the political force of innovative poetries lies not in their signification but the sensations they engender (10). In *Prior to Meaning*, Steve McCaffery similarly uses Deleuze and Guattari's adoption of "dissipative structures" as a way of thinking about how the material force of the protosemantic functions in poetics (xviii).[9] While I appreciate these critics' Deleuze and Guattari–informed confidence that innovative poems have a political force that is "potentially productive of changes" in readers (Clay 47), their focus on the poem as a block of sensation rather than meaning provides only a limited understanding of that political force. Sianne Ngai speculates that the affect of "stuplimity" generated by Gertrude Stein's poems results in an "open feeling," "a state of undifferentiated alertness or responsiveness" (283). Cognitive theories of the brain's response to nonsense bear out Ngai's theory. But what about the thinking that happens in the wake of that open feeling? What about the creative generation of meaning that the text enables, and that Ngai herself models in her readings of Stein? As William

E. Connolly notes, "Thinking itself can sometimes modify the microcomposition of body/brain processes" (8). "Thinking is not merely involved in knowing, explaining, representing, evaluating, and judging. Subsisting within these activities are the inventive and compositional dimensions of thinking" (104). As poet Rosmarie Waldrop writes in one of the epigraphs to this chapter, "The poem is not 'expression,' but a cognitive process that, to some extent, changes me" ("Thinking of Follows").

This inventive and compositional dimension of thinking offers another corrective to current materialist approaches to experimentalism, which tend to couch the effects of these texts in negative, even violent terms. As we have seen, Felski and Ngai insist on their paralyzing effects/affects of shock and stuplimity, and Steve McCaffery, in *Prior to Meaning*, representatively describes the Deleuzian dissipative structures of experimental poems as "informational excesses that in part impale and in part escape readers" (xx), effecting "the killing of speech in its capitalist, propositional embodiments" (186). A cognitive materialist approach to these poems allows me to explore how experimental modes such as the New Sentence, proceduralism, projective verse, sound poetry, and visual poetry can be generative rather than destructive, invoking active thinking and creation in readers, not just reactive negative feelings.

Avant-Garde/Experimental

Attentive readers might have noted in the opening pages a slippage in my use of terminology to describe the project's focus, starting with the language of the "innovative" and "experimental" and then referring to the "avant-garde" when I turned to affective approaches and their more negative, violent take on experimentalism's effects. This shift was calculated because I contend that this binary of destructivity versus creativity loosely maps onto some of the distinctions between the modernist avant-garde and postmodernist experimentalism. Among many others, Marjorie Perloff, in *21st Century Modernisms*, proclaims the growing inconsequentiality of this divide (1–2), but I find it useful to explore these differences, which are aesthetic and theoretical as well as historical.[10]

In Paul Stephens's helpful history of the term "experimentalism," he rightly notes that it is "typically less politically charged" than the modernist avant-garde (148). Experimentalism is generally defined by its methods and techniques, he finds, while the avant-garde is more of a situated response to its sociopolitical setting (158). He quotes avant-garde theorist Clement Greenberg, who in his famous 1939 "Avant Garde and Kitsch" writes, "The true and most important function of the avant-garde was not to 'experiment,' but to find a path along which it would be possible to keep culture *moving* in the midst of ideological confusion and violence" (157). If received bourgeois notions of art and aesthetics at the turn of the century led to that confusion and violence, then art's only possible response was to attack its own institutions, to explode the status quo, to shock and appall. As Tristan Tzara notes in his Dada manifesto, "We are like a raging wind that rips up the clothes of clouds and prayers, we are preparing the great spectacle of disaster, conflagration and decomposition" (8). Rather than ripping up clothes and burning down the house, the manifestos of postmodern poetry tend to describe their poetics as experimental methods aimed less at destruction and more at generation and transformation. For Charles Bernstein in *A Poetics*, experimentalism involves not shock but "antiabsorptive / techniques … used toward absorptive ends" (30). In their Language poetry manifesto on "Aesthetic Tendency and the Politics of Poetry," Ron Silliman et al. claim that the goal of experimental techniques is "to recharge [the] neurological scar tissue with some new synapses" (266). Joan Retallack in *The Poethical Wager* considers how experimental writing "helps form the direction and quality of attention, the intelligences, the senses we bring into contact with contemporary experience" (12). And Nathaniel Mackey finds that innovative Black art is constitutive, not destructive, of identity and community, with its methods "ranging from amorous touch to agonistic embrace, angelic rub. To don such wings and engage such resistances as though they were the stuff of identity and community is to have taken a step toward making them so" (239).

Though such experimental methods are often understood as inherently ahistorical, recent critics have begun to situate experimentalism's innovations within the post-1945 cultural moment in provocative ways. Margaret Ronda, for example, notes how the language of the "innovation paradigm" in postwar poetics has "analogical affinities with the logic of commodity production and liberal narratives of historical progress" of the time (16).[11] Peter Middleton examines experimental poets at midcentury who are inspired by the ascendency of physics in the American imaginary, particularly in the wake of the atomic bombs dropped on Hiroshima and Nagasaki. These poets "wanted to claim a right of experiment and inquiry for poetry"—one that might encompass what science can accomplish, and much more (2, 142). Relatedly, Natalia Cecire argues that the linguistic turn in critical theory at midcentury granted experimental poets a sense that language could not only represent reality but also intervene in it. Language becomes an active force "through which knowledge could be made to facilitate—or oppose state violence" (9). Postwar experimental writing takes on the era's epistemic virtues of "objective" science, according to Cecire, with the idea that a dehistoricized, abstracted method or set of techniques could cause political change in the world.[12] She ultimately finds the term "experimental" rather useless because of its abstraction of method. While Cecire's book does important work in situating experimentalism within the ideologies of its particular cultural moment, reading these methods and techniques as solely historical epiphenomena limits our understanding of the material work that experimental methods can accomplish. As Cecire herself writes of the epistemic virtues she examines in modernist experimentalism, they "all reveal something of this complicity, even as they also open up thrilling vistas of knowledge" (46).

By considering the aesthetic and theoretical differences between the modernist and postmodernist avant-gardes (which are always already historical), *Poetics of Cognition* works to explore those "thrilling vistas of knowledge" opened up by contemporary experimental writers. The modernist avant-garde often takes a macropolitical approach to its acts of resistance. This is Jacques Rancière's avant-garde defined as "the topographical and military notion of the force that marches in the lead, that has a clear understanding of the movement, embodies its forces, determines the direction of historical evolution, and chooses subjective political orientations" (29). Its goal was large-scale political destruction, to "topple banks and bureaucracies, museums and markets," as Felski writes (109). Postmodern experimentalism, on the contrary, adopts micropolitical techniques to effect more subtle acts of transformation and regeneration.

If power in postmodern culture is decentralized and plural, as Foucault and others have theorized, then resistance and struggle must be likewise. Foucault offers two possible avenues for this micropolitics: discourse politics, which involves speaking outside the rules and norms of hegemonic discourses, and biopolitics, in which individuals resist disciplinary power by reinventing the body itself with new forms of desire and pleasure (Kellner and Best 57–58). Critics have rightly noted a tension between these two modes of resistance, assuming a historically and discursively constructed body on the one hand and suggesting some extradiscursive aspects of the body on the other (Kellner and Best 58).

My cognitive materialist approach eases this tension, however, as it uncovers what we might call a biodiscourse politics at the heart of experimental poetics. It confirms the well-established theory that innovative poetic language makes familiar language strange by breaking the rules of normative discourse, but at the same time, as Proulx and Heine's studies of nonsense suggest, my approach reveals that this strangeness can reinvent or rewire the embodied mind for navigation and resistance within a postmodern environment and power structure. This is Rancière's second version of the avant-garde, which is "rooted in the aesthetic anticipation of the future … the invention of sensible forms and material structures for a life to come" (29). Though the focus on creating "innovative sensible modes of experience" may seem to depoliticize the avant-garde, the experiments that experimental poetry conducts on its subjects can have powerful micropolitical effects as they generate new forms of thinking.

Experimental Cognitive Poetics

By incorporating theory and results from studies in contemporary cognitive science and neuroscience, my approach clearly treats the idea of experimental poetry as more than a mere metaphor. My methodology brings together cognitive poetics and the phenomenological turn in literary study—two recent approaches that, when paired, overcome many of their individual limitations. On the one hand, cognitive poetics, as it has been practiced so far by critics such as Reuven Tsur, Mark Turner, and Peter Stockwell, has borrowed heavily from cognitive linguistics (particularly from George Lakoff), analyzing lyric poems by applying theories of conceptual metaphor, conceptual blending, figure/ground, prototypes, deixis, schemas, and so on. Such readings have been criticized, however, for generating familiar formalist readings of poems, just with new cognitive terminology.[13] Moreover, the conceptual framework of cognitive linguistics alone is inadequate to grasp the rich experiential range of experimental poetic language, which engages a great deal more of the embodied brain's anatomy than its left frontal lobe. *Poetics of Cognition* thus expands the cognitive poetics toolbox, using theories of embodied cognition, musical processing, reading, the brain's letter box, language development, visual perception, and the brain's response to nonsense. On the other hand, phenomenology, with its emphasis on thick descriptions of embodied experience, seems to offer a useful antidote to the limits of cognitive poetics, yet so far, phenomenological critics have focused almost exclusively on emotion and affect—another significant but also limited slice of our engagement with literary texts. Phenomenology also assumes an always already subjective field, imbued with human meaning,[14] which can elide consideration of the push of nonconscious cognition. This book thus attempts a hybrid phenomenological-cognitive approach, giving phenomenology a brain and cognition a body, so to speak, in order to chart a descriptive anatomy of experimental poetics and its possible effects.

Another field related to this book's line of inquiry is neuroaesthetics, which examines the neural bases for the experience of art and aesthetic judgments. This twenty-first century discipline is well represented by G. Gabrielle Starr's *Feeling Beauty: The Neuroscience of Aesthetic Experience*. Focusing on the "Sister Arts" of poetry, painting, and music, Starr uses functional magnetic resonance imaging experiments to show the ways that aesthetic experience across these arts relies on a distributed neural architecture involved in emotion, reward, perception, imagery, memory, and language. As some critics of neuroaesthetics have noted, however, a gap exists between the sophisticated machine rendering of physiochemical activity in the brain and the actual phenomenological experience that goes along with that activity. Furthermore, a field like neuroaesthetics needs to examine not only the brain structures that allow us to perceive the beautiful, but also how art, whether beautiful, interesting, or shocking, might change the landscape of the brain itself. By drawing on evidence from cognitive science, neuroscience, and phenomenology, my interdisciplinary methodology attempts to expand the purview of strictly neuroaesthetic approaches.

In attempting such an interdisciplinary approach, I consider not only what the sciences can teach us about literature and literary experience, but also the unique capacities that literary production and literary scholarship can bring to the sciences. Scholars such as Lisa Zunshine, Blakey Vermeule, and Elaine Scarry have used scientific models of cognition and perception to understand our engagement with fiction in particular.[15] However, as fascinating as this criticism is, it often ends up executing only a kind of matching exercise—science tells us X about how the brain works, and this literary text is reflecting that X capacity.[16] While some of my analyses might rightly be accused of using a similar methodology, the unique qualities of experimental poetry as a genre allow me to escape that trap. Unlike traditional fiction, the goal of which is to describe the world and human experience within it, experimental poetry runs its own experiments in order to transform the very cognition from which human experience emerges.[17] As cognitive neuroscientist and poet Jan Lauwereyns writes, "Good and demanding poetry may serve as our secret well of scientific hypotheses (or it may simply tickle our curiosity)," prompting new scientific questions to pursue (208). As a literary critic, I found that the poems in the chapters that follow raise just such questions for me, so I turned to cognitive science and neuroscience looking for answers, thereby practicing what Brian Massumi calls "shameless poaching" (20).[18] My goal is to use their theories and discoveries to make a difference in my field of contemporary poetry and poetics, but I do not want science to be wielded as an unquestioned universal tool to dissect passive poem specimens etherized upon a table. While cognitive science works to explain and map the brain's territory, experimental poems offer deterritorializing forms of thinking that recapitulate the embodied brain's structures and processes—and also work to reshape them.

My primary focus here is thus not a series of studies of avant-garde poetry but rather a series of tests of the hypothesis that poems written with experimental techniques can generate new practices of thought. The body of the book is divided into two sections, the first exploring the ways that experimental poems attempt to materialize the activity of the brain, and the second exploring how they consequently might inculcate new forms of thinking in their readers. Each chapter brings cognitive and poetic theory into conversation to illuminate a key concept in experimental poetics: intentionality, voice, projective verse, the letter, the protosemantic.

Intentionality might seem a strange place to begin, as it has become a critical commonplace that in experimental writing, the poet's attention takes the place of intention, the desire to convey a specific meaning. Jennifer Ashton is particularly critical of this "theoretical mistake," which she sees at the heart of both Language poetry and neuroaesthetics—the conflation of the meaning of the work of art with its causes and effects ("Two Problems"). Chapter 1 thus attempts to theorize the role of writerly intention and meaning in experimental poetics by deconstructing this attention/intention binary. New research into the mechanisms of perception confirms the philosopher William James's earlier theory that any act of attention is always already biased, shaped by memory, sensation, and imagination. Cognitive neuroscientist Jan Lauwereyns explains this "intensive approach" in perception: we are always tending toward (*in,* "toward" + *tendere,* "stretch, tend") some purpose or meaning. In this chapter, I read Lyn Hejinian's critically unexamined dialogue with William James in her seminal work of Language poetry *My Life* and its more recent addendum, *My Life in the Nineties,* to explore the ramifications of this intensiveness of perception both for writer and reader.

Along with intentionality, many theories of postmodern poetics similarly dismiss the central self or voice behind traditional lyric poetry, rejecting a naive notion of inspiration in favor of various forms of constraint or proceduralism. How then do we account for the uniqueness of style and even personality that emerges among different experimental poetries? This critical resistance to voice or identity has often led to the exclusion of writers of color who mix formal risk taking and experimentation with attention to a racially or ethnically marked voice; or when they are treated by critics, their identity-based content is ignored. Chapter 2 focuses on Harryette Mullen's abecedarian, *Sleeping with the Dictionary,* which itself seems to theorize this complicated interaction of the poet's mind, body, voice, language, and procedure in the act of experimental poetic creation. Placing Mullen's language games alongside cognitive theories of the mind's inner voices and the crucial role of constraints in launching creativity ultimately reveals a fresher, more comprehensive, and inclusive model for describing and understanding the complex material voice or voices behind experimental poetics than current models that focus solely on abstract language function and procedure.

Chapter 3 examines Larry Eigner's poems, which are often associated with the Black Mountain school and Charles Olson's influential "Projective Verse," but what Olson attempts in *Maximus,* Eigner pursues in minimus. As a result of a birth injury, Eigner had cerebral palsy, which made walking, speaking, and writing difficult for him; he composed on a manual typewriter, typing one key at a time with his right index finger. His poems are therefore not so much *projective* verse, sounding the speech force of the poet's mind, but objects *projected* into a three-dimensional field. Psychological studies of how the eye processes multistable images such as the Necker cube ground this claim. Traditional poems take place on a flat x/y-axis, but Eigner's drifting forms seem to project outward toward the reader or away into the distance, enacting a depth perception in their form as well as their content, as individual words similarly shift in their semantic purpose within the poem. Phenomenological approaches often assume a normalized body as the locus of experience, one unhampered by disability, prosthesis, or disease. This chapter expands the phenomenological approach by considering how the lived, embodied experience of a particular disabled writer creatively constrained and enabled his poetics. A new experimental organicism takes a significant turn toward a disability poetics in the case of Eigner, leading me to consider how he critically engages his unique form of embodiment within his poetics and how his poems become a kind of prosthesis for the reader, disabling ossified habits of mind and enabling new multistable forms of vision and thought.

Chapter 4 zooms in from the form of the words on the page to the shapes of the letters themselves, a central concern for many experimental poets in the international movement of concrete poetry and its heirs. Though this movement has been dubbed a failure by some, I join in a recent critical recovery of concrete poetry by exploring how these poems draw on and highlight the building blocks of reading in the brain. Using research from cognitive neuroscientist Stanislas Dehaene, I analyze poems in Emmett Williams's midcentury *Anthology of Concrete Poetry* alongside poems from the more recent movement of visual poetry, known as vispo. While the clean aesthetic of these concrete poems often works to expose and confound the brain's letter box and other cognitive quirks and tools that lie at the foundation of our ability to read, the messier vispo triggers some fascinating positive effects of disfluency on cognition.

Chapter 5 shifts focus from the brain's visual centers to its sound processors. Avant-garde sound poems have often been understood by their performers and critics to be adopting and engaging various protosemantic elements and energies as they work to transform their audiences. However, the effects of the protosemantic are often couched in negative, even violent terms: rupture, waste, expenditure, delirium, killing, loss. Two contemporary sound poets, Tracie Morris and Lisa Jarnot, reveal a different side of the protosemantic—one that is generative rather than deconstructive, inducing not delirium but human connection and development. To reveal some of the transformational potential behind this warmer avant-garde (more "mama" than Dada?), I turn to cognitive theories of the protosemantic origins and development of human language, particularly in the phenomena of infant-directed speech and infant language acquisition.

Finally, my investigation into the transformative cognitive effects of reading experimental poems leads logically into questions of teaching these difficult poems, which is the subject of the book's epilogue. Indeed, critic Alan Golding claims that the avant-garde poem is "always pedagogical, teaching us how to read it but also how to teach it" (15). Meanwhile, Joan Retallack and Juliana Spahr have bemoaned the fact that "contemporary literary pedagogy is chronically behind contemporary literature by about half a century" (xii). *Poetics of Cognition* thus closes by shifting from theory to praxis, extracting forms of teaching from the forms of thinking that experimental poems instill in order to better enable their transformative effects in readers and to bring poetry pedagogy into the twenty-first century.

Lyn Hejinian, the New Sentence, and the Matter of Intention

William James's *Principles of Psychology* (1890) begins by marveling at the variety and complexity of mental life—the seeming chaos of thoughts, feelings, perceptions, desires, decisions, and so on that make up an individual consciousness (1). With typical Jamesian poetic language, he poses a key question for the book: "This multitude of ideas, existing absolutely, yet clinging together, and weaving an endless carpet of themselves, like dominoes in ceaseless change, or the bits of glass in a kaleidoscope,— whence do they get their fantastic laws of clinging, and why do they cling in just the shapes they do?" (3). In an uncited reference, Lyn Hejinian quotes James's line in her work of Language poetry, *My Life:* "Such is the rhythm of cognition, a maudlin source of anxiety. We are ruled by the fantastic laws of clinging" (95). James goes on to answer his question by theorizing the intentional nature of consciousness: it is always about some object as well as always active and selective in its orientation toward the world. Hejinian began studying James in the 1960s,[1] and her engagement with his theories of memory, perception, and intentionality is evident throughout *My Life* in its various iterations: the original 1980 publication, the 1987 revision, and the ten new chapters added in *My Life in the*

Nineties (2013).[2] This experimental autobiography is constructed using the form of the New Sentence as Ron Silliman defines it: sentences are arranged paratactically, lacking a clear connection or subordination to the sentences around them. Reading *My Life* in dialogue with James answers an important question about the New Sentence: "whence do they get their fantastic laws of clinging, and why do they cling in just the shapes they do," for both writer and reader?

Intention/Attention

"Intention" at first glance might seem a strange word to associate with Language poetry, the most foundational premise of which is to challenge, even explode, the notion of a particular self at the center of creative practice (Silliman et al. 263).[3] Indeed, the paratactic form of the New Sentence becomes evidence of the fragmentation of postmodern identity for Frederic Jameson (28–29), with its "heaps of fragments" exposing the self's lack of agency within the world of late capitalism (29). Postmodern subjects, according to Jameson, are no longer able "to unify the past, present, and future of [their] own biographical experience or psychic life," and this breakdown in temporality "releases the present moment from all the activities or intentionalities that might focus it and make it a space of praxis" (27). Critic Jennifer Ashton, similarly bemoaning the shift from modernism to postmodernism, argues that meaning has become less a matter of someone's intention and more the matter of someone's attention, be it the writer's or the reader's (*From Modernism* 13). She accuses the Language poets of being interested only in a causal form of agency, "for it requires no intention at all" (*From Modernism* 24).

Indeed, many critics who are proponents of Language poetry and the New Sentence might agree with this assessment of its project. Steve McCaffery describes the form in causal terms—that it "provoke[s] in the reader the experience of a loss in meaning" (*Prior* 152), "an experience of delirium" (155) rooted in sensation and sensory impressions rather than semantics. McCaffery is right about one dimension of the New Sentence, but such analyses also prompt some important questions. Why these words? Couldn't any words, in any order, create this effect? If the New

Sentence is just about "switching on and off the phrasal continuum," as McCaffery writes (156), couldn't a computer program just generate the text? What exactly is the role of the poet's intention in creating the experimental poem?

Lori Emerson addresses these questions in an insightful essay on Erin Mouré's computer-generated poems. She engages with the work of Walter Benn Michaels, who, like Ashton, argues that contemporary experimental writing pits the materiality of the text against authorial intent, resulting in texts that generate effects rather than meanings (Emerson 54). She glosses his argument as follows: "if you believe that an author's intentions are important in the interpretation of the meaning of a text, then you do not believe that language can be approached as a material object, and if you believe that language can be approached as a material object, then you do not believe that an author's intentions are important—thereby believing in meaninglessness and the non-existence of texts" (55). Like Emerson, I find that critiques like Michaels's of experimental writing create a false binary. There is value in continuing to think through textual materiality and authorial intentionality alongside one another in our analysis of experimental texts—a premise that is at the heart of this book. Any text, even one produced by chance, is "in fact produced by humans using language, using words," as Emerson writes; "there is humanness and language all the way through" (61). The task, then, is to develop a methodology, a form of thinking, that allows for both the push of intent and the pull of materiality.

Hejinian attempts to create just such a form of thinking in the poetics of *My Life*, inspired in part by James's original ideas about the intentionality of a consciousness rooted in a material body and a material world.[4] She believes this poetics generates a "space of praxis," as Jameson calls for. "Am I, in my sentences ... in pursuit of change?" she writes. "Do I want to improve the world? Of course. If so, it will have to be *in* sentences, not *by* them. The sentence is a medium of arrivals and departures, a medium of inquiry, discovery, and acknowledgment" (*Language of Inquiry* 196). Hejinian's language of "arrivals and departures" here echoes James's theory of the stream of consciousness—a stream that is not a continuous flow but rather is made up of a "series of flights and perchings," "like a bird's life" (*Principles of Psychology* 236). "The rhythm of language expresses this" as well, James continues, "where every thought is expressed in a sentence, and every sentence closed by a period" (236). The mind "perches" on the matter of the sentence or on the sensory data coming in from the outside world, holding it still and contemplating its significance. Then it must "fly" to connect that significance to other sentences, ideas, or other sensory information, creating the "transitive parts" of the stream of thought (236). James, of course, is more interested in these "transitive parts" of thought and experience than in the "substantive parts" or conclusions. For James, such "flights" are the material of cognition and consciousness itself. "What interests James (as it interests me)," Hejinian writes, "are not so much the things, which simple conjunction leaves undisturbed, but the transitions between them and between them and us" (*Language of Inquiry* 136). She thus seems to take the phenomenology of his transitive parts of thought as an inspiration for the construction of her sentences in *My Life*.[5]

For example, the book begins with the tag line "a pause, a rose, / something on paper" followed by these sentences:

> A moment yellow, just as four years later, when my father returned home from the war, the moment of greeting him, as he stood at the bottom of the stairs, younger, thinner than when he had left, was purple—though moments are no longer so colored. Somewhere, in the background, rooms share a pattern of small roses. Pretty is as pretty does. In certain families, the meaning of necessity is at one with the sentiment of pre-necessity. The better things were gathered in a pen. (7)

This work might be read as an autobiography of Frederic Jameson's postmodern self.[6] The links in the signifying chain have snapped, resulting in "schizophrenia in the form of a rubble of distinct and unrelated signifiers" (Jameson 26); the self is thus "reduced to an experience of pure material signifiers, or, in other words, a series of pure and unrelated presents in time" (27). For Jameson, such sentences reveal the empty, ahistorical "joyous intensities" that postmodernism engenders—a feeling, he argues, that is ultimately ineffectual for any cultural critique or transformation (29). Hejinian seems to confront Jameson's description of the schizophrenic forms of postmodern art directly in a sentence from *My Life in the Nineties:* "The schizophrenic, gazing at something, watches it turn not only unfamiliar but unreal, but the artistic gaze (and the resulting defamiliarization) heightens a thing's palpability, sees it turn not only unfamiliar but real" (110). Indeed, Jameson's long quote from Marguerite Sechehaye's *Autobiography of a Schizophrenic Girl: The True Story of "Renee"* (1994), which he (problematically) appropriates as an analogy for what a postmodern aesthetic "feels like," supports Hejinian's point, as Sechehaye describes the "disturbing sense of unreality" generated by a schizo-phrenic episode (qtd. in Jameson 27). In an odd shift that underscores the problems with his schizophrenia analogy, Jameson acknowledges that the experience is described "in the negative terms of anxiety and loss of reality," "but which one could just as well imagine in the positive terms of euphoria" (27–28). As Hejinian's sentence suggests, perhaps the charged affective experience generated by the New Sentence is not due to a schizo-phrenic gaze, which makes things appear disturbingly unreal, but to the artistic gaze, which makes material things unfamiliar to us, and thus more real.

One of the material things made more real to us by the New Sentence is William James's "transitive parts" of thought, the "series of flights and perchings" executed by the stream of consciousness. When characterizing the "heap" or "rubble" of postmodern art and identity, Jameson focuses on the perception of "the material ... signifier in isolation" rather than the movement between the parts (27). Jameson's sense of the failure of postmodern art as a site of praxis and intentionality arises more from his understanding of the work and the postmodern self as a "heap" than from the text itself. The image of a heap made up of isolated signifiers does not account for "the fantastic laws of clinging" that occur among the fragments, both for the poet who formed the heap and the reader who excavates it.[7] The heap also offers a static, spatial orientation for under-standing the New Sentence, as well as postmodern art and identity more generally. Citing installations by artist Nam June Paik where television screens are stacked and scattered in lush vegetation, Jameson explains that the "postmodernist viewer ... is called on to do the impossible, namely, to see all the screens at once, in their radical and random difference" (31). If this is in fact what postmodern art and environments require, then

Jameson is correct that we would need to "grow new organs" to navigate them—an "impossible imperative" (39, 31). However, a new possibility and utility emerge if, following Hejinian's lead in *My Life*, we theorize the New Sentence and the fragmented postmodern self not as Jameson's heap but as James's stream. His stream theory of perception and consciousness allows us to take into account the transitive intention/attention of the artist and the active intention/attention of the reader, who experiences post-modern art not just spatially but also temporally.[8]

Building on James's foundational theories, new cognitive research into the mechanisms of perception reveals the ways that the embodied mind actively shapes and constructs what we perceive. Here I particularly focus on the work of cognitive psychologist Jan Lauwereyns, who, in *Brain and the Gaze: On the Active Boundaries of Vision* (2012), integrates theories and current research from neuroscience, psychology, and philosophy (including James) to illustrate that any act of attention is always already biased, shaped by the specific personality, culture, experience, psycho-physiological state, and imagination of the individual perceiver (154). The empirical evidence that Lauwereyns assembles in the book helps deconstruct Jennifer Ashton's binary logic that the poet's attention takes the place of intention in experimental writing. For, to put it simply, even the most basic acts of attention are suffused with intention. The gaze is inherently biased, he explains, always "tending toward" (*in* [toward] + *tendere* [stretch, tend]) "a particular purpose or plan" (147). In an interview with Larry McCaffery and Brian McHale, Hejinian makes a similar point about language. "You can't make nonsense with words," she insists; there is no such thing as nonreferentiality in language (138). Certainly Hejinian's authorial intent in *My Life* is not intentional in the same way as T. S. Eliot's or Robert Frost's; her poems are much more open to the peculiar stretchy contingencies of the language system, and most particularly to the attentions and intentions of the reader.

Here is where Lauwereyns's research can help. He finds that the term "intention" implies that perception involves a deliberate and purposeful choice on the part of the perceiver, when many of the operating biases and sensitivities are mostly unconscious.[9] Thus, in a terminology shift, Lauwereyns describes what he calls the "*intensive* approach" in perception.

The term "intensive" includes the idea of intention and purpose, but it also connotes concentration and efficiency (as in intensive planting in agriculture) and force (as with measurements of intensity in physics) (154). The intensive approach in perception acknowledges the significance not just of gaze position (what you're looking at) but also of gaze duration (how long you look) and gaze magnitude (how hard you look) (173). "When we keep information in active vision," Lauwereyns writes, "we increase our opportunities to analyze it, to see it in the context of what we know and what we remember, and to read new meanings into it" (173). Lauwereyns's theory of the intensive approach in perception offers a helpful rubric for analyzing both the intentionality of the writer behind the New Sentence and the intentionality of the reader, whose intensive reading gaze is always stretching toward making meaning.[10]

Hejinian's *My Life* similarly deconstructs the attention/intention binary, theorizing and enacting the poetics of the New Sentence as an act of intensive perception by both writer and reader. Let us return to James's question: "Whence do they get their fantastic laws of clinging, and why do they cling in just the shapes they do?" (3). I next examine how Hejinian theorizes the "fantastic laws of clinging" that emerge from her own acts of writerly perception and intention, enhanced by improvisation and the unpredictability of her myopic vision. Then I consider what potentially happens for readers when the object of active, intensive perception is the New Sentence itself.

"Vision determines the view," or Writerly Intention

Questions of intentionality emerge early in *My Life*. "So that if I tell you my intentions, I force myself to maintain those intentions," she muses in the ninth section of the book (20). A more rigid sense of intentionality, of top-down authorial control and determinism of a text, creates a closed text, "one in which all the elements of the work are directed toward a single reading of it," Hejinian explains in "The Rejection of Closure" (*Language of Inquiry* 42), whereas "when what happens is not intentional, one can't ascribe meaning to it," as she writes in the fifth section of *My Life* (12). At first glance, this formulation seems to play into some of the criticisms of

Language poetry made by Jennifer Ashton and Walter Benn Michaels cited earlier. Without intentionality, we are left with a text that generates not meaning but effects. "The reduction of expression to experience," Hejinian writes later in *My Life* (99). This evidence seems to support Ashton's claim that Language poetry "requires no intention at all" but rather emerges from a "purely causal" agency (*From Modernism* 24). "Vision determines the view," Hejinian writes (*My Life* 18). By analogy, the poet's attention, not intention, determines the poem.

Yet every act of vision itself is always already infused with intentionality, as William James first theorized, and as contemporary neuroscience is now confirming. Hejinian's important theory of description builds on this understanding of perception as active and contextual, offering a theory of intentionality more complex than these critics allow. It is worth taking an in-depth look at this poetics of description as she outlines it in her essay "Strangeness."

> By description I don't mean after-the-fact realism, with its emphasis on the world described (the objects of description), nor do I want to focus on an organizing subjectivity (that of the perceiver-describer); nor, finally, am I securing the term to a theory of language.
>
> I propose description as a method of invention and of composition. Description, in my sense of the term, is phenomenal rather than epiphenomenal, original, with a marked tendency toward effecting isolation and displacement, that is toward objectifying all that's described and making it strange.
>
> Description should not be confused with definition; it is not definitive but transformative. Description ... is a particular and complicated process of thinking, being highly intentional while at the same time, because it is simultaneous with and equivalent to perception, remaining open to the arbitrariness, unpredictability, and inadvertence of what appears. Or one might say that it is at once improvisational and purposive. (*Language of Inquiry* 138–39)

For Hejinian, description is "equivalent to perception," but this is not a passive form of attention wherein the describer/observer paints an "objective" vision of the world. It is also not purely subjective, divorced from the material world. Nor, finally, is this a perception/description determined solely by the language system. Hejinian's analysis sounds remarkably similar to Lauwereyns's James-inspired description of active vision, which involves "an intensive form of traveling back and forth between memory, sensation, and imagination" (xviii). Perception/description and the New Sentences that emerge from it are methods of invention, composition, and transformation—both highly intentional and open to unpredictability—reflecting the writer-perceiver's own flights and perchings of perception, memory, and imagination.[11]

The section in *My Life in the Nineties* with the tag line "along comes something, launched in context" thinks through some of these questions. The tag line reminds us that perception is always contextual; we can never perceive objects outside of the rich tapestry of sensation, emotion, memory, and desire that our consciousness provides at that particular space and time. Thus, as James originally asserted, perception is always active and selective within that context. Much of this intensive action and selection is outside of the perceiver's conscious control, so "the focus of one's work may lie somewhere other than where one thinks one is focusing. It seems from our methodical and even obsessive habits of attention" (*My Life* 130). She clarifies her point with a quote from James's *A Pluralistic Universe*: "As Gertrude Stein's one-time mentor William James observed, this is 'where things happen': 'reality, life, experience, concreteness, immediacy, use what word you will, exceeds our logic, overflows and surrounds it . . . — and by reality here I mean where things *happen*'" (131). Reality is a field "where things *happen*," and our experiences, perceptions, and actions (including sentences) within it often exceed any logical reasons or clear intentionalities that we might attempt to impose. Much of what happens in that field is lost to us as a result of the idiosyncrasies of our attention: "large parts of the day refuse to come forward, and, if they deposit themselves anywhere at all, it is certainly not in our minds, we are dispossessed of them, and they will never belong to us" (130).

Furthermore, even the perceptions that do stick in our minds and memories are deeply shaped by bias. "All that occurs does so in many ways," Hejinian asserts (131), depending on how it is perceived. "Things, being perceived, produce my reasons. There are an infinite number of sequences under way" (132). Hejinian's meditation on the active, intentional nature of perception in this poem accords with current research into the cognitive mechanisms behind acts of vision as Lauwereyns describes it:

> Every neural projection changes the information, takes care of a portion of the perceptual work. There is no recursion of exact copies; every echo is a variation, an abstraction....In the supreme fiction of vision (which we call "the truth"), a part of the poetry happens in the inner chamber of the thalamus. Here poetry means the art of making ideas. It happens not in a Cartesian Theater, but through a complex network of parallel projections that transform, convert, integrate, and/or combine information....There is no single place, no precise point where all these projections come together to trigger perception or consciousness. Instead, perception lives in the distribution of the activity, in the intensities of different neural responses across various regions in the brain. The only observer is the whole person, with his or her entire brain. (162)[12]

Here Lauwereyns aptly describes the intentionality of perception as a kind of poetics, but it is not the top-down intentionality of a single director/poet in a Cartesian theater aiming at a particular meaning. Instead, our perceptions are emergent phenomena, the result of the transformations, integrations, and projections of many actors distributed across the brain, such that "things, being perceived, produce reasons" and meaning (*My Life* 132). By this account, intentionality itself, at its most foundational level, is shrouded in mystery; it emerges from material processes outside of the perceiver-poet's conscious control. Hejinian hammers this point home later in the poem: "Who we are—it is only partly revealed in the patterns of our lives—something remains hidden in our intentions" (132–33).

While for Lauwereyns perception is a kind of poetics, for Hejinian, "the poem *is* a mind" that reflects that poetics of cognition (*Language of Inquiry* 44). In a final section of *My Life*, she "borrow[s] a phrase to say that the mechanics of perception turn psychology into aesthetics" (92). Hejinian's use of parataxis in her New Sentences reproduces the perceptual poetics of the brain, in which multiple and competing activities and neural projections come together to make a representation of the world. As Hejinian writes, "Only fragments are accurate. Break it up into single words, charge them to combination" (*My Life* 44). However, like the various pieces of information (Lauwereyns takes pains to say these are "not digital bits" [163]) that are charged into combination in the brain, the connections between Hejinian's sentences are ambiguous, offering a shifting field of possible and competing combinations and interpretations. Hejinian also enacts this field of variation and recombination with the book's tag lines.[13] Recurring phrases across *My Life* and *My Life in the Nineties* include "a pause, a rose, something on paper" (twenty-three times), "as for we who 'love to be astonished'" (twenty-nine times), and "a name trimmed with colored ribbons" (twelve times—thirteen if you count the pony with "his mane trimmed with colored ribbons" [*My Life* 10]). However, as in perception, with these repetitions, "there is no recursion of exact copies; every echo is a variation" (Lauwereyns 162). The tag line resonates differently each time, depending on the sentences around it.

One tag line, "the obvious analogy is with music" (repeated thirteen times), thematizes the connection between perception/cognition and aesthetics across its various iterations. "Seeing and hearing are activities rather than receptivities," Hejinian writes, continuing, "The obvious analogy is with music" (*My Life* 54). Hejinian also repeats the musical tag line in relation to language making: "When you speak you play a language. The obvious analogy is with music" (70) and "The obvious analogy is with music as with words" (78). In this analogy, Hejinian is not invoking the standard poetic trope of the musical sounds of language. Instead, the words emerge in the mind and on the page much like sounds are arranged and ordered in music (see also Quartermain). Her poetry, like the architecture behind human perception, does not have the sounds of music but rather its structure. Leitmotifs and echo variations offer shifting refrains that paradoxically hold the pieces together—as indeed she recognizes in another appearance of the tag line: "And the gaps began to stick. The obvious analogy is with music" (*My Life* 66). The gaps, the silences or rests, in a piece of music are not interruptions but an integral part of the structure and rhythm of a piece. Hejinian links this idea of musical rhythm to the rhythms of the mind: "The rejection of interruption—the only thing in its space at the time. Such is the rhythm of cognition, and the obvious analogy is with music" (*My Life* 89).[14]

Like the emergent symphony of perception in the brain, Hejinian's poems are not under the direction of an all-controlling intentional composer. Instead, Hejinian uses the language of collaboration and improvisation to describe their construction: "Collaborate with the occasion. The obvious analogy is with music" (21). A new tag line that appears in *My Life in the Nineties* explains the relationship between intention and improvisation: "Intention provides the field for inquiry and improvisation the means for inquiring" (131). The line is a direct quote from her introduction to *The Language of Inquiry*, where she elaborates, "Or, to phrase it another way, the act of writing is a process of improvisation within a framework (form) of intention" (3). Hejinian creates an intentional framework for *My Life*—the 45 × 45 sentence structure, the prose poem, the tag lines, the paratactical New Sentence, the act of description, the autobiography—but once that framework is in place, the writer begins to improvise within it, like John Coltrane within the melodic structures of "My Favorite Things." It is no coincidence that Hejinian's husband, who is referenced at several points in *My Life*, is a jazz musician. In one sentence, she seems to compare her poetic acts of improvisation to his musical ones: "It's hard to make a heart go pal pal pal at description but with that fat music on big feet I go beat beat beat and twitch containment" (55). It is difficult to provoke the same kind of emotional and physical response that listeners have to "fat music" with poetic acts of description, but Hejinian likely hopes that her improvised poetic "feet" will also "twitch containment," breaking her own cognition—and that of her readers—out of old ruts and routes of thought into new ones.

There are very few moments in these sentences where a regular meter with countable feet emerges, but one of them from *My Life in the Nineties* also references improvisation: "I thought I saw a crumpled blanket lying on the bed, but then I saw it was an improviser standing on his head" (129). The first clause of the rhymed couplet is a perfect fourteener, a line of iambs whose seven feet ease English readers into the familiar 4–3 rhythms of ballad meter. But Hejinian's feet "go beat beat beat and twitch containment" in the second clause (55), as the number of iambic feet shifts from seven to eight. If Hejinian practices improvisation in the rhythm of this sentence, then she theorizes it in the content. Interestingly, she connects the act of improvisation to a shift in perception, an error of vision (is it a crumpled blanket or a person lying on the bed?). Hejinian finds such ambiguities and perceptual mistakes to be productive, generative, and creative.[15] They add a welcome uncertainty and unpredictability. They are a means toward improvisation within the intentional field of description/perception.[16]

To return to the larger question of intentionality, our perceptions are thus actively shaped not only by context and by biases of memory and imagination, but also by the very vicissitudes of our sensory instruments. Hejinian is interested particularly in the condition of myopia, or nearsightedness, and the improvisational opportunities it affords. She explains in an interview with Craig Dworkin, "Meanwhile, because our models of perception are geared towards vision and sight, 'myopia' is a handy metaphor for uncertainties vis-à-vis perception, an awareness that what you perceive may not be what's there—that distortions are intrinsic to perception. I am myopic" ("Roughly Stapled"). She links all of these elements—myopia, active perception, and poetics—in two sentences from My Life: "Skies are the terrains of this myopic, eyes are the servants of perception. Of course, this is a poem, that model of inquiry" (90). To parse the first clause, which is also a tag line in the book, the details of the sky would be blurry to someone nearsighted because they are at a distance. Hejinian, however, suggests that this blurriness makes the sky more of a "terrain," a field of inquiry, for the myopic viewer-poet, offering more space for imagination, interpretation, and improvisation. As she writes elsewhere in the book, "But as I've said before, I am nearsighted, and there are many figures in this scene which might form different scenes" (84).[17]

Hejinian explores the shifting myopic perceptual terrain of the sky and its clouds more than thirty times across My Life and My Life in the Nineties, including two significant tag lines. First, she writes, "There is no 'sameness' of the sky" (70); even on a perfectly clear day, she can perceive "Blue mounds of a cloudless sky" (88). Second, "One begins as a student but becomes a friend of clouds" (72). In a poem from My Life in the Nineties, clouds become a metaphor for her New Sentence poetics: "The artist doesn't paint clouds she paints time, she paints with the eye of enduring. The sentence, an island only temporarily and tentatively colonized, sails, an aphorism on a page painted by a stranger" (117). The visual artist captures the shifting terrain of the sky and freezes one moment, one vision of it, for an eternity. Hejinian suggests that her sentences are actually more like clouds than such frozen images, for these briefly colonized islands on the page or in the sky "sail" for viewers, shifting in meaning because of their internal ambiguity and the unpredictability of the sentences around them. Interestingly, according to the *Oxford English Dictionary* (*OED*, www.oed.com), the word "myopia" comes from Greek *myein*, "to be closed," and *ōps*, "eye," which links myopia directly to the act of improvisation. As Hejinian writes early in *My Life*, "You could tell that it was improvisational because at that point they closed their eyes" (11). For Hejinian, the act of description/perception is best executed through the half-closed eyes of the myopic viewer. Indeed, even if one is not myopic, she advocates "moving to some harder way to see without blocking what's to see" (77). Jan Lauwereyns also touts the benefits of not-seeing, which, following Keats, he describes as a kind of negative capability:

> An important part of perception would be to resist discrimination, to try to remain in doubt or to accommodate multiple possibilities. Sometimes we need to keep options open, consider alternatives. On occasion we need to keep looking where there appears to be nothing at first. This requires an active blindness, an effortful, sustained not-seeing. If our basic visual biases are compulsively oriented to objects … then negative capability argues that these have to be kept in check to attain the highest achievement in perception.…Negative capability becomes a matter of voluntary control, down-regulating the perceptual salience of certain items in order to increase the powers of presence of subtler information. (233)

A rare definition of "nearsighted," according to the *OED*, is "close, careful," as in paying meticulous "near-sighted attention" to an object. The paradox inherent in this word well reflects the negative capability that Lauwereyns describes. Myopia creates a productive condition of "not-seeing" that also requires the viewer to gaze longer and more intensively at an object, revealing more of its nuances as well as the field of its shifting possibilities. Nearsightedness thus perhaps surprisingly enables "the highest achievement in perception" (233). There is evidence that *My Life* is itself launched with just such a myopic achievement. The "moment yellow" with which the book begins seems to be referenced later, in poem 13: "I may have started inexactly, I thought, nearsighted to a buttercup; I will begin again, and I rolled over into the next indentation" (30). Could that mysterious "moment yellow" be a nearsighted perception of a buttercup?[18] Hejinian's use of the preposition "nearsighted *to*" suggests the "close, careful" denotation of nearsightedness, but she also acknowledges that this myopic vision is "inexact"; she keeps her perception/description intensive and active as she "roll[s] over into the next indentation" (30), the next sentence, the next poem.

Hejinian's reference to the space of the page, along with her writerly and readerly movement among its various indentations, invites us to consider her sentences themselves as beneficent objects of "near-sighted attention." Three poems after the nearsighted to a buttercup reference, Hejinian elaborates: "Thus myopia may serve to dispel the pains of chronophobia. The obvious analogy is with music. Thought it through and through. The inaccessibility of the meaning intrigued me all the more" (37). She again associates myopic attention with musical improvisation, but here that improvisation is linked to the act of reading her sentences, which we must think "through and through," rereading them to parse their internal ambiguities, repeatedly "playing the language" as we encounter some of the same sentences repeated in different contexts throughout the book. Their "inaccessibility" begets a productive "not-seeing," a negative capability that enriches perception and experience, counteracting "chronophobia," or the painful, farsighted perception of the passage of time.[19]

In this theory of poetic intentionality, Hejinian's "vision determines the view." It is shaped by the internal mechanisms and biases of the individual poet-perceiver and her own improvisation. However, the condition of myopia also reveals the ways that the view determines vision. Myopia rates have been increasing in certain areas of the world, particularly in developing countries, and one of the reasons for this increase is the prevalence of near work, such as reading, among more educated populations (Foster and Jiang). The condition of myopia thus at least partly emerges from the repeated practice of close observation. The eye elongates, adapting to this repeated use, making this type of focus easier. How does the embodied mind adapt when the object of close observation is the New Sentence itself?

"Meaning reasons sentenced haply," or
Readerly Intention

As we have seen, critics of postmodern poetry such as Jennifer Ashton argue that the New Sentence has only a causal form of agency in relation to its readers. If the poem is just a "material effect" of the "material cause" of its writer's attention, then the poem cannot produce meaning but rather only material effects on its readers (*From Modernism* 167). Ashton asserts a restrictive and ultimately false binary here, for materiality and intentionality are not mutually exclusive but inextricably linked. Just as writerly acts of attention are always already infused with intentionality, so is the reader's act of attention to the text. As Jan Lauwereyns asserts in his theory of the intensive nature of our perception, our attention is always "'tending toward' a particular purpose or plan" (147). Whatever the author intended, readers search for and generate meaning in the texts they encounter, even in the most ambiguous texts.[20]

Lauwereyns introduces his chapter on the intensive approach with a selection from "Objects" in Gertrude Stein's *Tender Buttons*. Though he finds that it "pushes, perhaps crosses, the boundaries of the comprehensible," "it does so in a way that invites us to play along, to stretch toward the other side" (149). Lauwereyns takes us through his own attempts to make sense of the poem, tracing his semantic associations and efforts to fill in the gaps and generate meaning. He pays particular attention to Stein's ambiguous phrase, "to have a green point not to red but to point again." An example of a "garden path" sentence (named after Jorge Luis Borges's *The Garden of Forking Paths* [1941]), the sentence and its grammar confound readers here: is "point" a noun ("a green point") or a verb ("point not to red")? Cognitive psychologists have studied reader responses to such sentences and found that "readers' eye movements typically derail at such forks in the garden paths; the ambiguities are looked at longer and revisited more frequently than other words in the sentences" (150). The ambiguity in Stein's sentence beautifully occurs at the very point (literally the word "point") that asks us to look again, as Lauwereyns notes (150). Of course, this rich multiplicity only emerges for the reader willing to move beyond the sensory experience of the words and to intensify information processing, to forcefully stretch for meaning (150). Like the myopic viewer, the attentive reader gazes longer and more intensely at the sentence. As Lauwereyns reminds us, "When we keep information in active vision, we increase our opportunities to analyze it, to see it in the context of what we know and what we remember, and to read new meanings into it" (173).

Stein's mentor, William James, also writes about the effects of strange sentences in *Principles of Psychology*. "But if an unusual foreign word be introduced, if the grammar trip, or if a term from an incongruous vocabulary suddenly appear ... the sentence detonates, as it were, we receive a shock from the incongruity" (253). James's description here seems to anticipate Steve McCaffery's description of the New Sentence as creating "a loss in meaning," "an experience of delirium" (*Prior* 152, 155). But James doesn't stop there, with the reader in a state of shock and loss. He concludes his sentence, "and the drowsy assent is gone" (253). That is, the extraordinary sentence awakens the reader from her "drowsy assent" to the transparency of language and launches her into an active state of intensive meaning production. Though some readers might stop at the initial experience of loss and delirium, preferring the state of drowsy assent, James reminds us that "the essential achievement of the will, in short, when it is most 'voluntary,' is to ATTEND to a difficult object, and hold it fast before the mind" (1166). Indeed, attending to such an object can potentially reshape the mind itself.

One of the most significant ideas to emerge from James's discussion of "the stream of thought" is the notion that consciousness is not a separate entity with its own internal structures encountering objects in the world. Instead, consciousness takes its forms and structures from its objects (see Edie 42). James rejects the Kantian view that to know a thing, one must distinguish between the thing and one's self. He writes, "Thought may, but need not, in knowing, discriminate between its object and itself"; "O *per se*, or O *plus* P, are as good objects of knowledge as O *plus me* is" (265). Interestingly, James tends to use sentences as examples of objects of knowledge. For example, he insists that in the sentence "Columbus discovered America in 1492," the mind's object is not Columbus, America, or its discovery but the entire sentence itself: "Columbus-discovered-America-in-1492" (265). James's sentence has a clear meaning and a subject–verb–object structure, but consider what happens when the sentence, the mind's object, is something like Hejinian's tag line phrase in *My Life in the Nineties:* "meaning-reasons-sentenced-haply" (hyphens added, 134).[21] Hejinian seems to address this question, and allude to James, in section 24 of *My Life:* "A lot of questions, a few answers, the progress of questioning, the spot on the brain where these words will go....One thing beside another, or and then another, x times y, x dividing y, x plus you" (53). Hejinian's sentence leaves us with "a lot of questions," perhaps "a few answers," and a "progress of questioning" that engages not a stable "spot on the brain" where the words go, but an act of kaleidoscopic cognitive word processing. If x equals "meaning-reasons-sentenced-haply," then let us solve for "x plus you."

Or, perhaps more accurately, let us solve for "x plus *me*," because, as James writes, every reader-perceiver will have a particular "delicate idio-syncrasy" in her relationship to each object of thought, "with every word fringed and the whole sentence bathed in [a]...halo of obscure relations, which, like an horizon, then spread about its meaning" (266). To compli-cate the equation further, later in the section with this tag line, Hejinian suggests that "other combinations make sense, too: sentence reasons meaning and meaning sentences reason" (137).[22] Here, the first iteration implies a subject–verb–object structure (even though the word "reasons" does not usually take an object in English). A sentence, by its very struc-ture, reasons meaning; it makes us think that meaning is there to be found and is reasonable. James would agree: "Subjectively any collocation of words may make sense—even the wildest words in a dream—if only one does not doubt their belonging together" (254) and if it has a grammatical sequence (255).[23] The second iteration, "meaning sentences reason," could suggest that meaning inflicts judgment, even punishment, on reason, like a judge passing a sentence on a criminal. However, the verb "sentences" also has a more obscure meaning of "to put into sentences" and "to influ-ence by maxims," which might be appealing to a writer of poetic sentences like Hejinian. The *OED* gives an example of usage from 1685: "to sentence them into their Wits and good Manners again." In this light, the phrase reads that meaning puts reason into a sentence, or perhaps even attempts to influence reason.

As one gazes at this particular object of thought, the words of the sentence shift in definition, mutating from nouns to verbs to objects and back again.[24] Returning to the original tag line, then, "meaning reasons sentenced haply," brings us back to intention. For Hejinian, the meaning and reasons of the work are put into sentences "haply," which the OED notes means "perhaps, maybe" (is there even meaning there?), "by chance or by accident" (as with her writerly improvisation), and "luckily, fortunately" (for those readers who would gaze long enough). Hejinian's line haply suggests we might read the New Sentence not as a proper noun but as a transitive verb, as in, "The reader was New Sentenced into her Wits again; the drowsy assent is gone."

While my first example of readerly intention in *My Life* focused on a single ambiguous sentence, New Sentence praxis is best characterized by the ambiguity between sentences.[25] What makes them new is their lack of subordination to a larger narrative frame; they are arranged paratactically, but not randomly. As Bob Perelman explains in "The New Sentence in Theory and Practice," "The autonomous meaning of a sentence is heightened, questioned, and changed by the degree of separation or connection that the reader perceives with regard to the surrounding sentences" (26). For Jameson, such paratactic sentences represent the meaningless and powerless "heaps of fragments" that characterize postmodern experience and identity under late capitalism. For Perelman, however, the New Sentence is not merely a symptom of late capitalism. It also actively works "to fight the random parataxis of commodification with a more committed, oppositional parataxis—the positing of structural similarities across categories" (27, 43). If Hejinian's sentences resist any coherent narrative, then their praxis also demands "renarrativization" from readers, according to Perelman (44). The attentive reader enacts an intentional construction of meaning and purpose not from a static heap of fragments but within the active, intensive stream of meaning that is the New Sentence.[26]

While cognitive psychology offers many studies of reader responses to individual ambiguous sentences, such as the garden paths, it has far less to say about the ambiguity that exists between sentences. Indeed, some researchers have criticized the fact that most of the current knowledge about language processing in the brain has emerged from carefully constructed "textoids" in tightly controlled studies rather than from the rich complexity and ambiguity of real-world discourse in a particular context (Hasson et al.). Sadly, no intrepid scientist has yet taken up the question of how readers respond to the most ambiguous texts in the world: experimental poetry. However, there has been some work in the fields of psychology and neuroscience that speaks to this question of how readers or viewers approach and respond to ambiguity beyond individual sentences and how they work to construct meaning. Psychologists, for example, have studied the assumptions readers bring to texts and how they make inferences as they read; O'Brien et al. provide an in-depth tour of this field. Graesser et al. offer a constructionist model of inference making, considering (in a Jamesian way) how readers rely on their experience and background knowledge to understand narratives and construct inferences/meanings. They assert that readers bring a "coherence assumption" to texts and consequently work to (re)construct meaning at both local and global levels (293). Any gaps or ambiguities that emerge in the text create a state of "cognitive disequilibrium" and "stimulate the reader to think actively, generate inferences, and reinterpret the text in an effort to fill in, repair, or acknowledge the cohesion gap" (293–94). Such disequilibrium can apparently be salubrious for readers. By tracking the various affects that readers experience during learning, researchers have found that the "affective state that best predicts learning at deeper levels is confusion, a cognitive-affective state associated with thought and deliberation" (Graesser et al. 307).[27] Cognitive disequilibrium, confusion, creative construction, active learning: this is your brain on the New Sentence.

Of course, for the most in-depth theory of New Sentence processing and effects, we should turn to Hejinian. She explores the role and effects of parataxis in her poetics in the essay "Strangeness," in which she connects parataxis to metonymy, the figure of speech in which one thing is called by the name of another related thing.[28] The following examples from *My Life* illustrate metonyms in which the producer stands in for its product: "The dog was lying in the sunlight not the *sun*" and "I was reading *Montaigne*" (55, 82, emphasis added). Hejinian asserts that metonymy has a "paratactic perspective" because it moves the attention from thing to thing (from the sun to the sunlight, from Montaigne to his essays)—not through a kind of code like metaphor, as she describes it, but by foregrounding the interrelationships between things. Metonymy is also distinct from metaphor because it preserves context and the discreteness of particulars in the inter-relationship (the sun produces sunlight; Montaigne writes essays). Unlike the world of metaphor, which is based on conserving similarity between its objects, "the metonymic world is unstable," according to Hejinian, because "its paratactic perspective gives it multiple vanishing points" (*Language of Inquiry* 148). Gaps exist between the two objects or ideas that constitute a metonym, between the pen and the act of writing, between the "boots on the ground" and the soldiers they describe. Readers can fill in those gaps in multiple and various ways.[29]

Curiously, however, Hejinian does not generate many metonymic figures of speech in *My Life*. The examples I cite were the only two overt metonyms I found. Rather than using metonymy within the content of her sentences, she uses it as a formal device for sentence construction. In "Strangeness," she describes one of her inspirations for this metonymic form in William Warburton's eighteenth-century work on Egyptian hiero-glyphics. Instead of viewing them as symbolic code, like Roman letters, he considers hieroglyphs to be "based on forms found in nature and intended to convey information directly to the eyes"; "they are universal, condensed, and efficient" (*Language of Inquiry* 154–55). Hieroglyphs thus function metonymically, representing "as a fragment of concrete nature might." A "paragraph" of hieroglyphs must be organized paratactically, according to Hejinian, through a kind of "composition by juxtaposition" (*Language of Inquiry* 155). The reader of hieroglyphs must work to fill in the gaps between these condensed and efficient fragments, just as with the objects of metonymy and Hejinian's paratactic sentences.[30]

Hejinian ultimately connects metonymy and its paratactic perspective to perceptual processes: "The metonym, as I understand it, is a cognitive entity, with immediate ties to the logics of perception" (*Language of Inquiry* 151). Perception is an emergent, unstable construction that is distributed widely across various regions in the brain. Following the logic of the unstable metonym, each of these regions offers its own "echo variation" on what is perceived (Lauwereyns 162). As Lauwereyns explains, "perception lives in the distribution of the activity" across these regions; there is no place where all of the variations come together to trigger perception except in the "whole person" thinking "with his or her entire brain" (162). To study the dynamic nature of these echo variations in perception, neuroscientists deploy ambiguous figures such as the Necker cube or the duck–rabbit drawing; or they create binocular rivalry by introducing different images to each eye (165) (see chapter 3). Perhaps one of the most interesting examples of how perception dynamically fills in gaps is the phenomenon of afterimages. Fix your gaze at the small white dot on the left beneath the shapes in figure 1 for twenty seconds, and shift your gaze to the dot on the right. Then, as Lauwereyns writes, "Savor your wonderful visions" (166).

From *Brain and the Gaze: On the Active Boundaries of Vision* (166).
Courtesy of Jan Lauwereyns.

You might sometimes see complete disks without the pie piece cut out of them, and then the disks might disappear so that you see a complete hovering square. Even though you begin by looking at a static figure, these afterimages are dynamic, with different images moving in and out of consciousness beyond your control. Furthermore, the fact that you see multiple images suggests that the systems behind perception are offering parallel and competing representations. Finally, your perception of complete disks or a complete square suggests that some "filling in" is happening somewhere among the multiple brain regions involved in perception (Lauwereyns 167).

If the metonym is "a cognitive entity, with immediate ties to the logics of perception" (*Language of Inquiry* 151), as Hejinian claims, then it is interesting to think about the potential linguistic afterimages that the gaps between her hieroglyph-like sentences might generate under the intensive gaze of readers. Let me demonstrate my own intensive act of filling in the gaps of Hejinian's New Sentences, as well as the dynamic afterimages that result, with a section from *My Life* that also addresses metonymy.

Reason looks for two, then arranges it from there Where I woke and was awake, in the room fitting the wall, withdrawn, I had my desk and thus my corner. While waiting, waltz. The soles of our boots wear thin, but the soles of our feet grow thick. The difference between "he presented his argument" and "they had an argument." I still respond to the academic year, the sound of the school bell, the hot Wednesday morning after Labor Day. Must the physiologist stand apart from the philosopher. We are not forgetting the patience of the mad, their love of detail. The sudden brief early morning breeze, the first indication of a day's palpability, stays high in the trees, while flashing silver and green the leaves flutter, a bird sweeps from one branch to another, the indistinct shadows lift off the crumpled weeds, smoke rises from the gravel quarry—all this is metonymy. (48)

The tag line "reason looks for two, then arranges it from there" outlines the kind of antimetonymy of analytical thought, which likes to simplify things and to think in terms of binaries. The section begins in such a structure, with an "I" awakening into a space of rigidly drawn boxes and reasonable boundaries. The room "fits" its walls, and the "I" finds herself boxed in, "withdrawn" into her "desk" and her "corner." Yet the playful alliteration of the *w* sound in this sentence seems to allow her to break out of these rigid boxes as it is echoed in the next sentence, "While waiting, waltz," opening up the boundaries with a sense of musical flow. The next sentences capitalize on this deconstructive impulse by illustrating the slippery and paradoxical nature of language. Both boots and feet have "soles," but one grows thin with wear and the other grows thick. An "argument" can be a reasoned, rational speech but also an emotionally charged altercation. The body begins to assert itself here through the defense mechanisms of well-used feet and the feelings associated with having an argument. Finally, the disembodied, boxed-in "I" of the opening sentences becomes embodied, relating that her body "responds" to the rhythms and sensory details of the academic year—the sounds of bells and the feeling of late summer heat on her skin. If body and language were separated into their own rooms at the beginning of the poem, then the boundaries are now being tentatively crossed when Hejinian writes, "Must the physiologist stand apart from the philosopher." This is not a question for her; the love and study of wisdom and knowledge cannot be separated from the study of the body and its materiality.

In my intensive reading, these opening sentences accomplish a binary deconstruction, blurring the lines between body and mind, body and language, but Hejinian does not stop with this analytical exercise comprising only "two" ideas. Her metonymic "poetics of description" must strive toward an inclusive realism, a more "direct and sensuous contact with the concrete and material world" (*Language of Inquiry* 153). It must describe not just two but rather an infinite number of objects and ideas. The next sentence of the poem suggests that this kind of description can be viewed as unreasonable, even "mad," by an analytical world trapped in binary thinking, but the poet insists that we must not forget "the patience of the mad, their love of detail." The following sentence offers an example of her own "mad" metonymy. Instead of reasonably looking for two and arranging it from there, she juxtaposes multiple "palpable" descriptions of different objects in a scene around her—the early morning breeze high in the trees, the flashing of the leaves, the stop-and-go flight of a bird, the shadows on the ground, the smoke rising from a quarry. The reader is invited to put the pieces together metonymically, to fill in the gaps between treetops and weeds, between forest and quarry, between bird and observer, just as my interpretation fills in the gaps between her sentences.

By filling in the cohesion gaps and making inferences across sentences, I generated a highly specific and directed interpretation of these sentences, but the actual process of thinking through these sentences was more dynamic than that coherent reading implies. As a reader of poetry, for example, I experienced afterimages of other poems in it everywhere. The first line, "Where I woke and was awake," reminded me of the opening of one of Gerard Manley Hopkins's sonnets of spiritual despair, "I wake and feel the fell of dark, not day," which also plays with alliteration of the *w* sound (65). In contrast, I was struck by the abstractness and lack of emotion in Hejinian's evocation of the scene, which was more like an architect's conceptual map of the room. This religious connection affected my reading of the "soles" of boots and of feet that appear later. What would it mean for a "soul" to grow thin or thick? And which of these is Hopkins experiencing in his poem? "While waiting, waltz" evoked more poems in my mind, including Elizabeth Bishop's "In the Waiting Room," in which she writes of a momentary loss of self that happens while waiting in a dentist's office. I couldn't help but think of the tinny sounds of a Muzak waltz crackling from the speakers in my dentist's office. This sparked a connection to the tag line "the obvious analogy is with music." Perhaps in "the rhythm of cognition" of this abstract, emotionless state, "the obvious analogy is with Muzak" instead. The connections to music and to other poems also generated a new afterimage for the word "feet," which of course has a poetic as well as a physiological sense, and I was struck by how traditionally metrical the sentence was.

˘   ´   ˘   ˘   ´   ˘   ´

The soles of our boots wear thin,

˘   ˘   ´   ˘   ˘   ´   ˘   ´

but the soles of our feet grow thick.

Each line is a parallel march of iambs and anapests in trimeter, which, of course, is also the meter of a waltz. The more one slows down and allows the connections and afterimages to occur, the more vertiginous is the experience of the rich and unending potential of the mind's intensive ability to make connections and generate dynamic meanings. Hejinian concludes this particular prose poem by insisting, "Not fragments but metonymy. Duration. Language makes tracks" (49).

Rather than Jameson's static heap of fragments, the New Sentence is a temporal form of motion and duration. Its "language makes tracks"— sound tracks with music and "feet," but also a line or path for the reader's gaze to track (and retrack) across the page. Its sentences leave "tracks" in the reader's brain with the shifting linguistic afterimages that result from an intensive, intentional gaze. Hejinian seems to theorize this dynamic act of reading the New Sentence in a section from *My Life in the Nineties:*

> An analysis of details alternates with scenes, and there are pauses for these analyses, themselves scenes. It is a work of moments inserted.... Sentence by sentence, all these exertions (looping, jutting, and providing pleasure from numerous sources), these judgments and extensions, whose curves often repeat themselves, form a whole which, despite momentary pauses, is unbroken by the angles, shadows, and impeding particles included. But years are not pauses, not roses. (113–14)

The sentence, taken as a whole, creates a scene for readers, but its rich ambiguity requires some analysis of details within it.[31] To unpack the complexity and ambiguity of these dense, compressed, volatile sentences, the reader must pause to analyze, and that analysis itself creates a new scene, a new moment inserted into the text. The word "moment" originally derives from the Latin word *momentum,* with all its connotations of movement, force, particles, and expenditure of energy (*OED*). Hejinian's metapoetic passage here also emphasizes the action ("looping, jutting") and "exertions," but also the "pleasure," that reading these sentences entails. These moments of analysis also happen between sentences, as we have seen, "sentence by sentence," as the poem unfolds, loops, and repeats itself (with a difference), as with the reference to "pauses" and "roses" at the end of the quote, a gesture toward the first and oft-repeated tag line "a pause, a rose, something on paper."[32] Her description of the reader's exertions, judgments, and extensions forming a "whole" that is "unbroken by the angles, shadows, and impeding particles included" sounds much more like James's stream than Jameson's heap.

Readerly attention to the New Sentence is always already infused with intention, as we have seen, always tending toward a purpose or plan, stretching toward meaning (Lauwereyns 147). However, Hejinian generates some new implications for this model with her use of the word "extension." She was thinking about these terms even in 1974; as she wrote in her journal, "tend (as to take direction; also, to take care of) becomes tender and tense, as parents to a cluster of words which radiate, reciprocally a cluster of meaning, as with the sense of one who cares most deeply within and without; intend to extend, intense (intensive) to extensive, intent (intention) to extent (extension)."[33] Readers of the New Sentence stretch toward meaning (intention), but they also stretch out (extension), expanding their abilities and possibilities of language processing and cognition. Hejinian seems to equate this extension with an ethics, increasing not just readers' extent of meaning making but also of caregiving—care directed within, toward the self ("my life"), but also care directed without, toward the world. If the postmodern world of late capitalism piles up heaps of meaningless fragments, then the New Sentence teaches us how not to despair. Nothing is meaningless if we open and extend our capacities for attention and perception.[34]

To return to James: "Whence do they get their fantastic laws of clinging, and why do they cling in just the shapes they do?" To say that New Sentence and Language poetry more generally have material origins in the attention of the poet and material effects on its readers does not negate the role of intentionality in its production or reception, as Jennifer Ashton would have it. For Hejinian, authorial intention is most predominant at the level of form, within which she practices a looser but still purposeful mode of attention/intentionality through improvisation. These forms certainly have material effects on readers, as we have seen, but experimental poetics work to invoke action as much as reaction. That is, for the reader, these forms do not necessarily stop at the material effects/affects of shock or delirium; rather, they launch an intensive act of creation and meaning making. Thinking through the stream of the New Sentence helpfully keeps readers in transition and in active vision; it keeps them "not-seeing," lengthening the duration and magnitude of the gaze so that they increase their opportunities and abilities to analyze, imagine, and generate new meanings (Lauwereyns 173). Unlike the authorial intention of traditional lyric poetry, which asks readers to be passive knowers, the intentionality of experimental poetics invites readers to become active learners.[35]

Harryette Mullen, Proceduralism, and the Matter of Voice

> Choice voice noise.
>
> —HARRYETTE MULLEN, *MUSE & DRUDGE*

A quick perusal of the table of contents in Harryette Mullen's *Sleeping with the Dictionary* (2002) reveals that Mullen has left the letters *I, U,* and *Y* out of her abecedary. This erasure becomes the punning subject of one of the book's poems, entitled "Why You and I," which begins, "Who knows why you and I fell off the roster?" and ends, "who can stand to reason why you and I let / our union dissolve to strike the orderly alphabet?" (78). Though Mullen's barrage of punning questions in the poem is certainly playful, her choice of deleted letters is significant. These poems are not the product of a traditional lyric "I" shaping the language to evoke the epiphanies of an essential self. Instead, Mullen conspicuously puts that "I" under erasure. Confirming this goal, "All She Wrote," the first poem of the book, consists of a list of excuses for why she is *not* writing: "Forgive me, I'm no good at this [...]. By the way, my computer was stolen. Now I'm unable to process words. I suffer from aphasia [...]. I went to bed with writer's cramp [...]. Then *Oprah* came on with a fabulous author plugging her best-selling book" (3). If this is "All She Wrote," then the remaining poems in the book must be the products of something other than the writing "I."[1]

Mullen's erasure of the lyric "I" clearly reflects the influence of a Language poetics that dismisses the central "voice" of "workshop" poetry, rejecting its naive notion of inspiration in favor of various forms of proceduralism. In his typology of postmodern poetic forms, Joseph M. Conte explains that with procedural poems, "rule-dominated composition relieves the poet of the burden of the self, since the 'personality' of the artist is no longer called on to direct the creative process" (40). In chapter 1, I complicate this characterization by exploring the embodied improvisational intentionality at work behind Lyn Hejinian's New Sentence poetics. But how do we account for the uniqueness of style and voice that emerges even in a procedural poetics governed by constraint? As Marjorie Perloff points out, the "us-versus-them rhetoric" of experimentalism's founding manifestos has become complicated by many contemporary innovative poetries that seem to manifest a personality within the procedures ("Language Poetry" 433). As many critics have pointed out, this rigid binary often results in the exclusion of innovative minority writers like Mullen.[2] The theorists of lyric and experimental poetics have certainly drawn the battle lines: inspiration or systematization, lyric "I" or language function, voice or noise. However, contemporary experimental poetries often tell a different story. Perloff rightly wonders, "Must it be either/or?" (416). The complicated interaction of procedure and personality in experimental poetic creation remains to be adequately theorized.

As the paratactical construction of Mullen's line "choice voice noise" from *Muse & Drudge* suggests, her work certainly seems to complicate these lyric/Language binaries (65).[3] She began her career writing a voice-based, Black Arts–inspired poetry, represented in *Tree Tall Woman* (1981). Her next books, *Trimmings* (1991) and *S*PeRM**K*T* (1992), influenced by Gertrude Stein's *Tender Buttons* and Ron Silliman's *New Sentence*, illustrate a shift from writing the "I" to considering the subject and language itself "not as transparent but constructed."[4] In an interview with Cynthia Hogue, Mullen explains how these two approaches created different audiences for her; the former drew people of color in community readings, and the latter drew homogeneously white audiences on college campuses.

Muse & Drudge (1995) allowed her to bring these two approaches and audiences together, with its blues-inspired quatrains and experimentation with language and form. In the essay "Poetry and Identity," Mullen explores these difficulties of being a "Black" poet and an "experimental" poet, and insists on a more inclusive poetics that allows for both.[5]

Mullen's *Sleeping with the Dictionary* is her avant-garde ars poetica, offering a poetics of both/and: both experimental and Black, both procedural and inspired, both linguistic and embodied. In it, she figures poetic creation neither as a romantic epiphany of the poet's singular, authentic, racialized voice nor as pure experimental linguistic or procedural play. Instead, the book manifests an alternative poetics that incorporates the vicissitudes of the language system and the embodied consciousness of the poet. Theorists and practitioners of Language poetry have emphasized the materiality of the sign, insisting that the signs of language themselves have substance and presence (Andrews and Bernstein 34, 41). Mullen's experimental poetics offers an even more radical materialism of the sign by exploring the productive embeddedness of language within the whole embodied cognitive system. The title poem of the collection seems to theorize this alternative poetics, imagining the act of poetic creation as an event—a complex, dynamic, but unified process out of which the poem emerges. This creative event, as the gerund phrase of the title suggests, incorporates the push of language (represented by the dictionary) and the pull of the poet's own body and mind; indeed, "sleeping with" intimates the dreams of the unconscious mind as well as the bodily act of sexual intercourse. For Mullen, body, mind, language, and procedure are all inextricably linked in the emergent event of poetic creation.[6]

Mullen's insistence on the fully embodied nature of poetic creation offers a helpful complication of current theories of Language poetry–oriented poetics built on a poststructuralist foundation. Clearly Language poetry's explosion of the traditional lyric "I" and free play with signifier and signified reveal the influence of poststructuralism. However, understanding experimental poetics solely within this paradigm provides a reductive picture of many experimental poetic projects that seem, like Mullen's, to reveal not only a discursively constructed subject but also an embodied person or persons at work behind the poem. Models of embodied cognition and theories of emergence from contemporary cognitive science offer a useful corrective to abstract, linguistically determined, poststructuralist models of the subject while still avoiding a return to an essentialized or biologically determined notion of self. These theories insist on the inseparability of mind and body in the emergence of human consciousness, just as Mullen seems to assert this connection in the process of poetic creation.[7]

To understand the embodied event of poetic creation that Mullen's book explores and enacts, one helpful cognitive theory is that of emergence. Cognitive theorists Francisco J. Varela, Evan Thompson, and Eleanor Rosch describe human consciousness and the identity built on it as an emergent phenomenon because it is autopoietic, self-making, and self-organizing. As we saw William James theorize in chapter 1, these connections are not hardwired into the brain but emerge and evolve as the organism has experiences in the world. That is, instead of a top-down construction, emergent phenomena are built from the bottom up with no director or governor, like the intricate honeycombs of an individual beehive, the multiuser construction of a digital information repository such as Wikipedia, or the movement of a school of fish or a flock of birds. Individual units within these complex structures are generally ignorant of the larger structure that they help to construct. This larger organization emerges as a gestalt, with the whole greater than its parts. In this chapter, I make the case for experimental poetry as one of those emergent forms.

Poets have long described the art of poetry as involving a kind of possession, and another cognitive theory, that of the mind's inner voice, or inner speech, helps to explain the source of this possession and poetic emergence. Inner speech is defined as the "talking" going on inside our heads, the intermittent but persistent voices in our minds that we hear with a kind of inner ear. In an essay bringing together philosophical and scientific explorations of this phenomenon, Denise Riley finds that because of inner speech, we are all to a certain degree in a perpetual state of "mild possession," owned by the voices streaming through us (64, 70).[8] The experience of the inner voice is thus often passive in nature; Riley characterizes it as a kind of "ventriloquy," a sense that one is "a vehicle for words from elsewhere" (72). Yet despite our possession by these voices, we maintain some agency; we can react by ignoring or disagreeing with certain linguistic arrivals, or by affirming them. Riley claims that the capacity to write is therefore "far more of a capacity to *edit* than it is to originate" (77). The act of editing the inner voice, whether for verbal or written communication, is thus both passive and active, as well as constituted by forces inside and outside the subject. (Think of the earworms of advertising jingles, or pop songs that seem to infect and reproduce themselves in the mind.)[9] Finally, the phenomenon of the inner voice does not imply a kind of semiotic soup that denies the presence of the body and its senses, for the inner voice implies an inner ear with which we hear it. As Riley asserts, "meditating on inner speech throws us hard back on the materiality of words"—that is, the aural qualities of the voices we hear in our heads (95). Thus, the poetic interpreter of the inner voice is possessed not only by its semiotic signs but also by the sonority of its sounds.[10]

Mullen's conflation of the influences of mind, body, and the sounds and semiotics of language into a single phrase, "sleeping with the dictionary," suggests that separating out the parts of poetic emergence is an impossible task—and perhaps beside the point. The act of creation is a kind of "experiential confound," as philosopher of science Brian Massumi describes it, an "unsplittable relationality" in which all these influences work together to form a gestalt (168, 163).[11] As Riley's notion of writing as editing suggests, artistic making is not a detached, objective, artist-centered process but an "integrally experienced emergence. It is a creative event" (Massumi 174). But if a poem is not constructed from the top down, what exactly is the role of the poet in its emergence? Massumi's explanation of the visual artist's activity is relevant here: "Yielding to the complexity of variation, the artist's activity *joins* the confound [...]. The artist's activity *becomes* one of the encompassed variations of the confound. The artist can still act. But her action is more an experimental tweaking of an autonomous process than a molding of dumb matter. The artist's joining the confound helps catalyze a particular co-emergence of color, illumination, form, and space-time. This is still a 'creative' process—all the more so because it modulates an actual emergence" (173).

The artist's role, then, is that of a catalyst. If we shift Massumi's description from the production of visual art to poetic making, then the creative event looks something like this: the poet's inner voices, composed of aural and semiotic information from inside and outside, along with the dreams and visions of the unconscious mind as well as the bodily experiences of language, generate what I call a linguistic confound, the "unsplittable relationality" of the poet's embodied experience of language. The poet yields to the push of these multiple influences while at the same time adding her own activity and procedures to the mix, an "experimental tweaking" of this overdetermined confound through which the poem emerges. *Sleeping with the Dictionary* illustrates this emergent poetics through its creative use of constraints and ultimately theorizes it in the body talk of its metapoetic title poem.

Creative Constraints

Mullen's erasure of the lyric "I" and play with constraints reflect the influence of Oulipo and the group's devaluation of classical notions of the inspired writer in favor of a "voluntary" or "conscious" literature with rules that the author herself imposes (Motte 18).[12] She was obviously inspired by the "lipogram," in which, like her erasure of *I, U,* and *Y,* an author strictly excludes a particular letter of the alphabet.[13] Another technique is the N + 7 game, in which one replaces a noun in a given text with the seventh noun following it in a particular dictionary. While Mullen uses many of these Oulipean games in the book, she often modifies them, allowing for more choice within the noise of a procedural poetics.[14]

Mullen applies the constraint of the dictionary form itself to *Sleeping with the Dictionary,* organizing poems alphabetically, beginning with "All She Wrote" and ending with "Zombie Hat," and including a varying number of entries for each letter. Mimicking the appearance of the book's namesake, the majority of the fifty-seven entries are prose poems with justified right and left margins. Along with the constraints of alphabetical order and the N + 7 game, Mullen uses and modifies many recognizable poetic forms and word games to compose the book's poems. "Ask Aden" is an acrostic; "Fancy Cortex" and "Present Tense" use anaphora, the repetition of a word or phrase at the beginning of each line;[15] "The Lunar Lutheran" and "Zen Acorn" play with anagrams; "Any Lit" and "Coo/Slur" are structured by homophony. Puns proliferate but are especially prominent in "Music for Homemade Instruments" and "Resistance Is Fertile." Finally, Mullen uses well-known texts as constraints for parodies, such as Shakespeare's Sonnet 130, known as the "dark lady" sonnet ("Dim Lady"), the story of Goldilocks ("European Folk Tale Variant"), and the language of "Junk Mail" and of corporate disclaimers in "We Are Not Responsible."[16]

By imposing constraints so ubiquitously in the book, Mullen highlights their important role in the act of poetic making. Similarly, cognitive scientist Margaret A. Boden explains that such restrictions are actually what make creative thought possible (58). Seeking to demystify the idea of inspiration, she analyzes several famous examples of innovative thinking to argue that new knowledge and art do not arise out of a vacuum. Creative thinkers work within established maps within their disciplines, and these maps become "generative systems that guide thought and action into some paths but not others" (59). At the same time, those maps may prove overused, so the thinker, out of boredom or curiosity, may tweak the map in order to explore new ground (60). Chemist Friedrich von Kekulé, for example, had a dream about a snake biting its tail that led to his discovery of the benzene ring—a moment of inspiration he reached essentially by altering the generative maps of his discipline, dropping the constraint that molecules must combine in strings only. Boden suggests he may have accomplished this shift, consciously or unconsciously, by using the heuristic device of "considering the negative," or negating some aspect of the problem in order to see it in a new light (66). The brain's constraining semantic maps also offer a useful tool for developing new ideas. Memories of concepts are linked in semantic nets in the brain, according to Boden, which become associative systems, much like the dictionary, wherein one idea can lead to many other ideas, whether linked by concept, sound, or sheer coincidence. Disciplinary maps, heuristics, and semantic nets have powerful generative abilities for the event of creation, and Mullen's book illustrates this fact through her parodies, play with disciplinary forms, and N + 7 word games.

Like Kekulé, however, and like the Oulipeans, Mullen tweaks the disciplinary constraints that she uses. The poetic results of Mullen's application of the N + 7 game are not as nonsensical as one might imagine because she modifies the form, permitting herself more choice. She uses a free-style version of the game in "Variation on a Theme Park," replacing words from Shakespeare's Sonnet 130 with words that begin with the same letter rather than words strictly seven entries below the original in a dictionary (Mullen, interview with Kane). Thus, instead of beginning "My mite's eyecups are nothing like the sunburn" (using N + 7), her poem reads, "My Mickey Mouse ears are nothing like sonar" (75).[17] Mullen's freestyle modifications of such constraints result in a kind of soft experimentalism. Her goal seems to be to revel in the ludic pleasures of Oulipean construc-tions while maintaining an accessible, often political, theme. "Variation," though humorous, can ultimately be read as a critique of the false, whitewashed perfection of Walt Disney "World": "I have seen roadkill damaged, riddled, and wintergreen, but no such roadkill see I in Walt's checkbook" (75). Even her choice of dictionary reflects this dual poetic goal. The *American Heritage Dictionary*—her sleeping companion, according to the book jacket—was composed with the assistance of African American poets Langston Hughes and Arna Bontemps, as well as feminist theorist Gloria Steinem.

Mullen's application of constraints and political modifications of the results illustrates the interplay of poetic agency and the push of the language system in the act of poetic creation. This interaction is espe-cially evident in "Swift Tommy," which makes use of Tom Swifties, a word game in which there is a punning relationship between a speaker's quotation and the adverb describing how he said it—for example, "I've struck oil!" Tom shouted crudely. Mullen's prose poem begins with a traditional, though lengthy, example of the genre. "'I grew up with a lot of punctuation myself, so I can understand your nostalgia for paren-theses,' the dashing Sister Ka exclaimed to her dingbat friend across the periodic table" (70). There are many punctuation puns in the sentence, including "Sister Ka," an anagram of "asterisk," and "dingbat," referring to typographical symbols. The next sentence relies on synonyms (as well as puns) to connect the two pieces. "'Is a pink collar worker a redneck who came in from the sun?' a bloody European quizzed the ruddy Fulbright scholar during the in-depth Q and A following her profound lecture on the abysmal fried tradition of deep southern chickens" (70). Pink, red, bloody, ruddy; in-depth, profound, abysmal, deep—the dictionary provides a kind of semantic net here for Mullen as the definitions for particular words include and link to other synonyms, offering an associative system for creating the Tom Swifty.[18]

As the poem continues, the sentences begin to break out of the constraints of the form as Mullen shapes them into a critique of consumer capitalism. "The old crock tearfully confided to the young salt, 'A wave of mock cashmere turtlenecks swallowed my ethnic pride, and I can't believe it's not bitter'" (70). The quotation satirizes images from mail-order catalogs like those of Lands' End or J. Crew, in which models of all races conform to a specific white bourgeois look and seemingly bond over their shared love of turtlenecks.[19] Mullen emphasizes the superficiality of the images by including "*mock* cashmere turtlenecks." The following clause continues this critique with a send-up of the margarine with the ecstatic brand name "I Can't Believe It's Not Butter!" In the spirit of the Tom Swifty form, the interlocutors here also embody her commentary on consumerism. They are identified not as persons but as products; one is an "old crock" (also a tub of butter) and the other is a "young salt." The poem "Swift Tommy" thus emerges from Mullen's play with the constraint of a particular cultural form (Tom Swifties), from the language system itself (dictionary), from the detritus of advertising caught in the stream of her mind's inner speech, and from her own experimental tweaking and shaping.

Though the previous examples might seem to imply that poetic creation is a purely cognitive, disembodied act, Mullen quickly disabuses the reader of that notion. The heteroglossia of language in our heads and in the world around us, her poems insist, is not only semiotic and syntactic in makeup but also acoustic. The seemingly silent affair of "sleeping with the dictionary" turns out to be bedlam, a cacophony of sound. Mullen's use of traditional poetic sound techniques such as alliteration ("Do dragons dream?" [8]) and assonance ("My ass acts bad" [9]) offer one way of calling attention to this cacophony. Most important to the book, however, is homophony, the use of words that are spelled differently but sound the same, or similar, to one another. The third poem in the book, "Any Lit," introduces her affection for reveling in the sounds of language, as well as her both/and, Black and experimental poetics. The phrases of the poem are modeled after a traditional African American courtship ritual, in which a courted lady finds herself unable to respond to the complex figurative language of her suitor and states, "You are a huckleberry beyond my persimmon" (Henning 47). Mullen tweaks the form to emphasize its sounds:

You are a ukulele beyond my microphone
You are a Yukon beyond my Micronesia
You are a union beyond my meiosis
You are a unicycle beyond my migration (6)

The poem continues in this form for thirty-three lines, the *u* sound repeated in "You" and the fourth word, and the "my" sound doubled in the second half of the sentence.[20]

Mullen emphasizes the phonic nature of this constraint by including many different letter combinations that create the same sound: "u-," "Yu-," "eu-," and "yoo-"; "my-," "mi-," "mei-," "mai-," "mae-," and "May-" (as in "Mayan"). Moreover, the "litany" intimated in the title "Any Lit" reminds readers of a resonant and repetitive chant or prayer, often in a call-and-response format—hence the "you, you," "my, my" back-and-forth within the poem's lines. But if this is a chant-like litany, what is it that Mullen is invoking? The semiotic meanings of the word pairs are tacitly related. Someone with a ukulele might sing into a microphone; Yukon and Micronesia are geographical names; union and meiosis are opposites; and one might use a unicycle for some kind of wacky migration. However, Mullen's litany seems to be an attempt to decenter the semiotic meaning of words and to emphasize instead their phonic possibilities, their feeling and resonance within the body itself—an emphasis that is significant to many of the book's later poems.[21]

Mullen's acoustic play here reflects the emphasis on the phonic aspects of the sign among poets and writers of the Language tradition. Charles Bernstein, in his introduction to *Close Listening: Poetry and the Performed Word,* makes an important distinction between aurality and orality for understanding the function of sound in poetry:

By *aurality* I mean to emphasize the sounding of the *writing,* and to make a sharp contrast with *orality* and its emphasis on breath, voice, and speech—

an emphasis that tends to valorize speech over writing, voice over sound, listening over hearing, and indeed, orality over aurality. *Aurality precedes orality*, just as language precedes speech. Aurality is connected to the body—what the mouth and tongue and vocal chords enact—not the presence of the poet; it is proprioceptive, in Charles Olson's sense. (13)

Language poets often cite a goal of calling attention to language as language, of slowing down the reader's leap to rapid interpretation and unquestioning consumption of words' semiotic meanings. Bernstein's distinction here also illustrates a similar goal for the sounds of words. Rather than leaping immediately to "listening" through words for their meanings, we should try "hearing" their sounds first—that is, attend to the building blocks with which we create meaning and presence. Bernstein, like Olson, suggests that we hear them not with the ear alone, but proprioceptively, with the entire body.

Bernstein makes this distinction in the context of his larger argument about the significance of the poetry reading/performance, but his idea of aurality as "the sounding of the *writing*" and its connectedness to the body is helpful for understanding the role of sound constraints in Mullen's book. The constant, uniform repetition of sounds in "Any Lit" begs that the poem be read aloud, causing the mouth and tongue to repeatedly move in the same ways. Each phrase begins with the back-close vowel sound of the "You" and moves to the open vowel sound of "are" to the lip-smacking labial stop opening "beyond" that ends with the tongue humming on the teeth for "n," followed by a quick flick for the "d." The phrases culminate with the nasal humming of the two "m" words. Mullen's seemingly nonsensical poem is proprioceptive, its repetitions making you meet your mouth, feel your face, and hear the hum in your head as you pronounce each word. As the poem's title also suggests, this bodily sounding of language is ultimately true of "Any Lit," and perhaps we should be open to hearing it more often.

"Any Lit" prepares us for more proprioceptive sound constraints to come, such as "Blah-Blah," another interesting litany of words that one reviewer of the book remarkably deemed "forgettable" (King 536). The poem consists of an alphabetical list of words with doubled sounds. It begins,

Ack-ack, aye-aye.

Baa baa, Baba, Bambam, Bebe, Berber, Bibi, blah-blah, Bobo,
    bonbon,

booboo, Bora Bora, Boutros Boutros, bye-bye.

Caca, cancan, Cece, cha-cha, chichi, choo-choo, chop chop,
    chow chow, Coco, cocoa,

come come, cuckoo. (12)

The poem continues in this vein through the alphabet.[22] This tempting
tongue twister is difficult to resist reading aloud. Slips of the tongue are
nearly inevitable, whether on a shift in consonant sound (from "Cece" to
"cha-cha"), a shift in the number of syllables (from "Sing Sing" to "Sirhan
Sirhan"), or a shift to an unfamiliar language ("ylang-ylang"). Reading
this poem aloud is like calisthenics for your mouth; it truly leaves your
face muscles a bit sore.[23] As for the poem's sounds, the combined effect
of the echoing words is a kind of baby talk, mimicking an infant's prelinguistic babble, her playful discovery of the many different sounds she
can make with her mouth. (Mullen even includes the stereotypical baby
words "Gaga" and "googoo.")[24] The poem results in a kind of regression,
returning the reader both in body movements and sound effects to a
time before the sounds of words were connected to concepts. Here is the
aurality that precedes orality that Bernstein writes about, the experimental
cacophony that precedes the voice, speech, and presence of a human self.

It is impossible, however, for readers to regress completely to this
prelinguistic moment of pure embodied sound. We cannot escape the
leap to semiotic meaning when we hear a sound concept from a familiar
language (like the old paradox, "Don't think of an elephant"). This
multiplicity of acoustic and semiotic elements ultimately makes up the
linguistic confound of inner speech from which a poem emerges. In
"Blah-Blah," Mullen applies a particular alphabetical and sound constraint,
but the poem it engenders is far more than just silly nonsense, as the title
might imply. Though the list of words, read semiotically, seems random
at first, patterns begin to emerge. "Ack-ack," originally British slang for an
antiaircraft gun or antiaircraft fire, is a helpful word to begin the poem,
for it is both semiotic (being a kind of abbreviation for "antiaircraft") and

onomatopoetic (mimicking the sound the gun makes). The *B* list contains another example of onomatopoeia with the sheep's sound "Baa baa," the women's clothing brand "Bebe," two Indian words "Baba" and "Bibi" (terms of respect for an old man and a wife), two African peoples ("Bobo" and "Berber"), a French Polynesian resort island ("Bora Bora"), and the Egyptian former UN secretary general, Boutros Boutros-Ghali.

Mullen's litany, including as it does Indian words, words from several African languages, European words, words from Asian nations, as well as English and Spanish, is revealed to be multicultural in scope, reflecting the cacophony of sound and semiotics created by the information age and contemporary globalization.[25] I was unfamiliar with many of the words in the poem, and because so many were not in the English dictionary, I searched the Internet to find their meanings. In this process, I was struck by a sense that I was exploring the streaming inner voices of a global culture, for many of the words that Mullen chose reflect the linguistic cross-pollination that results from globalization.[26] Take two words from the *Z* list, for example (13). "Zizi" is the word for "owl" in several African languages, a name for a lodge in South Africa, an art gallery in London, and a baby talk name for "penis" in French. The famous Black actress Josephine Baker starred as Zouzou, a Creole laundress, in the eponymous 1934 French film. But Zouzou is also the name of a 1960s French film, a French fashion celebrity, and a Mediterranean deli in Chicago. These transglobal and translinguistic conjunctions reflect a fertile connectedness across cultures, as well as the overdetermined nature of any linguistic utterance in a global marketplace.[27]

Mullen's heteroglossia goes beyond a mere postmodern reveling in the joyous intensities of the information glut of globalization, however. She explains in an interview with Daniel Kane, "In *Sleeping with the Dictionary,* I'm concerned with the direction of what's called globalization. Are we members of a global village, or just consumers or investors in a virtual global market?" Her word choices within the echoing constraint reflect this political valence, emphasizing the conquests of European and American empires that were the instigators of the process of globalization (e.g., Bora Bora, Pago Pago, Palau Palau) and focusing on the African diaspora in particular. Words associated with the voodoo religion such as "grisgris" (a charm or amulet) and "veve" (a symbol used in rituals) evoke voodoo's origins in Africa and its diasporic practitioners in Haiti and the United States. Mullen also includes multiple words from African languages, from food ("dindin" and "foofoo") to religious objects (the Yoruba's "juju"). Several words also evoke the problems they face, from the "tsetse" fly, widespread carrier of malaria, to "Tingi Tingi," a refugee camp for Rwandan Hutus in Zaire.[28]

Mullen's distinctly multicultural inflection in "Blah-Blah" seems to reflect the fact that the English language is itself a product of globalization and colonization, absorbing words indiscriminately from its speakers' colonies and conquests over the centuries. In fact, several of the "colonized" words cited in the poem actually appear in the *American Heritage Dictionary*. Mullen therefore calls attention to the history of despotism and exploitation contained within that linguistic heritage. Indeed, this poem might explain *Sleeping with the Dictionary*'s close resonation with the phrase "sleeping with the enemy."

These political valences are confirmed by Mullen's incorporation of the word "yari yari." Yari Yari Pamberi was a conference, first held in 1997, that highlights the work of Black women writers from around the globe and the consequences of globalization on their lives. The term *yari yari* is from the Kuranko language of Sierra Leone and means "the future," and *pamberi* means "forward" in the Shona language of Zimbabwe ("Yari Yari Pamberi").[29] Paradoxically, perhaps, Mullen views "Blah-Blah" as a kind of participation in this dialogue—a dialogue meant to empower not only Black women writers but also citizens of the global culture more generally. One way the poem does so is by calling attention to the glut of noise and information that daily courses through and echoes in the mind's ear. Mullen's comment on her long poem *Muse & Drudge* equally applies to this poem: "The culture is always babbling at us. And so I was capturing some of the babble and turning it this way and that to see how it could be told" (interview with Frost 409). Instead of "telling" it for us, however, the babble of recycled words in "Blah-Blah" teaches the reader how to tell for herself—to look for and focus on particular patterns in that noise out of which meaning and connection, and potentially action, can emerge. Like Charles Bernstein, Mullen wants us to get "a nose for the sheer noise of language," but unlike Bernstein, Mullen doesn't want us to "stop decoding" (*Close Listening* 22). "Blah-Blah" lets us hear and enjoy the noise; it teaches us to sniff out the semiotics and politics embedded within it.

"Blah-Blah" ultimately embodies the multiple and overdetermined elements of the stream of language coursing through our minds' ear— elements that we experience sensually, semiotically, and politically. Moreover, this rich poem reflects an important aspect of the act of poetic creation itself: echo. Mullen could have chosen any constraint to capture the babble of global consciousness, perhaps some kind of N + 7 game with Google or with several different language dictionaries. Instead, Mullen's litany reminds us of the echoing tendency of the mind's passive inner ear or voice. Critic Jed Rasula characterizes the act of poetic creation in these terms as well: "writing assumes control of an echo … [it] is, in effect, the ventriloquial means of transposing an acoustic event onto an optic event" ("Poetry's Voice-over" 280). What results is the poet's sense that she is "inspired" or "possessed," with the poet transcribing words coming from elsewhere.

Rasula suggests that the nymph Echo is therefore a prototype for the inspired poet's possession by language.[30] Punished by Juno with the inability to initiate speech, Echo can speak only through compulsive repetition of the words that she hears. Interestingly, however, she is not without some agency in her responses to her love, Narcissus. When Narcissus speaks a sentence with which she agrees, she responds with a direct echo, as with "Come! Come!" and "Let's meet." Ovid's version of the story explains that on hearing these sentences, "with the happiest reply / that ever was to leave her lips," she repeated him (92). Yet when Narcissus pushes her away, exclaiming, "Don't cling to me! I'd sooner die than say / I'm yours," Echo replies only with "I'm yours" (92–93). Fated to repeat only the sounds of other voices, this mythopoetic prototype for the inspired poet is nevertheless still able to modify and edit those voices in her reply. She is mastered by the linguistic confound but still retains some agency within the constraints of her echoing technique.

Though echoing poems like "Blah-Blah" and its companion poem, "Jinglejangle," certainly represent a Language-influenced procedural poetics, they also illustrate the catalytic choice of the poet in shaping the noise of the linguistic confound into a distinctive, if multiplicitous and shifting, poetic voice that emerges from editing and constraining the "blah-blah" of language that her mind both takes in and echoes back to her. Unlike the nymph Echo, however, whose body slowly shrank away until she was only a voice, Mullen's echoing poetics throws us hard back on the embodied materiality of words—their feeling in the mouth, their resonance in the head and in the mind's ear. The poet's body becomes an echo chamber, giving shape to the sounds and voices resonating within it.

Body Talk

Mullen's title poem, "Sleeping with the Dictionary," offers a metapoetic perspective on the playful poems of the collection, theorizing the act of poetic creation as an emergent process involving mind, body, and language as well as the procedures and experimentation of the poet herself. Using "I" and "my," the opening sentences emphasize the personal nature of the poetics she describes; however, as the poem continues, the "I" drops away and her language becomes more inclusive, describing "the poet's [...] mission" and using "we" and "our" (67). Indeed, Mullen's poems throughout the book reflect her embodied connections to multiple subcommunities—Black, female, consumer, academic ("Quality of Life"), even Southern Californian ("Bilingual Instructions"). In the title poem, she relates to the community of poets and a more universal experience of the human body's fertile intimacy with language.[31]

The poem begins, "I beg to dicker with my silver-tongued companion, whose lips are ready to read my shining gloss" (67), stressing the inextricable connection between language and embodiment. The language system itself, represented by the dictionary, is anthropomorphized, given a body with a "tongue" and "lips." Elsewhere in the book Mullen writes, "I've been licked all over by the English tongue" (57); here too the poet's body and the body of the dictionary are ambiguously mingled. Instead of the poet reading the dictionary's lips, the dictionary's lips are reading the poet's "shining gloss," suggesting a gloss on her lips as well as the gloss of a dictionary entry, as if her body is constituted by both flesh and language itself. Underscoring this fleshy connection is the poet's verb choice, "to dicker," which means to haggle, bargain, or barter, but which originally came from the fur trade, where it meant a quantity of ten hides or skins. The poet's role of "dickering" with the dictionary implies a kind of give-and-take, a combination of mastery of and being mastered by the linguistic corpus of her companion. Yet this bargaining is also a transaction of and within the flesh. The ten skins of her dickering are ultimately reflected in the poem's ten sentences, the product of the confluence of the "tongue," "lips," and "gloss" of the poet's body and the corpus of the dictionary.

Mullen consistently figures this mingling of the body of language and her own body as a kind of sexual encounter: "Retiring to the canopy of the bedroom, turning on the bedside light, taking the big dictionary to bed, clutching the unabridged bulk, heavy with the weight of all the meanings between these covers, smoothing the thin sheets, thick with accented syllables […], groping in the dark for an alluring word, is the poet's nocturnal mission" (67). In her meticulous unfolding of gerund phrases here, Mullen self-consciously mimics the language of bodice rippers. She clasps the bulky body of her heavy partner, smooths its skin, which seems to bristle with a hirsuteness of "accented syllables," and begs for it to talk dirty to her. Mullen's light-hearted dictionary porn also emphasizes a more serious point: the ways that language penetrates our bodies in the resonance of its sounds, and the feeling of its movements as we hear it and speak it. Words are not abstract entities for Mullen; they have heft and flesh. In her "nocturnal mission," the writer therefore "gropes" for words—not with her mind alone but with her entire body.[32]

Because the writer's body and the dictionary's body are of the same species, so to speak, their nightly coupling can be productive; her "nocturnal mission" also implies a nocturnal *emission*. Mullen suggests that this coupling ultimately breeds poetry itself through her play on the word "verse." "A versatile partner, conversant and well-versed in the verbal art, the dictionary is not averse to the solitary habits of the curiously wide-awake reader" (67). The Latin word *vertere*, "to turn," is at the root of all these "verse" words. The poet's active "turning" of the pages of the dictionary makes her partner versatile and conversant, yet she also describes her actions as a "habit," a compulsive bodily repetition. The poet's paradoxical active yet passive "turning" and conversing with the dictionary lead to more oxymorons in the next sentence: "In the dark night's insomnia, the book is a stimulating sedative, awakening my tired imagination to the hypnagogic trance of language" (67). In her nightly habitual act, is the poet awake or asleep? Stimulated or sedated? Conscious or unconscious? Mullen's answer seems to be all of the above.

We have already encountered this notion of poetic inspiration as passive and active, but Mullen in this poem also highlights the importance of habit and even "exercise" to creativity. Of the list of gerund phrases, she explains that "all are exercises in the conscious regimen of dreamers, who toss words on their tongues while turning illuminated pages." "To go through all these motions and procedures" is ultimately the poet's "mission" (67). The model of inspiration that emerges here is far from metaphysical; the poet does not passively wait for the Muse's voice to speak through her. Instead, she goes through a "regimen" of "exercises" and "procedures" from which a poem might emerge. Mullen certainly intends the embodied valence of these terms. More than just mental exercises, these are embodied "motions and procedures" that involve touching and turning pages, "toss[ing] words on [...] tongues," and "groping in the dark for an alluring word" (67). Mullen's foreplay/wordplay culminates in another reference to a regimented practice: "Aroused by myriad possibilities, we try out the most perverse positions in the practice of our nightly act, the penetration of the denotative body of the work" (67). Part of the act of poetic creation involves the poet's own techne, her making and shaping of language. This techne necessitates some techniques, as Mullen suggests here: mental and bodily constraints, "procedures," or "practices," even "positions," that generate creative thought.

The poet's exercises and procedures reflect the importance of constraints to creative thought that cognitive scientists such as Margaret Boden have theorized. Mullen's habitual practices, like the disciplinary maps, heuristic devices, and semantic nets in the brain that Boden describes, can have powerful generative abilities for the act of creation. Mullen cites the constraint of alphabetization as one helpful procedure in the poem: "The alphabetical order of this ample block of knowledge might render a dense lexicon of lucid hallucinations" (67). In part, the restriction of a particular order or procedure renders or produces creative ideas and their "dense lexicon." *Sleeping with the Dictionary* itself exemplifies this rendering, being a kind of ordered lexicon or dictionary, but a "dense" one, crowded with different forms and sounds and meanings, and demanding concentration from its readers. The lexicon of the book is made up of the products of these exercises—or, as Mullen oxymoronically describes them, "lucid hallucinations." Creative thought is both rational and irrational, a seemingly false perception dredged up from the depths of the unconscious.[33] A "lucid hallucination" well describes Friedrich von Kekulé's irrational dream of a snake biting its own tail that yielded a rational theory of how carbon atoms combine. Boden too considers the role that the irrational unconscious must play in the emergence of creative thought (29).

Mullen's model of creative emergence, however, moves beyond Boden's more brain-centered, cognitive interpretation of constraints to emphasize the role of the whole embodied cognitive system. Mullen deliberately chooses words that have exclusively mental and bodily connotations: an "exercise," a "position," the acts of "groping" and "penetration" and being "aroused." Boden's favorite examples of creative thought in her book are Archimedes's "Eureka!" moment in his bathtub, Kekulé's dream by the fire, and Henri Poincaré's mathematical discovery as he was boarding a bus (25), which lead her to speculate about the role of constraining abstract thought processes like heuristics and the unconscious. In *Sleeping with the Dictionary*, however, Mullen suggests that the positions, exercises, and movements of the thinker's body are also important to creative emergence. A body resting by a fire, a body boarding a bus, a body taking a bath— surely these corporeal positions and practices (all of them habitual) also play a role in the thinker's mental positions and practices as well as the ideas that they engender.

Mullen even suggests trying out "perverse positions" to stimulate creative acts. The word "perverse" (note the play on "verse" again) literally means "turned away from normal," and these "perverse" positions can be mental, as when Kekulé turned away from the theory in his discipline that molecules must combine in strings only. But why not also try out a new body position to experience the world or consider a problem in a new sensory way? These positions and procedures, both mental and physical, both habitual and "perverse," serve to stimulate creative thought. The final sentences of the poem highlight the ways that these constraints set poetic emergence in motion. "Beside the bed, a pad lies open to record the meandering of migratory words. In the rapid eye movement of the poet's night vision, this dictum can be decoded, like the secret acrostic of a lover's name" (67). Like a brook whose contours and meanderings emerge from the landscape around it, Mullen's poetics is shaped by the constraints within her own embodied consciousness, within the language system itself, and by those that she imposes on it from without.

Her choice of the word "migratory" also sheds light on the notion of an emergent act of creation, as Mullen imagines it here. A migratory flock of birds has no leader or center. Rather, each bird within it follows certain instinctual rules or constraints, and what emerges is a beautifully fluctuant and multiplicitous entity. Similarly, the poet's nighttime practices precipitate the emergence of a shifting flock of words out of the language system of the dictionary and the poet's own babble of inner voices. The poet's "rapid eye movement" can therefore be understood as her eyes' quick saccades as they read the words of the dictionary, as well as her eyes' movements during REM sleep—the kind of sleep in which dreaming takes place. The creative event emerges from the multiple influences of language, the poet's passive submission to the push of her body and unconscious mind, and her active tweaking and shaping, or simple "recording," of the "dictums" of these influences on the pad by the bed.

Following the cardinal principle of Language poetics, Mullen rejects an authoritative voice as the foundation of her poetry, but this does not mean that the art of experimental poetry is finally unrelated to the poet's identity. Mullen reminds us that writing a poem is a fully embodied event—something that happens to her as well as something that she does. The poem emerges from the complex interplay of bodily systems and structures, environmental and cultural systems and structures, and the poet's own catalytic editing and shaping. Though Mullen's methods of poetic making are certainly unique, her emphasis on the constraints and procedures of the poet's body, along with those imposed from without, suggests a way of explaining and considering the differences among experimental writers without resorting to an essentialized, monolithic notion of self or voice behind poetic making. This emergent post-Language poetics that

Mullen explores and enacts in *Sleeping with the Dictionary* ultimately offers a fresher, more comprehensive model for describing and understanding experimental poetic making than current models that focus solely on language function and procedure. Her poems illustrate an emergent poetics arising from the constraints of a body whose flesh is possessed by language itself.

Larry Eigner's Projected Verse

Chapter 2's central conception—the poet's body as a constraint that launches creativity—takes on a compelling new dimension in the case of Larry Eigner. As a result of a birth injury, he lived with severe cerebral palsy and spent the first fifty years of his life in his parents' home in Swampscott, Massachusetts, before moving across the country to Berkeley and becoming an essential figure in the San Francisco Renaissance and the emergence of Language poetry. In this chapter, I am interested in considering how Eigner's lived, embodied experience creatively constrained and enabled his poetics. Here I respond to Michael Davidson's call for a disability poetics that theorizes "the ways that poetry defamiliarizes not only language but the body normalized within language" and that reads the embodied poetics of midcentury writers against their actual bodies ("Missing Larry" 7, 8). By taking Davidson's methodology one step further, we can explore how disability poetics becomes for the reader a defamiliarizing prosthesis that enables new forms of vision and embodied cognition.[1]

Language poet Clark Coolidge writes in his poem "Larry Eigner Notes,"

I see . . .
    the noun states accent in air

so much that an "on" or "hard" takes on
solidity of noun at line-end

the prepositional phrases: a thought he's
using only one unit, over & over again
                    (Cézanne?) (224)

Coolidge recognizes the objectivist nature of Eigner's poems, the way that
words take on a materiality and solidity of their own within his lines. He
concludes by connecting this objectivism to the work of postimpressionist
painter Paul Cézanne. Cézanne famously attempted to paint the "lived
perspective, that which we actually perceive," rather than a geometric or
photographic perspective, as phenomenologist Maurice Merleau-Ponty
explains (64). For Cézanne, "the object is no longer covered by the reflec-
tions and lost in its relationships to the atmosphere and other objects: it
seems subtly illuminated from within, light emanates from it, and the
result is an impression of solidity and material substance" (62). Coolidge
implies that Eigner has an analogous understanding of words, as things to
"see," "in air," with "solidity and material substance" of their own—objects
illuminated in minimalist lines within the white space of the page.

Interestingly, Cézanne's perception was also affected by a disability,
schizothymia, which is a mild form of schizophrenia that reduces the
world to frozen, expressionless appearances (Merleau-Ponty 71). Merleau-
Ponty points out that as Cézanne grew older, "he wondered whether
the novelty of his painting might not come from trouble with his eyes,
whether his whole life had not been based upon an accident of his body"
(59). However, like Lyn Hejinian's myopia, which I discussed in chapter 1,
Cézanne's visual impairment and Eigner's cerebral palsy become creative
constraints that allow the artists and their work to incorporate, question,
and extend the reigning aesthetic paradigms of their times.

Indeed, Eigner seems to extol the originality of Cézanne's vision in a
1971 poem with the parascript "c e z a n n e a / c a t h o l i c // u p / o l d /
h i l l s," which begins:

an original

        eye

                    a reverent

                              eye

          wild

          discipline

                              eye

                              eye

          what you

                    see you

          settle

                    on

                    moves

          do something (*Collected Poems* 1021)

Eigner reads the "wild discipline" of the painter's eye as capturing how the
eye and mind work together to create what we see. Jonah Lehrer suggests
that Cézanne's paintings "show us the world as it first appears to the
brain"—that is, abstract angles and forms that the mind fills in to form a
coherent scene (98). The paintings illustrate how "what you // see you //
settle // on," as Eigner writes. The eyes "settle" on the world, in the sense
of bringing into a permanent form, fixing one's attention, making a home,
and making up one's mind to "do something" (*OED*). Interestingly, Eigner
places the word "eye" in two pairs that float along the poem's right edge. It
is, of course, the twoness of the eyes, binocular vision, that creates depth
perception, providing to the viewer a three-dimensional world. (To get
even more objectivist, even the shape of the word "eye" seems to reflect
this twoness: two circular letters divided by a triangle.)[2] The artist Alberto
Giacometti claimed that "Cézanne was seeking depth all his life," not depth
as a mere "third dimension" that could be invoked by the geometrical
tricks of perspective art, as Merleau-Ponty explains, but depth as a "*first*
dimension that contains all the others*," the experience "of a global 'locality'

in which everything is in the same place at the same time, a locality from which height, width, and depth are abstracted, a voluminosity we express in a word when we say that a thing is *there*" (140).

In this chapter, I argue that Larry Eigner uses a similar poetics of "depth," evoking the "voluminosity" of images and words themselves in poems that are seemingly projected into a three-dimensional, even four-dimensional, space—an open field "in which everything is in the same place at the same time." I thus must engage with Eigner's relationship to Charles Olson's theories of projective verse and an open field poetics; indeed, Eigner's work often seems to embody the poetics of Olson's famous manifestos even more fully than Olson himself did in his oeuvre. This depth poetics was certainly enabled by Eigner's limited mobility and his deep attention to the patch of world framed by his screened-in porch in Swampscott, but as Michael Davidson insists, we must not read the poems as merely a "compensatory response" to his disability ("Missing Larry" 11); furthermore, we must acknowledge Eigner's relative poetic silence on the topic of his cerebral palsy. As Merleau-Ponty writes, "Although it is certain that a person's life does not *explain* his work, it is equally certain that the two are connected. The truth is that *that work to be done called for that life*" (70). Eigner's work, like Cézanne's, offers a poetics of the "lived perspective"—a fusion of a particular body and world rather than an attempt at a more universal, normalized imitation. It is a work that invites another set of eyes, those of the viewer-reader, to "take up the gesture which created it" (Merleau-Ponty 88).[3] Eigner's poems thus become a unique prosthesis for the reader, enabling an unfamiliar gesture that calls into question normative forms of embodiment and vision as well as normative language use.

Non-Euclidean Poetics

In 1993, the lines of Larry Eigner's poem "Again dawn" were arranged on the large, fragmented faces of the Berkeley Art Museum. Inspired by poetry and architecture collaborations such as the John Ashbery inscription on the footbridge of the Walker Art Museum in Minneapolis, the museum's designer worked with Eigner to create the layout on its multiple facades. This collaboration highlights some important effects of Eigner's poetics of the two-dimensional page—the way his lines work to create and invoke a perception of depth in a shifting, multidimensional field in what I call his non-Euclidean poetics.

Eigner's work is often associated with the Black Mountain school, especially Charles Olson's notion of "composition by field" as laid out in his 1950 essay "Projective Verse" (*Collected Prose* 243). Ron Silliman rightly suggests that Eigner provides the ultimate test of Olson's emphasis on breath, speech, and voice ("Who Speaks" 372); Eigner's cerebral palsy made speech difficult for him and difficult for others to understand.[4] (When he began to give public readings once he moved west to Berkeley in 1978, the poems were handed out or placed on an overhead projector to aid the audience.) Reading Olson's statement of his embodied poetics alongside the unique poetics and embodiment of Larry Eigner highlights some tensions in "Projective Verse" between its emphasis on the ear

Eigner installation of "Again Dawn" on the Berkeley Art Museum in 1993.
Courtesy of the Berkeley Art Museum and Pacific Film Archive.

and speech and a more multisensory, often visual, notion of an open-field poetics. For example, Olson describes the lines and syllables of a poem as "OBJECTS" inside a "FIELD" (243), but he then insists that it is only through "speech-force of language" that they are given "solidity" (244). He highlights the advantages of the typewriter's "space precisions" for the projective poet, but not so much for the visual effects as for the ability to "record the listening he has done to his own speech," so that the reader might revoice it (245). While he praises the ear-based work of "the sons of Pound and Williams" who were writing verse "as though not the eye but the ear was to be its measurer" (246), he later offers a lovely visual and tactile image, describing the poem or the line "to be as shaped as wood can be when a man has had his hand to it" (247). Olson leans toward a more objectivist poetics when he states that the projectivist act takes place "in the larger field of objects, lead[ing] to dimensions larger than the man," but he determines that the act emerges only in "the moment he takes speech up in all its fullness" (247). Can objects in a field generate a force without the act of breath or speech?[5]

Some of these tensions begin to be reconciled in Olson's study of Mayan glyphs. In 1951, the year after he wrote "Projective Verse," Olson spent several months in Central America. The letters he wrote to Robert Creeley during that time illustrate a subtle shift in his poetics under the influence of the glyphs. As Steve McCaffery argues, the "*Mayan Letters* expose a dense interest in the silence of a graphic economy and a system of writing irreducible to either speech or breath" (*Prior to Meaning* 53). While he was writing to Creeley, Olson also submitted a project proposal to the Viking Fund to begin site investigations of the glyphs. In it, Olson claimed that the previous "decipherers" of the glyphs focused only on their abstract "lexicon," whereas his emphasis would also include "the live stone, for all the value of its 'relief'. . . its force as carved thing" (96). It is this glyph-like ability to convey meaning both through an abstract lexicon and by concrete objecthood and shape that comes to fruition in Eigner's projected poetics of the page. Eigner's poems are not three-dimensional objects like the glyphs; instead, they convey a multidimensionality, a "thing-force" to the viewer of the page, much like the pen-and-ink drawings of the Mayan glyphs that Olson so admired. Olson's description of these sketches well conveys the visual effects I perceive in Eigner's typewritten poems: "the very dimensional advantages of relief have been carried over successfully by pen on to paper" ("Project" 98).

Indeed, Eigner's work brings a role for the "dimensional advantages" of the eye back to projective verse. His poems are not so much *projective,* sounding the speech-force of the poet's mind, as they are *projected,* launching the thing-force of the poet's vision into a three-dimensional field, exploring depth in both content and form. While projective verse implies a speaker having the power to project his voice, projected verse makes the verse itself into an object, something "thrown or thrust forward; placed so as to protrude; cast upon a surface" (*OED*). In a June 1969 poem likely inspired by the run-up to the moon landing in July, Eigner seems to confront Olson's vococentrism, pointing to Olson's later piece "Proprioception," with its more fully embodied, multisensual phenomenology.[6]

       synaesthesia   proprioception

sight-seeing

  the moon

tourists

the eyes are more than the lungs (*Collected Poems* 914)

Instead of only "sight-reading" the musical "stave and the bar" of the typewritten page, as Olson called for (*Collected Prose* 245), Eigner advocates a "sight-seeing" of the poem written from his uniquely constrained experience in the world, wherein "the eyes are more [projective] than the lungs."[7] Eigner takes Olson's emphasis on the breath and replaces it with the eye, as I illustrate here by tweaking Olson's famous lines: "verse will only do in which a poet manages to register both the acquisitions of his ear *and* the pressures of his [eye]" (241); "the line comes (I swear it) from the [eye]" (242).

There is no more distinctive visual feature of Eigner's poems than his lines' subtle shift across the page to the right as they unfold down the page; rarely does a line return to the original left margin.[8] These drifting lines have been read as a manifestation of Olson's poetics of "kinetics" and "movement," a "dance" or "speech-force" on the page that Eigner could never execute with his body (*Collected Poems* 240, 244). In the poem, Williams's machine made out of words, thus becomes for Eigner "a machine for walking" (*Collected Poems* 195), so that he can write "o i walk i walk," and mean it as the words leap across the page (113).[9]

The actual kinetics of Eigner's writing process is relevant here: he painstakingly typed each poem using only his thumb and right index finger on a manual typewriter. Olson focused on the ear because "it has the mind's speed" (242), allowing the poet to "keep moving, keep in, speed, the nerves, their speed, the perceptions, theirs.... One perception must must must MOVE, INSTANTER, ON ANOTHER!" (240). Clearly Eigner's typing finger could not keep up with "the mind's speed." Read in this context, Eigner's poems generate a tension as the words punctuate the delay and skip across the timescape of his perception.[10] Perhaps, though, his bodily constraint generated a distinct poetics, a different relationship of thought to typed word. Instead of constituting a hyperactive catalog of perceptions, the poem is more like Olson's Mayan glyphs or block of wood: a three-dimensional object shaped slowly by the man who puts his hand to it (247), a poetics of whittling, a poetics of layers, of depth—the depth of space and the depth of time. It is a non-Euclidean poetics.

Traditional verse happens in two dimensions: the *x*- and *y*-axes, with horizontal and vertical orientation and movement. However, Eigner's poems create the visual effect of a diagonal, a *z*-axis, as they drift across the page.[11] Diagonal lines famously create the illusion of depth on a two-dimensional surface, as in the Necker cube. Gestalt psychologists were fascinated by such 3-D images because of their multistability; one can see the upper square as the back of the cube and the lower as the front, closer to the viewer, or vice versa. Background and foreground shift depending on the eye's focus.

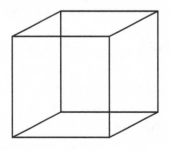

A Necker cube. Public domain.

There is evidence that Eigner, a self-professed lover of geometry (*areas* 128), may have thought about such shapes and effects. He mentions Euclid in an early poem that seems to explore depth perception with the play of apple trees against a "background" of "radiant light" (*Collected Poems* 85); he describes a "disorganized gestalt, dead? / flat" (200) and "gestalt concentrate" (699) in later poems; elsewhere, he determines that "zigzags outline / the // n dimensions // the world" (1093). The less one returns to the left margin, he explains, "the more easily a piece can rise up off the page" (*areas* 150). The reader might thus perceive these drifting lines not merely as reaching horizontally along the *x*-axis of the page ("what kind of poetry is / a horizontal line" [*Collected Poems* 1172]) but also, as in the Necker cube illusion, reaching out toward the viewer, or even receding, as if his poems' words were floating away on the omnipresent "wind":

> twigs
>
> barrels
>
>   rubbish
>
> junk
>
> relations
>
> forwards
>
>   changes
>
> the wind
>
>   blows
>
> on (*Collected Poems* 1195)

Eigner's poetics thus literalizes Olson's well-known quotation of Robert Creeley that "form is never more than an extension of content," as his lines can perceptually extend out toward the viewer (Olson, *Collected Prose* 240).

The content of the lines themselves often highlights this three-dimensionality along with the lines' orientation on the page:

>   twig stick
> A line of trees hard
>   branches above the roofs

                    the sea fog
press backward, down to water

                    every way slightly rocked

    paths   infinite
3 dimensions
                    direction of the sun
                        past the sight

                    emanate
    in time dense,   travel
        around   the sap
                        risen

            the wind blows (*Collected Poems* 560)

Eigner rarely used capital letters in his poems, particularly outside of the first line. He explained in an interview, "If you start a poem or a line with an upper-case letter it's like the big beginning of all speech, not just a piece of language" (*areas* 150). The capital letter *A* in line 2 thus stands out to Eigner's diligent readers as an object. Like a pictographic Mayan glyph, it may even elicit the shape of a treetop, making the line of words evoke a "line of trees" for the reader. The twigs and trees visually hover over the line "above the roofs" in the poem, "the sea fog" does settle (on) "down to water," and the phrase "press backward" presses backward toward the left margin. The reader is thus "every way slightly rocked" in the "3 dimensions" of the poem, such that the word "risen" almost seems to push up the word "sap" by the end. While reading his poems, I have found myself drawing arrows up, down, left, right to follow the visual and semantic movements of the lines.[12]

Like the 3-D planes of the Berkeley Art Museum or the illusionistic 3-D of the Necker cube or pen-and-ink glyph drawings, the arrows also reach along the z-axis, toward or away from the reader, invoking depth:

        beautiful
    storm clouds,
            the sun
    shines underneath (*Collected Poems* 587)

"The sun" is centered underneath the "clouds" on the page, but it is behind them in the imagined visual imagery. The lines take a cross section of the depth of sky stretching before the viewer and turn it on its side in two-dimensional space. Many of Eigner's images ask to be superimposed almost atop one another, as in these fragments:

blackbird
blue sky (*Collected Poems* 621)

the sill ducks moon
  clouds trees (*Collected Poems* 593)

The images convey a depth of space, as well as the "drift of perception" within it (*Collected Poems* 655), over the windowsill to the flying ducks above the trees, which are perhaps outlined against the more distant clouds and the even more distant moon. The depth of the scene exists all at once, as in human perception, with objects superimposed and competing for attention.

Merleau-Ponty finds a similar depth in Cézanne's paintings, contrasting them with the Euclidean perspectives of classical painting, which uses vanishing points and vanishing lines in an attempt to create a "true" representation of a scene. But this perspective is far from true. To look at a classical painting, he explains, is to "cease to see like a human being, who is open to the world because he is situated in it": "Before I had the experience of a world of teeming, exclusive things which could be taken in only by means of a temporal cycle in which each gain was at the same time a loss. Now the inexhaustible being crystallizes into an ordered perspective within which backgrounds resign themselves to being only backgrounds ... and objects in the foreground abandon something of their aggressiveness, order their inner lines according to the common law of the spectacle" (87). However, Cézanne's paintings—and Eigner's poems—reject such "monocular views" for a lived perspective (87), a depth perception in which background and foreground are multistable, with words, images, and lines vibrating with possibility. Traditional poetic syntax and lineation, like classical painting, tend to crystallize language and meaning into an ordered perspective, with clear background and foreground. In Yeats's famous lines, "Turning and turning in the widening gyre / The falcon cannot hear the falconer," the three iterations of the word "the" are clearly meant to be background to the main action, the nouns and verbs of the sentence. In Eigner's paratactic lines, "the" can easily float to the foreground—another object in the list of "sill ducks [and] moon" (unless "ducks" is a verb here, which makes the line even more multistable).[13]

If Cézanne offers the "physiognomy" of objects in his paintings (Merleau-Ponty 66), then Eigner offers the "physiognomy" of words, even the least of these—the *a*, the *on*, the *to*. Eigner's is a "dancing / alphabet," where "the aim / of words" can be their semantic meaning but also the direction they seem to point in space; poems become "something to see" as well as to read (*Collected Poems* 1108). However, a dance happens not just in space but also in time—a fourth dimension that Eigner also attempts to capture in the depth perception of his poems.

The Fourth Dimension

In Euclidean geometry, distance is always spatial and positive, and time is considered universal and constant. In contrast, non-Euclidean geometry factors the variable fourth dimension of time into its equations, measuring not distances between points but intervals between events situated in space-time. Just as Eigner projects his poem/object into a three-dimensional perceptual space, so do his non-Euclidean poems take on a fourth dimension when reader meets poem. They become poetic events that project time's unfolding in a uniquely spatial way, "in which everything is in the same place at the same time," as Merleau-Ponty describes Cézanne's work (140).[14] Eigner's poems seem to create an enfolding of space and time, cleverly evoked in the line

$s_t P_i {}^a_m {}^c_e e$ (*Collected Poems* 1650)

Charles Olson also admired non-Euclidean geometry; he found its elliptical mechanisms reflected in the projective space-time of Herman Melville's work. For Melville, time "had density, as space had, and events were objects accumulated with it, around which men could move as they moved in space" (Olson, *Collected Prose* 88).[15] Gary Grieve-Carlson helpfully outlines Olson's theory of history that emerges in his prose. Influenced

by Alfred North Whitehead, Olson believed that time has depth as well
as length, as "the past retains a 'presence' in the unfolding of any event"
(109). Olson thus likens an event in space-time to a sphere, "round and ...
multiple in its planes," but claims that a writer can describe the event only
"by selecting from the full content some face of it, or plane, some part"
(qtd. in Grieve-Carlson 106, 107). Rather than selecting some part of an
event, Eigner's poems work to become a kind of spherical event in their
own right, with the poem an object projected in space-time that readers
can move around in, just as they move around in space.

For Olson, "history is the practice of space in time" (*Special View* 27),
and he plumbs the depths of lengthy histories—of Gloucester, Massachusetts, as well as the early peoples of Central America. What Olson attempts
in *Maximus,* however, Eigner pursues in minimus, with poems that strive,
conversely, for a practice of time in space:

a   d o t

a glimpse is space
    a time is a long
        thing to see (*Collected Poems* 1495)

Olson's sprawling lines and forms reveal the layers of a particular "space
in time" and thus make time "a long / thing to see" for readers. In some
of Eigner's earlier poems, he tries out that longer line, allowing the poem
to "extend itself, naturally, quietly, and be like taking a walk" (728). In later
poems, particularly during the Berkeley years, as Robert Grenier writes,
"he learned that he could 'stop, any time' (instead of pushing the eventu-
ality 'onward'/ beyond itself)(without denying 'ongoingness' of what could
be said/'written next')" (1350). Eigner's compact lines often function more
like "a dot" for the reader, a chunk of "space" able to be taken in by "a
glimpse," revealing the layers of time in space.

Perhaps especially because of his slow writing process, Eigner acknowledges in one poem that "words / split / seconds" as the finger types them
or the eyes pass over them, yet "how instantaneous is / the same time in /
actual thought" (*Collected Poems* 1478). Some of his poems try to capture
that instantaneousness of thought and vision as a singular, split-second
event in space-time:

Instantaneous

out the house
from the back (*Collected Poems* 1501)

The spread-out letters of the first line constitute a kind of visual oxymoron, slowing down the eye, evoking the tension between Eigner's thought/ vision and his writing process. However, the closeness and shortness of the next two, deliberately lined up beneath one another, make the implied action seem to happen simultaneously, as the eye can almost take in the six words in one glimpse—much as Eigner may have held them, like objects, in his mind as he typed the poem.

Eigner goes for a similar effect to convey an even longer stretch of time in another poem:

a p e r s p e c t i v e on the p a s s a g e of t i m e

the sky at one
            branch and another

      nut   nut   nut
         eat eat eat
      scramble scramble (*Collected Poems* 1475)

Rather than convey the long, stretched-out passing of linear time, as the opening line implies, this poem creates a literal "passage" of time, as in a segment of words whose layers portray in a compressed visual format a squirrel's movement (another "passage") through the yard and through time.[16] The poem functions more like Olson's spherical model of an event in space-time as the eye takes a nonlinear path through the final three lines of the poem: "nut / eat / scramble / eat / nut." Indeed, the poem seems to take on the peculiar "double-nature" that Olson sees in Mayan writing: "it is at once object in space (the glyph) and motion on stone in time (the glyph-blocks)" ("Project" 96). Once again, Eigner's work leads us back to the concept of "depth": his "passages" embody time's depth more than its length, a vertical time that reveals time's layers, rather than a linear time with its vanishing present.[17]

Actual historical events appear rarely and often only implicitly in Eigner's oeuvre, but when they do, they get the four-dimensional treatment.[18] For example, "A m s t e r   d a m !" considers the plane crash of El Al Flight 1862 into a high-rise apartment building in Amsterdam on October 4, 1992. In that particular moment of space-time,

the plane crashed
                    (into the building)
    Bodies, charred, buried

        deep (ly) ,   ground ,   volatized (*Collected Poems* 1650)

Though the lines move down the page, taking time to unfold as we read, they attempt to capture a catastrophic event that happened in a split second. The first line crashes into the second with no intervening white space along the vertical axis, with those rare closed parentheses creating a feeling of compression. Conversely, the expanding blank spaces of the fourth line—growing from a one-pica space to two, to three, to four— illustrate the horrific occurrence of human flesh "volat[il]ized" in both time and space.

After recreating the crash in these lines, Eigner includes a large blank space before turning to the cosmic forces behind such events:

living

dying

instants

                eclectic

    m c ^{2} collaging

            super−

                $s_t p_i a_m c_e e$ (1650)

A body can go from "living" to "dying" in an "instant," but here, this occurs not linearly but vertically. The "dying // instants" of the past still remain buried beneath the "living" in Eigner's poetics of space-time. Albert Einstein was not the first to propose that energy is equal to mass times the speed of light squared, but he was the first to use this formula to propose the intertwining of space-time in his theory of general relativity.

By placing terms describing his poetics within this context, Eigner gives them the force of a cosmic event: "eclectic" and "collaging" suddenly evoke the energy of "electricity" and atoms "colliding"; his superimposed images explode into supernovas; his lines curve as space-time curves in the presence of matter (energy).[19]

According to the theory of general relativity, the rate at which time passes for an object depends on the relative position and velocity of whoever is watching. Eigner begins his exploration of plane crashes and cosmic forces in the poem by positioning the event's observer "in the hotel, / the room, the / bed" (*Collected Poems* 1650). The observer is not separate from the event but caught up in it, implicated in its unfolding, as in this poem: "garage // diamond // windows // fence // eyes // tree // shadows // branches" (*Collected Poems* 1476). By including "eyes" among the objects in the poem, Eigner acknowledges what Merleau-Ponty suggests about the phenomenology of space. For Merleau-Ponty, space is something "reckoned starting from me as the null point or degree zero of spatiality. I do not see it according to its exterior envelope; I live it from the inside; I am immersed in it. After all, the world is around me, not in front of me" (138).[20]

The embeddedness of the observer in Eigner's multidimensional poetics of projected space-time reminds us that the body itself is a non-Euclidean space, curved and complex. Indeed, the body is perhaps best illustrated by non-Euclidean topological forms such as the Klein bottle or the Sierpinski sponge, which have no clear interior or exterior. Critic Michael Jonik connects such forms to Charles Olson's beloved Melvillean whale, to its blowhole and other points of discharge and projection that are neither outside nor inside (146). He quotes Olson in "Letter 27" of *Maximus:* "No Greek will be able / to discriminate my body. / An American / is a complex of occasions / themselves a geometry / of spatial nature" (146).[21] Despite Olson's admiration of these forms, his practice of capturing space in time in projective verse often reinscribes a subject–object split, as Eugene Vydrin argues, "separating the receiver from the stimulus received" (179). Even in the later piece "Proprioception," in which Olson tries on more of a depth sensibility, decentering the ego within the cavities of the body, he still concludes that "projection is discrimination (of the object from the subject)" (*Collected Prose* 183).

Eigner's poems seem to better enact the non-Euclidean embodied poetics that Olson outlines in his prose. Olson strives to avoid "the self as ego and sublime" in favor of "the self as [a multistable] center and circumference" (*Special View* 45), but he clearly struggles to decenter that ego in his work.[22] Eigner's unique embodiment may have aided in such a decentering. As a result of his cerebral palsy, Eigner had what he describes as a "wild left arm and leg" until they were quieted by cryosurgery when he was thirty-five. Before the surgery, he had to practice a sort of proprioceptive double vision: "in order to relax at all I *had* to keep my attention partly away from myself, *had* to seek a home, coziness in the world" (*areas* 26). "Yet not too far away either" (128); the doctor advised him to keep his "free-from-jitters leg raised" to avoid a circulation problem and to "sit up straight to avoid squashing my liver a few yrs farther down the road" (39). Eigner describes an instructive form of attention here, a proprioception that acknowledges time's depths imbricated within the depths of the body, but also that body's embeddedness within the space-time of the world around it.[23] The body is not separated from objects but is a "thing among things," "caught in the fabric of the world" (Merleau-Ponty 125).

Eigner's poems are thus not just three-dimensional objects but also four-dimensional events. They capture moments of his vision and of his bodily experience in the world, an effect intensified by his poems' lack of titles. The poems thus also become an object or event for others to encounter and experience within the fabric of their world. The reader gets caught up in the event of the poem, taking on its double vision.

Multistable Reading

Unlike the singular perspective and linear time of classical painting and poetics, four-dimensional work like Eigner's or Cézanne's is also more open to collaboration with the viewer or reader. Maurice Merleau-Ponty writes, "The accomplished work is … not the work which exists in itself like a thing but the work which reaches its viewer and invites him to take up the gesture which created it" (88). "I" don't look "at" the work, the painting, or the poem, but "my gaze wanders within it as in the halos of Being. Rather than seeing it, I see according to, or with it" (126). Merleau-Ponty describes the reader or viewer's interaction with the work in four-dimensional terms: it is a "gesture," an expressive bodily movement in time and space. Furthermore, the work becomes a kind of tool, even a prosthesis, for the viewer, whose vision alters as she sees "with it" and looks through it. What happens when the reader takes up the gesture of a poem like Eigner's? What new visions does it create, and what forms of experience does it enable?

Rita Felski's 2008 manifesto *Uses of Literature* explores four different modes of textual engagement: recognition, enchantment, knowledge, and shock (14). As I discuss in the introduction, Felski places avant-garde works in the final chapter on shock and argues that this affect needs to be rescued from its abuse by these artists, questioning in particular their utopian aesthetics and politics, as well as the notion that shocking works of art could somehow "topple banks and bureaucracies, museums and markets" (109). She thus leaves the avant-garde behind in order to explore shock in the Dionysian drama *The Bacchae* and the Romantic poetry of Baudelaire. I agree with Felski that the art of the avant-garde and its contemporary experimental heirs has not yet achieved radical world transformations, but I am interested in exploring a more complex phenomenology of these texts. The following "thick description" of my experience of reading an Eigner poem attempts to uncover his more subtle gestural politics of transformation.

I know that if my students were to write such a description, they might offer a version of the affect of "stuplimity," which Sianne Ngai defines as a paradoxical synthesis of shock and boredom (2–3). This analysis could be useful, but I am more interested in the experience of a reader open to the complexity of the text, to the "artifice of absorption" that Charles Bernstein describes.[24] According to Bernstein, seemingly impermeable texts can generate their own feelings of enchantment as antiabsorptive techniques are used for absorptive ends (82). The shifting syntactic patterns in Leslie Scalapino's poetry, for example, create a disorienting play of attentional focus yet ultimately cohere into a mesmerizing, almost musical rhythm (81). Bernstein compares the affective experience to observing ambiguous figures (like the Necker cube): "The refusal to be absorbed / in any single focus on a situation / gives way to a / multifocused absorption that eerily / shifts, as an ambiguous figure / from anxious to / erotic to diffident /

to hypnotic" (81–82). It is in this experience of "multifocused absorption," of enchantment more than "shock," and of thinking as well as of feeling that the transformative possibilities of experimental poetics such as Eigner's lie.

Eigner's non-Euclidean poetics enables this multifocused absorption, or what cognitive scientists call multistable perception, which occurs when a visual pattern is too ambiguous for the eye to recognize a unique interpretation.[25] Like the sides of the Necker cube, Eigner's diagonally drifting poems appear to rise up from the page or shift to reach away into the distance. Cognitive scientists have suggested that the analogy between multistable visual perception and multistable linguistic perception is so strong that the same methods and models may be used to study both visual and linguistic ambiguity (Wildgen 221). In a similar toggling of focus, then, the reader's attention switches from the dignified nouns and verbs to the short, menial words that hold them up, and from the meaning of words to their shape and position on the page. Even the semantics of a single word can be multistable: is "ducks" a verb or a noun? In the four-dimensional environment of an Eigner poem, there is no right answer, no single focus, no clear background and foreground.

Perhaps one good analogy for "seeing with" an Eigner poem would be looking through the lens of a stereoscope, a tool by which two images of the same scene, taken at slightly different angles and viewed separately by each eye, produce a three-dimensional effect for the viewer. (The View-Master toy is a stereoscope.) Eigner puts it more succinctly: "stereoscopic, / dimensional" (*Collected Poems* 1279). Watch how he plays with the analogy in this poem:

a hole in the clouds moves
     the hole in the sky (*Collected Poems* 542)

The visual imagery here creates a vertiginous experience. Are the clouds moving against a stable background of sky, or does the sky itself move? Yet along with the imagery, Eigner's playful use of the space of the page invites readers to consider the lines themselves as visual images. With its large indentation and repetition of opening words, the second line enacts the movement of the "hole" as the reader's eye shifts from left to right across the page. Imagery and form thus give us two different "holes" to look through, for a stereoscopic experience of the poem. Barrett Watten contends that "in Eigner form and content are the same" and likens his poems to a "hologram" rather than an enclosed box (177). The multistability of vision evoked by Eigner's poems seems to prove this claim almost literally.

Eigner came up with the neologism "considerateing"—from the Latin *con* plus *siderare,* derived from *sider,* "star" or "constellation"—to describe poetry's thought. A constellation, a helpful analogy for Eigner's poetics, appears two-dimensional when mapped onto the page of the sky, yet in reality, it is four-dimensional, stretching across light-years of space-time. He writes in a 1970 poem, "spread-out constellations / dark / areas / all / together // far and near // points" (*Collected Poems* 976).[26] A constellation is also a projection of meaning onto that space; its connections could easily be redrawn in different configurations. Eigner invites readers to "stop anywhere, anytime" in his poems (*areas* 25), so things can come together to be assessed, but he warns, "You can't expect anything in particular that you've got to last, any integration or assay." All that endures is "the big conglomerate, the universe" (148). In this multistable projected world of images and words integrating and disintegrating before your very eyes, you can only "play and feel your way by ear and eye," as Eigner writes (150).

A good example of this multistable poetics is a poem that begins

to open your ears
            real music

    on the wire sparrows

or any other birds
      sit still

      their world dimensional

            more than dogs or cats
        or perhaps men (*Collected Poems* 600)

The perspective in the poem shifts to the more "dimensional" world of the sparrows, but this dimensionality also extends into the semantic world with "still," which could be temporal (the birds are "still" sitting on the wires) or spatial (the birds are not moving), so that when the next lines say "and listen / a moment of stillness / stick in the ear // a beginning and origin," the word "stillness" is paradoxically unstable, in motion.[27] The poet's words "stick in the ear" as the reader tries to nail down their semantic meaning, but they also serve as a "stick in the ear," a thrust or stab, a penetration that works to create new "origin[s]" of thought in the mind's eye and ear—a "dífférĕnt týmpănŭm," as Eigner writes in the poem's penultimate line. The two metrical dactyls become two "fingers" to "stick in the ears." Watten rightly argues that Eigner's poems "do not create an illusionistic space" of stable images but proceed instead "word to word, line to line" (176). Yet his projected verse does seem to create an illusionistic lexical space for the reader in which individual words can be experienced in their multidimensionality. Watch the word "it" later in the poem: "or stormy as it may be // an afternoon rain // how long it can seem to last // I think it's over there / the sky through the trees" (600). The use of "it" without an antecedent in the first line is known as a "prop" it ("it is stormy"). The second use seems to have a direct referent in "rain," but the very next line points ahead to a new referent in "sky." The poem concludes in this projected space where individual words glow with possibility and depth: "I imagine it shining" (*Collected Poems* 600).

The multidimensional form of poetic perception that Eigner's poems invite mimics the brain's methodology in multistable visual perception. As cognitive scientists David A. Leopold and Nikos K. Logothetis explain in a review of studies of multistability, when the eyes encounter a truly ambiguous figure, one that cannot be locked into a single solution, the brain persistently offers new perceptual hypotheses about the image. One staple of these exploratory behaviors is the introduction of randomness, such as saccadic eye movements, into the timing of perception in order to create variability. The reviewers state, "Perception might benefit from such randomness by constantly 'shaking-up' the organization of the input to allow for solutions that are not the most probable given the functional–anatomical constraints imposed by the visual pathways" (261).

Eigner illustrates and invokes such a process not only with individual ambiguous words but even with entire poems. He explains, "Accuracy of the moment is there in my pieces and others', and flimsy as mine often seem, there's a perfection too: they're petrified or frozen; artifacts. While a few times I've gotten two versions of a short thing I've been unable to decide between and couldn't resolve the dilemma, either, by thinking of a third—so I've put both versions side by side, with not indeterminate space between them, ahh!" (*areas* 151). The poem is shifting, unstable, offering two hypotheses that cannot be resolved into a coherent whole. In normal binocular vision, "you sniff / and smell a rose / and two get in your eyes," as Eigner writes (*Collected Poems* 1140). With a stereoscope, however, two quite different images can be shown to each eye, creating what is known as binocular rivalry. Though the brain processes both images, a higher-level selection process ensures that only one image is perceived at a time. The viewer thus experiences another multistable effect: the images fluctuate from one to the other (Leopold and Logothetis 262).

Eigner seems to play with this rivalry effect in his many two-columned poems, one of which begins "o n e o r t w o // t h i n g s c a n b e // s p e c u l a t e d" (*Collected Poems* 1663). Reading these poems, the eyes shift among the different versions. Again the effects of tiny words become apparent:

sun	sun some
walls	walls
years	white now
now	years (1293)

The more open poem on the left captures the sense of time's depth—how this moment, "now," in this room, is built on many other moments of sun shining on walls and, alternatively, on how the sun itself portions out time, "walls years." The addition of "some" and "white" in the version on the right considerably narrows our semantic understanding of the poem: the sun has made "some walls white now" after years of shining on them.[28] Yet this version is able to play more with sound, with the humming slant rhyme of "sun some," the alliteration of "walls / white," and the addition of the /i/ sound, making this tiny poem showcase all five vowels.[29]

Vision researcher Randolph Blake explains that the experience of binocular rivalry does not always mean that one image is dominant and the other suppressed. Many times, particularly after a long exposure, there is a "fluctuating patchwork" effect in which pieces of both views are intermingled (9). Eigner invites readers to "see each // thing // one // combination / or // another" (*Collected Poems* 1241), so if we read across the columns of the poem, the lines create an echo-chamber effect that highlights the repetitive nature of time: "sun sun some / walls walls / years white now / now years."[30] Another of Eigner's two-column poems can likewise be read as two separate columns or intermingled:

Steel mill out   in smokestacks

basketry and airshafts

Persepolis off the wall

ah!

one side to the other

faint shapes

back and forth

sound or

these dimensions to   time absorption

what other (*Collected Poems* 1443)

According to Eigner, the poem's structure was inspired by the artist Ronald King's plates in the poet's 1981 collection *earth / birds* (*Collected Poems*, note xxi), which create a three-dimensional effect with blind-embossed images of woven straps, ropes, and wood, punctuated by nails and holes at different intervals. (Blind embossing uses no ink, so the image is raised but uncolored.) In a similar fashion, Eigner's poem uses two columns to interweave the smokestacks of a contemporary steel mill with the columns of ancient Persepolis, creating a constellation of columns across the page and across space-time. The columns (historic and poetic) can and do exist separately from one another, but through the interweaving "basketry" of the lines, through the movement of the reader's eyes "back and forth" between them, their "faint shapes" emerge stereoscopically, bringing the two images together across time and space in a kind of "time absorption"—a phrase that, in floating outside the poem's established grid, crosses the horizontal lines of both columns.[31]

Just as the brain introduces "randomness" to visual perception in order to create new hypotheses, Eigner's poetics "shake up" the reader's perception, keeping his poems' meaning and form multistable. "Like a Dog Bark in Music," as he titles a prose piece in which he describes this poetics, "a poem *should* gain a reality capable of being renewed always, or an illusion of reality, by evoking, dragging in, or referring to something beyond the poem" (*areas* 27). Eigner's poems continually introduce randomness, leading a reader's brain to generate endlessly renewable hypotheses about them. Herein lies Eigner's sense of the transformative possibilities of an experimental poem: "no poetry can raise anyone's hopes for a medical cure, say, or any sort of miracle. Just 'refresh the eyes / against the abyss'" (*areas* 155). This quotation comes from a poem that Eigner wrote for Cid Corman that reads in its entirety, "how read it / line after line // given / one look // refresh the eyes / against the abyss" (*Collected Poems* 354). Experimental poems such as Eigner's are not going to "topple banks and bureaucracies, museums and markets," but the visual and linguistic multistability they produce refreshes the eyes and the ears, keeping the vibrant instability of language at the forefront of perception. Larry Eigner defines poetry, or at least "certain poems," as "pieces of language, nodes of language risen in thought out of the general continuum to prompt or orient us" (*areas* 27). The paradox of his multistable vision is clear here. Poems "orient" readers, but within a four-dimensional field whose reference points are projected and unstable; thus they also "prompt" readers, inciting and inspiring them to new forms of thinking, reminding them, like an actor's prompt, of how perception—both visual and lexical, abled and disabled—involves, at heart, a phenomenology of instability, oscillation, and creation.

Lighght Reading

CONCRETE AND VISPO

On June 30, 1970, the United States House of Representatives had their first debate over an experimental poem, which reads in its entirety:

lighght [.]

This concrete poem, written by Aram Saroyan, was selected by Robert Duncan to appear in a 1969 anthology funded by the newly formed National Endowment for the Arts. Like all the chosen writers, Saroyan was paid $500 for the entry, and the magazine where it first appeared received $250 (Daly).[1] It became the poster poem for Republicans eager to expose what they saw as the extravagancies of the NEA and the National Endowment for the Humanities.[2] Representative William J. Scherle, Republican from Iowa, was particularly offended by the poem and launched the analysis: "Has anyone figured out what 'Lighght' means? Can anyone even pronounce this poem?" He then quipped, "At that price,… it is certainly not free verse" (US Congress 22122).

Interestingly, Mr. Scherle was not the only detractor inspired into such punning and wordplay by the poem. He read several newspaper articles

and editorials about the offending text into the record, including one entitled "Taxpayers foot $750 'Lighght' Bill" (US Congress 22122) and another
"Things are Getting Verse and Verse" (22124). Several critics were inspired
to write their own experimental poems in response, including "DARARK"
and "Shockockock!" (22124). The poem also launched quite a few creative
efforts into interpreting the word's meaning. An article in Iowa's *Waterloo
Courier* explained in a mocking mise en abyme, "Obviously, there is only
one meaning for 'lighght.' It is a word for something so stupid that there
is no existing word in the language capable of expressing the stupidity"
(22123). Two other congressmen did some research. Representative
Randall "looked it up in every dictionary in our office" and couldn't find it,
"not even [in] the big 3,270-page Merriam-Webster unabridged volume"
(22145). Representative Hall turned philosophical, wondering, "In connection with the so-called word which has been bandied about today so much,
I would like to ask first of all what is a word?" After also consulting "the
biggest dictionary I can find," he ultimately determined "lighght" is
"a group of consonants and one lonely vowel" that "is very much like a
word." Consequently, he tried out some creative etymology of his own:
"Maybe it is related to the old Scotch song about: 'It's a braw bricht moon-
light nicht, tonicht'" (22131).

Like these congressional critics, I am interested in the nature of letters
and words and how we "read" poems like "lighght." Their response,
though derogatory, offers some potentially new ways of thinking about the
transformative effects of experimentalism and visual poetry more specifically. The literary critical response to Saroyan's poem and to concrete
poetry as a genre has generally emphasized that it is meant to be seen
rather than read (Solt 7). Saroyan himself says that "it doesn't have a
reading process.... Even a five-word poem has a beginning, middle, and
end. A one-word poem doesn't. You can see it all at once. It's instant"
(qtd. in Daly). But just because you see it in an instant doesn't mean that
you're not reading it. Even the tiniest words involve a "reading process"
in the brain. Indeed, given the poem's placement in an anthology of other
works to be read and its grouping of letters of the same size and font into
the spacing of a single word, a viewer's initial, unavoidable response would
be to attempt to "read" the word, as the congressmen did. What happens

when "lighght" enters the brain through the eye (or, perhaps more accurately, the "eyeye"—another concrete poem by Saroyan) (E. Williams)?

According to cognitive neuroscientist Stanislas Dehaene, the adult brain has two unique pathways for processing language that "coexist and supplement each other while we read" (38). The "phonological route" is used for new or unfamiliar words and neologisms. We first convert the letter strings into speech sounds and then attempt to access the meaning of the sound pattern (38). The "lexical route" takes over for frequently used words and those words whose pronunciation does not match their spelling (a common phenomenon in English). In this more direct route, we recall the identity and meaning of the word and use the lexical information to recover its pronunciation, if necessary (38).[3] Children first learning to read rely heavily on the phonological route. As their expertise grows, they are able to stop sounding out familiar words and can read more quickly via the lexical route. Dehaene explains, "It takes only twenty or thirty milliseconds of word viewing for our brain to automatically activate a word's spelling, but an additional forty milliseconds for its transformation into sound, as revealed by the emergence of sound-based priming" (29).

The word-poem "lighght" seems to engage and then confound both of these pathways. It looks initially like a familiar word whose spelling is unhelpful phonically, so we want to quickly recall the word "light" via our soundless, letter-to-meaning reading. However, those extra consonants perplex that easy lexical route, sending the word down the phonological route for unfamiliar words. How do we pronounce this word? What sound does *gh* make in the familiar word "light"? In other words? We tell new readers of English that the *gh* in such words is silent. Does this mean that "lighght" should be pronounced with more silence? Or, as in the different double g's in "suggest," is the second *gh* pronounced? If so, how? Like the hard *g* in "ugh," or the soft /f/ sound of "rough" and "enough"? Or perhaps, as Representative Hall intuits, it should be pronounced as a voiceless velar fricative, the rasp at the back of the throat in Old English that the *gh* once represented, a vestigial tail that words such as "bright," "light," and "night" still bear.

Maybe the brain's reading processors give up and begin to see the word more as "sculptural," as Saroyan hopes (Daly). But the poem definitely highlights the ways that reading visual poetry can work to activate the brain's reading mechanisms with revolutionary potential. Rosmarie Waldrop describes the power of concrete poetry: "it presents a text (and thereby 'reality') not as something given, fixed, to be accepted, but as a structure that can be seen differently from different perspectives and can therefore be changed" (56). Indeed, contemporary brain science reveals the ways that this revolutionary potential of processing ambiguity is built into the brain itself. Dehaene writes, "When our nervous system is confronted with ambiguity, its fundamental strategy is to leave all possibilities open— something that is only feasible in a massively parallel system where multiple interpretations can be simultaneously entertained" (50). This chapter will explore the ways that concrete and visual poetry can work to expose, confound, and even reshape these various cognitive mechanisms behind the act of reading—not only through the destructive affect of shock but also through the generative acts of meaning making that they initiate.

Concrete in Context

A simple definition of concrete poetry is poetry that is meant to be seen. While everyday texts allow us to see *through* words to the meanings they represent, concrete poems disrupt that act, forcing us to look at the word itself—its letters and syllables, its shape on the page (Waldrop 47). Yet it remains a hybrid genre, both visual and verbal, both seen and read.[4] This multimodal text allows us not only to see words but also the act of reading itself. If, as Rosmarie Waldrop writes, "concrete poetry is first of all a revolt against [the] transparency of the word" (47), then it is also a revolt against the transparent, easy fluency of reading.

Critics and taxonomists of visual poetry often describe a kind of continuum of the interplay of visual and verbal elements in the poems, with differing conceptual approaches behind that relationship (Higgins; Barry). The founder of the genre of concrete poetry, Eugen Gomringer, a Bolivian-born Swiss artist, began writing what he called constellations in 1951. For Gomringer and many early practitioners, the goal was to write a poem that was startlingly simple, understandable by readers of many languages, "as easily understood as signs in airports and traffic signs"

```
silencio silencio silencio
silencio silencio silencio
silencio         silencio
silencio silencio silencio
silencio silencio silencio
```

"Untitled [silencio]" (1954). Courtesy of Eugen Gomringer.

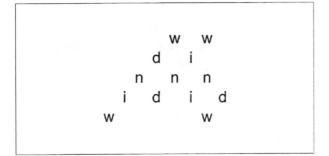

"wind" (1953). Courtesy of Eugen Gomringer.

(qtd. in Solt 70). They rejected the insular transparency of word meanings for a native speaker in favor of the universality of word as object. Marjorie Perloff suggests that this early concrete poetry may have been a reaction against the linguistic and national borders being drawn and reasserted in the postwar era. Here was a poetry that ostensibly transcended such borders (*Unoriginal* 64).

In an odd coincidence, many poets around the world were also writing poems in this mode at midcentury, often unbeknownst to one another. Gomringer's book *constellations* came out in 1953, the same year that Öyvind Fahlström of Sweden published his "Manifest för konkret poesie" (Solt 8). The Noigandres group—Haroldo de Campos, Décio Pignatari, and Augusto de Campos—were publishing similar "verbivocovisual" poems in Brazil.[5] By the 1960s, American poet Jonathan Williams could write, "If there is such a thing as a worldwide movement in the art of poetry, Concrete is it" (qtd. in E. Williams vii). Concrete poetry was thus a diverse international art movement with practitioners who often worked in three dimensions and made extensive use of the material processes of publishing; its cultural work relied on its embeddedness in particular publications and art venues. Craig Dworkin, for example, in *Radium of the Word* offers an analysis of the work of Russell Atkins, who wrote at the intersection of the Black nationalist movement and the concrete poetry scene in Cleveland in the 1960s. Though the concrete movement was never as energetic in the United States as it was internationally, it was well represented by two influential anthologies from American presses at the time: *An Anthology of Concrete Poetry* (1967), edited by Emmett Williams, and *Concrete Poetry: A World View* (1970), edited by Mary Ellen Solt, both of which include more international poets than American writers. My analyses here focus on poems from these anthologies, so my claims are about the effects of reading this particular version of concrete aesthetics, not necessarily about concrete poetry as a whole.

Solt's comprehensive introduction connects the movement to projective verse, noting the similarities between the concrete concept of "form = content / content = form" and Olson/Creeley's assertion that "form is never more than an extension of content" (48). Both seek a "composition by field," using the space of the page to convey "the kinetics of the thing" (Olson, *Collected Prose* 243, 240). While projective verse is launched from the breath and speech of the poet's body, as we saw in chapter 3, concrete poetry's lines of force emerge from the body of the word itself. As Emmett Williams writes in his anthology's introduction, "The visual element in their poetry tended to be structural, a consequence of the poem, a 'picture' of the lines of force of the work itself, and not merely textural. It was a poetry far beyond paraphrase, a poetry that often asked to be completed or activated by the reader, a poetry of direct presentation" (vi). Rather than words as "representation," pointing toward a signified, these are words of "direct presentation," pointing at their own inherent lines and structures. I appreciate the fact that Williams still calls the "activator" of concrete poems the "reader," not just a "viewer." What role does reading play in an encounter with a concrete poem, and what impact can these verbivocovisual lines of force have on readers?

Interestingly, many writers consider concrete poetry to be a failed experiment. In an oft-quoted line, French critic François Rigolot dismissed it as a "frivolous pastime" (qtd. in Bohn 13), and Caroline Bayard finds its doctrine of isomorphism, the potential fusion of sign and object, to be problematic, even dangerous (15). To its detractors, at its best, concrete poetry is too obvious and naive, like an elementary school project; at its worst, it is ideologically suspect—too much like ad copy.[6] However, concrete poetry is currently experiencing a renaissance among contemporary artists and scholars. Kenneth Goldsmith, for example, reads concrete poetry as a protodigital poetics, a genre that has finally found its true medium on the web.[7]

Marjorie Perloff makes a compelling argument for concretism as *arrière-garde,* the rear guard to modernism's vanguard of visual experimentation—completing its mission, ensuring its success (*Unoriginal* 53); she is right to point out concrete poets' indebtedness to their modernist predecessors. Gomringer borrowed the term "constellations" from Mallarmé (Webster 142). The Noigandres group took their name from a line in Pound's "Canto XX" (Perloff, *Unoriginal* 65). Indeed, the origin of the term "concrete poetry" seems to be from Ernest Fenollosa's book on the Chinese ideogram, so significant to Pound (Bayard 18).[8] According to Perloff, while avant-garde visual poetry at the turn of the century represents a rejection of its nineteenth-century predecessors and an act of "discovery" of a new poetics, concrete poetry at midcentury demonstrates a "respect bordering on veneration" in its act of "recovery" of the old (*Unoriginal* 56). Perloff acknowledges the differences between modernist and midcentury visual poetry, interpreting concrete poetry in relation to its particular historico-cultural moment, but ultimately, the major distinction she cites is their contrasting relationship to the past. The avant-garde started the war to break with its "stultifying" past, while the *arrière-garde* wholly embraces and carries on the fight of its predecessors (*Unoriginal* 55). Yet distinctions exist between the modernist and postmodernist avant-gardes in visual poetry, which are aesthetic as well as historical.

Modernist visual poetics often refers back to an authorial intention and the politics *in* the poem, while Concrete aesthetics, and its vispo heirs, aim more at readerly attention and the politics *of* the poem. Take, for example, F. T. Marinetti's *Après la Marne, Joffre visita le front en auto* (After

F. T. Marinetti, *Après la Marne, Joffre visita le front en auto* (1915).

the Marne, Joffre visited the front by car), a poster poem from his famous futurist book *Zang Tumb Tumb* (1915). An account of Marinetti's work as a journalist at the battle of Adrianople in the Balkan war, the poem uses *parole in libertá* (words in freedom—creative typography, onomatopoeia, etc.) to convey poetic impressions of the battle.

Michael Webster emphasizes Marinetti's clues to readers to figure out his intent, including the title and the description at the lower right of the text, "Dynamic verbalization of the route." The large *M* and *V* shapes thus act pictorially as mountains with the curving *S*'s of Joffre's route winding through them. The onomatopoetic "tatatatatata" and "TOUMB TOUM" create the soundscape of the battle.[9] As for the numbers and mathematical signs, Marinetti explains in a manifesto that they are "fit to render the mechanical shifting of gears in an automobile" (qtd. in Webster 39). Marinetti expected readers to intuitively grasp the meaning of his complex semiotics, relying on "the indestructible correspondences of sensibility" (qtd. in Webster 40). Though a viewer could certainly read against the grain of his system of signs, Marinetti clearly has a representational, even political, intent behind the text. Webster's close reading of the details reveals its unsubtle politics. It begins:

> With … a careful reading of those parts of the text that form recognizable words, the reader can gather that the poem celebrates the beauty of war ("BELLE," and "GUERRE" appear at the left), that it endorses the French side over the Germans, and that it celebrates the speed and power of the automobile that carries Joffre to the front. (At the upper right, words "vitesssss" [speed], "spirale pneumatique" [pneumatic spiral, or flying wheels?], "virer" [to turn], and "coup de volant" [turn of the wheel] appear.) (36)

When it comes to politics, literary critics of the avant-garde have suggested an important differentiation to be made between the politics *in* and *of* the poem.[10] The politics *in* the poem indicates poetry with political content—Marinetti's take on the war in "Apres" or Adrienne Rich's feminist lyrics, for example. In contrast, as Craig Dworkin explains, the politics *of* the poem is "what is signified by its form, enacted by its structures, implicit in its philosophy of language, how it positions its reader, and a range of questions relating to the poem as a material object" (*Reading* 4–5). The formal aspects of Marinetti's poster poem seem to work in service of the politics *in* the poem. The poem positions its reader to intuit the author's intent. As Webster argues, "Never interested in the word as symbol, [Marinetti] valued intuitive comprehension, quick syntheses, spoken declamation—in short, propaganda" (40).[11]

Postwar visual poetry signifies through its form and positions its reader not so much to convey a particular meaning or writerly *intention* but rather to engage the reader's *attention* toward the material and the act of reading itself. However, in calling attention to form, these poems do not take their place alongside the New Criticism–influenced verse also being written at midcentury. Instead, visual poetry positions its reader for a radical formalism, as Craig Dworkin describes it, "pursu[ing] the closest of close readings *in the service of* political questions, rather than to their exclusion" (*Reading* 5).[12] The formalist notion of close reading is something the reader does to the poem, but in the case of visual poetry, I argue that radical formalism is something the poem does to the reader, allowing us to see the readingness in close reading. Some changes occur as this poetry shifts from "clean" concrete forms represented in the Solt and Williams anthologies to a "dirty" aesthetic in the 1970s that continues into twenty-first century vispo.[13] Clean or dirty, all of these poems rely on and ultimately work to confound the various brain processes associated with reading. Clean concrete poems play on the material limits of the brain's letter box, while the messier vispo triggers some fascinating positive effects of disfluency on cognition.

Concrete Poetry and the Origin of Letters

The first phase of visual poetry at midcentury that emerged in the Solt and Williams anthologies had a clean aesthetic that often aimed for isomorphism, the fusion of word, shape, and meaning, as in Gomringer's "silencio" and "wind" poems. The Noigandres poets wrote in their "Pilot Plan" manifesto: "In a first moment of concrete poetry pragmatics, isomorphism tends to physiognomy, that is a movement imitating natural appearance (*motion*); organic form and phenomenology of composition prevail" (Solt 72). This was Pound and Fenollosa's dream for the Chinese ideogram—which proved untrue, of course; only about 2 percent of Chinese characters have pictographic content. Japanese concrete poet Seiichi Niikuni's ideographic poem in the Williams anthology is a good example. The kanji character composed of three lines on the left side is *kawa*, "river," while the character on the right side, which adds three marks to the original symbol, is *sasu*, "sandbank."[14] The ideograms take on the atomistic structure of what they represent; one is more open and liquid, the other more dense and solid.[15]

Seiichi Niikuni
kawa = river
sasu = sand-bank

"River/Sandbank" by Seiichi Niikuni (1966). Courtesy of Kenjiro Miura.

This dream of the fusion of linguistic matter and the real world it represents may have a basis in brain physiology. Dehaene explains the cognitive origins of the alphabet and how these origins affect the brain's reading processes. His book begins with a paradox. Our ability to read is a cultural activity that was invented only a few thousand years ago, yet the literate brain contains "specialized cortical mechanisms that are exquisitely attuned to the recognition of written words. Even more surprisingly, the same mechanisms, in all humans, are systematically housed in identical brain regions, as though there were a cerebral organ for reading" (4). This "organ" is too recent in human history, however, for it to have evolved for this purpose. Dehaene argues that these neuronal networks, having evolved to do other things, are now being "recycled" by the brain for the purposes of reading (2), noting, "Our cortex did not specifically evolve for writing. Rather writing evolved to fit the cortex" (171).

Japanese neuroscientist Keiji Tanaka has discovered a possible evolutionary source for our alphabets in his research on the monkey brain—an area dedicated to fragments of shape that can be combined to understand any complex form (Dehaene 133). Many of the preferred shapes of this area of the brain closely resemble our letters, symbols, or elementary Chinese characters (137). But where did these protoletters come from? Dehaene's hypothesis is that they were selected and preferred because these are shapes that are essential to parsing scenes in the real world (137). Line combinations such as the Roman alphabet capital letters *F*, *Y*, and *T*, for example, are also important forms that help apes (including

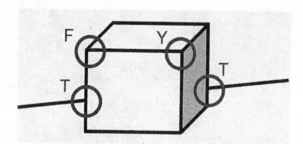

us) to determine 3-D-ness—what's in front of what. Our memory does not store extremely detailed images of these configurations; instead, "it merely extracts a sketch of their non-accidental properties," the lines, for help when encountering other similar combinations (138). Dehaene explains, "We did not invent most of our letter shapes: they lay dormant in our brains for millions of years, and were merely rediscovered when our species invented writing and the alphabet" (139).

The characters in worldwide writing systems also seem to have evolved into an optimal form that can be grasped by a single neuron, usually three strokes (plus or minus one). Marc Changizi and Shinsuke Shimojo at Caltech discovered this regularity in their cross-cultural analysis of 115 writing systems (Dehaene 177). Changizi also determined that the arrangement of individual strokes had a similar pattern, following "a universal distribution that closely parallels the features of natural scenes" (Dehaene 178). Inventors of alphabets around the world seemed to intuit that the characters they designed should be the easiest to read, so they modeled those signs after shapes found in the environment (178).

Concrete poets also seem to intuit these traits of writing systems, calling attention to them by breaking the cognitive rules. Aram Saroyan's poster-poem violates the brain's preference for 3 ± 1 strokes. The Roman letter *M* maxes out at four strokes, but Saroyan adds two more. With its unfamiliar extra strokes, this letter-poem confounds the translation of image to meaning in the brain's letter box.[16] The letter becomes an object again, expanding the cognitive work into surrounding areas of visual

Untitled poster poem (1965). Used by permission of Aram Saroyan.

analysis in the cortex. When I showed this poem to my students, they began by talking about *M* and *N,* but they quickly began to see it as a representation of an object in the real world—arches, doorways, even a camel or a cow (which makes a sound like "mmmmmm," they pointed out).

Hansjörg Mayer plays with this principle in a different way in his *alphabetenquadratbuch 1.* Originally published as a thirteen-page portfolio, its sequence of squares is condensed to four pages in the Williams anthology. The first square is empty; in the second, an "a" appears, followed by "b c d" in the third and "e f g h" in the fourth. The letters (in Futura font) initially appear to be placed randomly; like Gomringer's constellations, they might be stars slowly emerging in the night sky. The remaining letters of the alphabet emerge, scattered across the following squares, until by square seven, all twenty-six are accounted for.[17] The next page in the Williams anthology contains six squares that continue to fill up with more and more letters, and now the viewer can see that the letters are not naturally configured like stars in the sky but laid out in a 26 × 26 grid. By square twelve, each space in the grid is filled, with the horizontal lines containing every letter of the alphabet in various seemingly arbitrary combinations. Though this square looks like a giant word-search puzzle, Mayer appears to have avoided putting letters together that would combine to make words. In this way the letters become legible as objects in a system, although this English reader couldn't help but notice the significant poetic word "lyre" at the beginning of the sixth line and the word "jailer" at the exact center of the block. If Mayer finds the now rigid system of the alphabet (and the lyric?) and its limited combinatorial possibilities to be a "jailer," then he works to explode that system in square thirteen. In this final square, which is also enlarged and reprinted on the fourth page, the block has been printed four times on itself, each time turned one quarter, effectively effacing the lines of each letter with too many strokes. The resulting characters, composed of ten to twelve strokes each, put the brain's letter box on cognitive overload. The stacked letters look like the alphabet of an alien civilization, too complex for our simple brains to comprehend.

The fact that the world's writing systems are "recycling" older visual processes in the brain can also lead to some interesting problems in the act of reading. Take the issue of symmetry. When we learn a visual

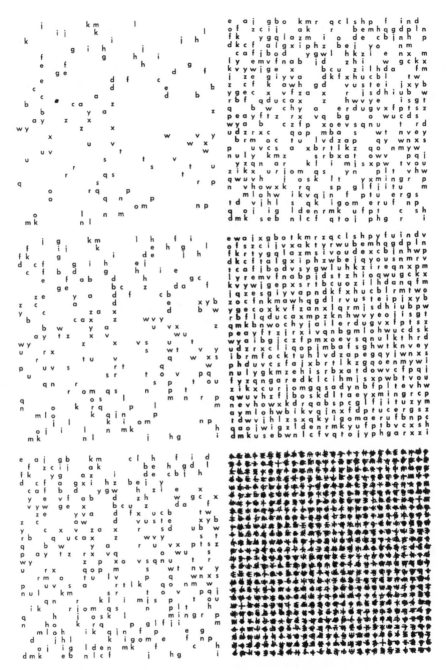

Image from *alphabetenquadratbuch 1* (1965). Courtesy of Hansjörg Mayer.

shape in the real world, we extend that knowledge to its mirror image. Distinguishing left from right is thus not so important, evolutionarily speaking (Dehaene 267). For example, the F-shaped junctions that help us make sense of 3-D objects in the real world can face right or left, and even up or down. This explains why new readers and writers often go through a "mirror-writing" stage, according to Dehaene, where their letters are flipped backward (265).

Illustration from *Reading in the Brain: The Science and Evolution of a Human Invention*, copyright 2009 by Stanislas Dehaene. Used by permission of Viking Books, an imprint of Penguin Publishing Group, a division of Penguin Random House LLC. All rights reserved. For UK version, used by permission of Stanislas Dehaene. All rights reserved.

The poet Diter Rot, in "Some variations on 4^4," plays with this deficiency/ability of the reading brain by having us mind our p's and q's—literally. The poem consists of different spatial configurations of four /p/ shapes, lined up in eight rows and sixteen columns. The effect of taking in the entire poem is initially pictorial, a dance of filigrees, cloverleafs, bracelets, and water spiders. Zoom in fractally on individual clusters, however, and the brain's letter box kicks in. When the letters appear in their usual vertical orientation, they are easily identified, as in the top left-hand corner "db/db." But the letters' shifting position along multiple axes disorients the Roman alphabet reader's ingrained left–right methodology, asking us to mind our d's and q's as well. When the letters turn horizontal, the poem takes the reading brain back to its childhood confusion with a new mirror-reading effect. Are those four d's or four p's lying on their side and back to back, or two of each? Is this one made up of two b's and two q's, or is it a quadruple exposure of a single letter b rotated around an axis? In a sense, the letter shape becomes four dimensional in this poem, flipping up, down, left, and right, pivoting and twirling in space and across time.

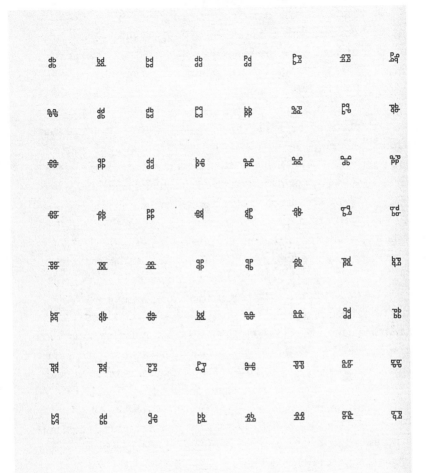

"Some variations on 4⁴" (1957). Copyright Dieter Roth Estate, courtesy of Hauser & Wirth.

Though our brain's letter box is deeply connected to its visions of the real world, Dehaene's research undercuts the traditional belief that writing systems began as solely iconic pictograms. "In most painted caves," he writes, "drawings of animals cohabit with a rich set of nonfigurative shapes: series of dots, parallel lines, checkerboards, abstract curves" (183); "From the start, writing was used to express abstract ideas" (185). Editor Emmett Williams also references cave painting in his foreword to *An Anthology of Concrete Poetry,* but only in order to resist the definition of concrete poetry as a return to "poem as picture," as merely the opposite of "abstract" poetry (v). He would appreciate that even cave paintings may have functioned more like concrete poetry, with an interplay of visual picture and abstract code. One good example of this interplay appears in José Lino Grünewald's poem "dois bois" (Two oxen). It begins "bois / bois," using the word (oxen) as abstract code, representation. The next "stanza," "dois / dois," can be read as even more abstract, as the word "dois" is itself representing an abstraction, the number two, and yet with the doubling of the lines, the poem begins to concretize that twoness, so the reader sees it. The "two oxen" appear paired together in the next couplet "dois / bois," and then the two are concretely linked in the final iconic line, where the *d* and *b* are merged along a shared vertical line creating an image of a yoke ("dbois"). The editor includes an explanatory note from Grünewald's fellow Noigandres poet, Haroldo de Campos, beneath the poem: "From digit to ideogram, d and b like two yoked oxen." But even de Campos's comment here involves abstraction. The *d* and *b* are yoked together *"like* two oxen"; this is an ideogram, not a pictogram. The two letters, back to back, form the shape not of two oxen but of a yoke—what connects the two oxen, but never the oxen themselves. Paradoxically, then, concrete poetry can work to highlight the abstract code behind reading and the alphabet.

The act of reading begins in the brain's letter box, and it makes sense that many writers of concrete poetry would focus their visual experiments on its cognitive quirks and abilities. But reading doesn't stop there. The letters have to be put together to make phonemes, words, and meaning. Using fine-grained magnetoencephalography, researchers at MIT have been able to watch in real time how a word lights up the brain. After about 250 milliseconds, the act of reading stops being exclusively visual and begins to connect to spoken-language networks on the way to making meaning (Dehaene 104). Semantics uses a widespread array of regions scattered throughout the brain, none of which is exclusive to the written word (Dehaene 109). Dehaene gives the example of reading the word "bite." Areas associated with the mouth and teeth are engaged along with associations related to eating or pain. "All of these fragments of gesture, motion, and sensation are bound together under the heading 'bite'" (112). Dehaene chooses the interesting metaphor of a tidal bore to describe how a word can activate these fragments dispersed throughout the brain. At high tide, the rivers and estuaries leading into the ocean are subject to this phenomenon whereby a massive wave can raise the water level in the entire system (though no saltwater ever reaches that far inland) (113). Much like this natural phenomenon, Dehaene explains, "a known word resonates in the temporal lobe networks and produces a massive wave of synchronized oscillations that rolls through millions of neurons. This tidal bore goes even as far as the more distant regions of the cortex as it successively contacts the many assemblies of neurons that each encode a fragment of the word's meaning" (114).

A concrete poem by Bob Cobbing offers a nice visual analog to this tidal bore effect of a word in the brain.[18] Michael Davidson sees the poem as conveying a downward movement, similar to Apollinaire's famous raindrops in "Il Pleut," that converges on the word complex "w ow r om wro rmm" at the end. Cobbing double strikes the letters of the words dripping down the page, creating, for Davidson, a visual sense of decay that is reflected in the semantics of the words themselves ("crumbling," "corpse," and "mouldering") (*Ghostlier* 16). The starting point of this poem may also be read as the strange word complex itself. Indeed, as the clearest letters in the poem, and the only ones placed in a traditional left-to-right format, this is where my gaze was first drawn. Cobbing confounds both the lexical and the phonological routes for reading with his strange, elongated evocation of "worm." But like "pseudo-homophones" such as "hed" or "wimen" that Dehaene mentions (115), the letters eventually evoke a familiar word for readers. The estuaries of blurry words radiating out embody the multiple strands of associations evoked when that familiar word is finally deduced. Each individual "stream" consists of words linked to one another,

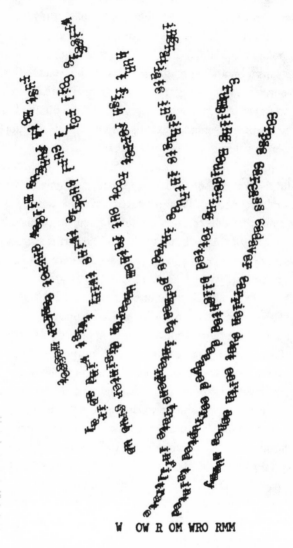

W OW R OM WRO RMM

"W OW R OM WRO RMM" (1966). Courtesy of the Estate of Bob Cobbing.

thesaurus style, as synonyms organized by different parts of speech. One line of nouns contains synonyms for a dead body ("corpse," "cadaver," "mummy"), another includes things that can cause decay ("rust," "mildew," "maggot"), and a line of participles conveys how we might describe these objects of decay ("rotted," "blighted," "corrupted"). Other estuaries wriggle with verbs we associate with "worm-ing," both literal ("coil," "twist," "wind") and metaphorical ("ingratiate," "intrude," "infiltrate"). Cobbing's poem shows us the massive tidal bore of fragments of meanings and associative links that a single word can set off in the brain. Reading the poem from bottom to top in this way reveals not "the mortal end of letters," as Davidson writes (*Ghostlier* 16), but the massive generativity of letters. Waves of blurry words vibrate with life, motion, ambiguity, and possibility.

Interestingly for the purposes of a cognitive study of experimental poetry, Dehaene's research suggests that a nonword such as "croil" doesn't initially trigger the same waves of activity in the brain that a word like "worm" or "cheese" will. "An unknown word,... even if it gets through the first stages of visual analysis, finds no echo in the cortex and the wave it triggers is quickly broken down into inarticulate cerebral foam" (114). Yet what cerebral Aphrodite might arise from that foam? What happens after that quarter second of nonrecognition if the nonword is encountered in the real world outside the laboratory? What if readers are told that it is a word, and they have to figure out the meaning? What if they are told that it's a poem? "Croil," for example, could generate many semantic possibilities: a portmanteau noun meaning a creek tainted by oil, or a verb meaning to toil in a crawling position. In fact, the Urban Dictionary says it means to "cry oil," as a Transformer robot might. As Dehaene notes, sometimes only the context of the sentence where the word appears can help us grasp its meaning. Without that context, the brain's "fundamental strategy is to leave all possibilities open" (50).

To return to the concrete poem "lighght" with which we began, this nonword seemed to have interesting generative effects on its experimental subjects in the US House of Representatives. While these congressmen were focused on the politics *in* the poem, the money from the National Endowment for the Arts that funded it, they unwittingly fell victim to the politics *of* the poem. They created puns, definitions, speculative etymologies, and even their own concrete poems in response. Representative Randall complains, "There is no text to the poem; no explanation as to what these letters mean as they are strung together … and when they are all strung together, capitalized and highlighted, they make no more sense than 'zQxQzQ'" (22145). He is wrong that "lighght" makes no more sense than his string of consonants. Dehaene even did an experiment with such consonant strings and found the brain's orthographic filter quickly separates them from "legal" letter strings that do not violate spelling rules (114). Still, the representative's poem shows the generative possibilities of reading concrete poetry. Visually, his poem creates a nice balance of angles and circles; including three capital Q's in one word highlights the unusualness of its little tail among the letters. Indeed, we might read his poem as a celebration of the three least utilized letters of the alphabet—and the keyboard. Mr. Randall wrote a poem that is perhaps the most difficult word to type of all time.

Though the clean forms of some midcentury concrete poetry may initially appear to be mere formal exercises scrubbed of political content, some attention to the politics *of* the poem reveals a new and powerful utility. A concrete aesthetics offers an even more radical materialism than its culture-jamming avant-garde predecessors by calling attention to the evolutionary roots of the sign in the material world itself and the resulting constraints on the embodied act of reading. Concrete poems play on and test those limits—not just to shock and destroy old ways of thinking but also to open the mind for what new forms of thinking and meaning making may come in their wake.[19]

Vispo and the Demolition of Letters

While concrete poets wholly embraced the modernist avant-garde, contemporary poets writing vispo clearly want to avoid associations with their concrete forebears. The most comprehensive collection of this work to date, *The Last Vispo Anthology: Visual Poetry, 1998–2008* (2012), edited by Nico Vassilakis and Crag Hill, is filled with flat-out rejections—concrete poetry is "technique without tectonics" (11), a "failure" (203)—and alternative genealogies in "the plastic arts" (201) and objectivist poetics (11). In the 1970s, visual poets began to shift from a clean to a dirty, more disfluent aesthetic. (Cobbing's worm poem offers a good transitional example.) If concrete poems were universal semiotic artifacts meant to be read, then contemporary vispo texts are phenomenological, meant to be experienced; indeed, the operative verb in the essays in the *Last Vispo* is "stare" (8). The following two "she/he" poems offer an instructive study in this contrast. At left is Pedro Xisto's "Epithalamium II" from the Solt concrete anthology (114). With the orderly arrangement of crisp typography (and a helpful legend), the Brazilian poet tells the story of the marriage of Adam and Eve. John Vieira's vispo "(S)HE" contains the same three letters, but they appear in different fonts and are placed more haphazardly (*Last Vispo* 194). While Xisto's poem celebrates the balanced unity of the traditional "epithalamium" marriage, the messy hand-drawn cartoon figures in the vispo poem make its meaning much more ambiguous. The

LEFT: "Epithalamium II" by Pedro Xisto (1969). Courtesy of Lia Robatto.
RIGHT: "(S)HE" (*Last Vispo* 194). Courtesy of John Vieira.

ABOVE: "The Message" (*Last Vispo* 24). Copyright Oded Ezer (2001).

RIGHT: "Fusion Series No. 1531" (*Last Vispo* 58). Courtesy of Cecil Touchon.

male figures on page 117 appear defiant in their facial expressions and body language, perhaps as they stand atop the more female-looking figure beside the *s* below them. At the same time, the lines of the male bodies seem to grow more feminine and/or blend with the female body's lines. The poem can suggest both the isolation and domination of the "she" by the "he," as well as the complexity and fluidity of gender identity.

While midcentury concrete poetry, as represented by Solt and Williams, used its fluent forms to call attention to the material act of reading, contemporary vispo often plays with the disruptive and generative possibilities of disfluency on the brain's reading processes. Concrete poets break language down into what they see as its smallest elements—words and letters[20]—but vispo writers find that even these seemingly basic elements can be atomized, decomposed. Many poems in the *Vispo Anthology* can be described as asemic writing—that is, writing with no semantic content, subverbal and subletteral. Reed Altemus's "Asemic Detail" looks like an ancient script engraved on a tomb, its meaning worn away by time and the elements. Illegible typescript appears to loosen itself from the page in Oded Ezer's "The Message." In his "Fusion Series," Cecil Touchon makes a similar move with found letters, fragmenting them to disguise their identity and collaging them together.

While concrete poetry stimulates and confounds the brain's letter box by violating various cognitive rules and expectations, contemporary visual poetry blows up the box. Intriguingly, the brain's letter box lies between areas in the ventral occipitotemporal region that show peak responses to seeing faces and tools (Dehaene 74). Moreover, such visual preferences overlap; the regions that respond most to faces also show some activity when responding to letters and tools (76). This placement and overlap make sense; our letters are as familiar and alive as faces, as useful and valuable as tools. Indeed, the first stage of reading for children begins in a logographic or pictorial stage, where the visual system recognizes words by their shape, as though they were faces or tools (Dehaene 200). By fragmenting letter shapes, vispo texts seem to return readers to this pictorial stage of reading as they hunt for and fail to synthesize the familiar shapes that help make meaning. Though both of the brain's hemispheres are initially stimulated in this visual analysis area when seeing a face or a string of letters, words quickly get funneled to the left and faces to the right (Dehaene 77). Like sound poetry, addressed in chapter 5, visual poetry can potentially prevent the expert reader's easy shift to the left hemisphere for word processing as the image crosses and recrosses the corpus callosum, the bundle of nerves connecting the two parts of the brain. Is it a letter or a meaningless line? Is it read, or is it seen?

Christian Bök's series of *Odalisques* seems to intuit the close cognitive relationship between faces, letters, and tools. Using the twenty-one shapes that can form every letter of the alphabet, Bök composed drawings that resemble lounging nude women. In keeping with the feats of poetic constraint that characterize much of Bök's work, each figure must use all twenty-one shapes in various configurations and scales, but without repeating. Permit me a historical digression to illuminate this work. In *The Alphabetic Labyrinth*, a study of the alphabet in history and art, Johanna Drucker describes how the rise of printing during the Renaissance led to a standardization and rationalization of the alphabet (161). Prominent artists, mathematicians, and printers of the time created "constructed alphabets" alongside treatises for "the just shaping of letters" (163).[21] One of the most significant of these alphabets, Champfleury (1529), was constructed by French printer Geoffrey Tory, whose basis for the formation and proportion of each capital letter was the human figure itself (164).

LEFT: From *Odalisques* (*Last Vispo* 227). Courtesy of Christian Bök.
RIGHT: From *Odalisques* (*Last Vispo* 229). Courtesy of Christian Bök.

Whereas the early modern printer projects the idealized human body and the indecomposable majuscule onto a rational, proportional grid, the postmodern poet takes the exploded fragments of the alphabet to rebuild a body. Moreover, unlike Tory's robust, fleshly male bodies mapping cleanly and holistically onto the thick lines of each letter, Bök's female bodies emerge as a gestalt effect in the white spaces between the letter fragments. Their borders elusive and slippery, their existence a mere trick of the brain, they highlight the body's constitution within language and the body of language itself. Named "odalisques" or concubines, they are both pretty faces and tools for those who would exploit them.[22] The rational forms of these constructed alphabets and type "faces" at the origin of printing were constructed to be clear and endlessly repeatable, unlike the messy and unique manuscript forms created by human scribes. Bök's deconstructed

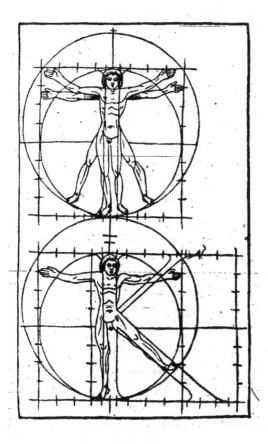

Geoffrey Tory's constructed *T* and *K* based on human proportions; from *Champfleury* (1529) (Drucker, *Alphabetic Labyrinth* 163).

alphabets and those of other vispo poets find aesthetic, even political, value in the broken, blurry, fragmented, and illegible.[23]

Cognitive science is beginning to uncover the power of such disfluency on the brain. The reading brain is a cognitive miser, preferring fluent letters that are easy to read. This preference is so strong that it can even translate into a reader's assessment of the material's content; people consistently rate easily processed stimuli to be more likable, valuable, moral, and accurate (Alter 437). The brain is thus seduced by easily formed conclusions. Here is an example. How many of each kind of animal did Moses take aboard the ark? In one study, 90 percent of people wrongly answered two. Did you? The correct answer is none. It was Noah, of course, not Moses, who sailed on the ark. The brain quickly glides over the name to the question about the number of animals. However, when this same question was asked in a disfluent font (twelve-point gray Brush Script), the error rate fell to 53 percent (Alter 438). In a literature review of "The Benefits of Cognitive Disfluency," Adam L. Alter compiles many recent experiments demonstrating this increased performance premium again and again. He theorizes that disfluent texts introduce a cognitive roadblock that forces readers to process information more deeply, carefully, and abstractly.[24] This phenomenon has important social as well as cognitive implications. Alter cites several experiments showing how disfluency counters xenophobic tendencies by encouraging people to delay their impressions of strangers, avoiding stereotypes before gathering more information (440). Another related study found that disfluency disrupts the confirmation bias, by which people tend to selectively seek evidence that is consistent with their prior beliefs and expectations. In two studies, participants' attitudes on a political issue became less extreme after reading an argument about it in a disfluent format (Hernandez and Preston 178).

These cognitive studies reveal a potent politics *of* the poem within the disfluent forms of contemporary vispo. Creating a text that infects the reader's brain so that it thinks more deeply and carefully, and inoculates it against xenophobia and stereotyping? A powerful avant-garde indeed. Poet Gareth Jenkins seems to thematize this power of disfluency in one of his texts created by overlapping letters and words he originally photocopied on acetate as a university lecturer.[25] Framed and marked by the dark, blurry

"check you" (*Last Vispo* 105).
Courtesy of Gareth Sion Jenkins.

vestiges of its origins as a copy (of a copy of a copy?) in the Xerox machine, this poem has you read '[b]nɒʜ ɿiǝʜɟ bɒǝɿ' disfluently backward and reversed in order "to check you" and your brain's lazy tendencies.

Jenkins's admonition to "read their han[d]" brings us to another disfluent methodology by which contemporary vispo calls attention to and confounds the brain's reading processes. Interestingly, most contemporary visual poetry tends to utilize type (even if it's blurred, broken, or exploded) rather than handwritten or cursive writing.[26] But *The Last Vispo Anthology* does include a chapter of "Handwritten" works, including two from someone who is probably among the best-known poets in the anthology: Robert Grenier. His "drawing poems" certainly activate the vispo effects

"AFTER/NOON/SUN/SHINE" (2004) (*Last Vispo* 172). Copyright Robert Grenier.

of disfluency we have been tracking as readers painstakingly attempt to decipher the scrawled and overlapping letters of his four-line poems.[27]

At poetry readings, Grenier even performs a kind of struggle to decode his own handwriting: "Is that an O or an R?" "Can you read that?" "Oh, look, the E is made out of the M and the W" (qtd. in Ackerman 140). As Ondrea E. Ackerman argues, "the drawing poems are literally about picturing the letter and learning to read" (133). Yet they ask more of their readers than just picturing the letter visually. Because Grenier includes the printed text of the poem in the title, the reader's job becomes less to "read" than to trace the motion of the line to find the *A*, the *F*, the *T*, etc. These handwritten words thus seem to engage what Nakamura et al. describe as "gestural reading." In addition to the letter shape recognition system ("reading by eye") used with clear type, the brain has a kinesthetic recognition system ("reading by hand") that is activated by cursive and difficult handwriting (Nakamura et al. 20766). This gestural system seems to play an important role in the act of learning to read. Recent research shows that children learn to read more effectively when they are taught to write or finger-trace the letter shapes rather than just matching letter to sound (Bara et al.). Grenier's childlike scrawls take readers back to this kinesthetic method of "reading by hand" as they slowly follow the pen stroke of each line to decipher the letter and word. Indeed, Grenier's questions and comments to the audience during his performed reading highlight the pedagogical nature of this work. As we saw in chapter 3, this is work that invites the viewer-reader to "take up the gesture which created it" (Merleau-Ponty 88), enabling an unfamiliar gesture that calls into question our normative ways of seeing, writing, and reading language.

Jesse Glass's handwritten poem "Shout Speak Whisper" explores one last piece in the experiential puzzle of reading disfluent writing, and that is the phenomenology of the frown. Reading a clear and well-designed text generates what psychologist Daniel Kahneman calls "cognitive ease" (59). Primed by a clear display, readers/viewers tend to show relaxed brows and a faint smile on their face (66), and as discussed earlier, they have a tendency to believe what they read, finding it comfortably familiar and intuitive (Kahneman 60).[28] In contrast, people frown and furrow their brow when they experience the cognitive strain of a disfluent text. Though in our happiness-obsessed culture people are often admonished with the poor poetry of "turn that frown upside down," experiments have shown important benefits to frowning. When subjects are told to shape their face into a frown (by squeezing their eyebrows together, for example), they become more vigilant and analytical in their thinking (Kahneman 60) as well as more empathetic. One experiment showed that frowning created "an enhanced emotional response to upsetting pictures—starving children, people arguing, maimed accident victims" (Kahneman 59).

In keeping with the disfluent vispo we've seen, Glass's piece works actively to prevent such cognitive ease and to engage the phenomenology of the frown. At first glance, the poem appears to be a fuzzy, twisted glyph, like an *H* and an *N* got into a wrestling match. With closer scrutiny, however, the fuzziness of the glyph emerges as cursive writing following the lines—a poem—written in what Glass calls his "ants on a string" style.[29] *"Begin by frowning of the Entrance of the senses,"* the first "line" of the poem commands, and the reader/viewer realizes that in order to decipher this disfluent cursive wrapping around a curvy line, she is in fact "frowning," or furrowing her brow in concentration.[30] We also frown to shield our eyes ("the Entrance of the senses") from overhead light, as Glass references next, but as Kahneman's research suggests, even a "primed" frown or forced frown can have salubrious effects on cognition.[31] *"Begin by frowning at the sun and dance the deviation of the vowels ooooh. Polish this monument to Pain with bags of pulverized Teeth AAAAAAAAAAAAOOOOOOOOO-AAA,"* the line painfully continues. *"Be each level of suffering defined by its sound, each level of pain + uncertainty + despair a sound."* Glass celebrates the suffering, uncertainty, and even despair that "reading by hand" engenders in his "monument to Pain" that contains its own vowelly "shouts" of readerly agony. Then the line shifts from cursive to print as "We fall into the body of the alphabet[,] the ignorance of the word. Yet when the lie is properly spoken we are released. Restrain yourselves, receive the imperishable seed." With the ease and clarity of print and type, we often "fall into the body of the alphabet" and the false transparency of the word. "Yet when the lie is properly spoken"—or in this case handwritten—"we are released." We are cognitively strained and restrained by the disfluency of the word.[32]

The final words of this "string" of the poem, "receive the imperishable

"Shout Speak Whisper" (*Last Vispo* 178). Courtesy of Jesse Glass.

seed," have crawled full circle back to the beginning and thus appear printed across the top of the earlier line "frowning at the sun." This juxtaposition suggests a bit of a utopian vision of the effects of the frown of poetic disfluency, as Glass alludes to the Bible verse: "For you have been born again, not of perishable seed, but of imperishable, through the living and enduring word" (1 Peter 1:23). The apostle refers to "the living and enduring word *of God,*" but Glass's poem points to another source of redemption and hope. In a new biblical reference, this time from the Old Testament, Glass writes that "the Blessed Lie of literature" is "a fiery cloud we follow through the night of our being." By that blessed lie, when "told correctly," "we are released & the vessels are Mended"; it is "repeated repeated repeated in the void in which every bird's an oracle in evening sky" (178). The words that are repeated in this poem appear on the connecting lines (labeled "Chorus"), and they read, "the Shells the Shells the Shells." According to the *OED,* a shell is "an empty or hollow thing; mere externality without substance"—the "lie" of language and the alphabet. Significantly, however, it is also a word for lyric poetry, as the first lyre, according to legend, was "a tortoise shell stringed" ("shell").[33] The "blessed lie" here, then, is poetry itself, the original sounding (and sighting?) of the lyre/liar that restrains, releases, and mends its readers.

The "imperishable seed" of visual poetry may leave its viewers frowning at the "lighght," so to speak, but as we have seen, the symptoms of this implantation move well beyond the paralysis of "shockockock!" (US Congress 22124). Shock begets inaction, stupefaction, insensitivity, and detachment. However, the radical forms of visual poetry stimulate a frenzy of cognition, launching the brain into acting, generating, deciphering, and learning. A powerful politics *of* the poem emerges in concrete poetry's tinkering with the material origins of the alphabet, activating the brain's capacity for play and openness to multiple interpretations. It materializes in the potent effects of vispo's disfluency, which prompts readers to think more deeply, fairly, and even empathetically as they evaluate the world around them. Whether read by eye, ear, or hand, visual poetry squeezes not just the abstract language system but also the elements (*stocheia,* "alphabet"), the very concrete materiality that comprises it, and through which our material minds process and produce it.

"The First Form of Communicating"

THE PROTOSEMANTIC IN SOUND POETRY

A group of hominids gathers around the carcass of a horse on the muddy banks of a lagoon. Some are working to cut its tendons with hand axes; others tend to children nearby. As they work, they communicate using a language of gestures and mime, as well as holistic utterances that are highly musical in nature (Mithen 192). These are the Singing Neanderthals that archaeologist Steven Mithen theorizes in his multidisciplinary book. Mithen hypothesizes that music and language coevolved from a single precursor with characteristics shared by both (26).[1] He names this early method of communication "Hmmmmm language," with the "Hmmmmm" referring to holistic, multimodal, manipulative, mimetic, and musical. It was holistic in that it functioned as a complete message or experience in and of itself, rather than combining specific words to generate meaning. It was multimodal in that it used other corporeal gestures besides or alongside the voice. Some of these gestures and sounds may have mimicked specific people and animals. Significantly, the language was musical (rhythmic and melodic) and used that music for manipulative purposes, working to shape the emotional states and behavior of others in the group (172).

We know that the Neanderthals were an evolutionary dead end, but Mithen thinks that this type of language was also used by the immediate ancestors of *Homo sapiens* in Africa, though in "a form less highly evolved than among the Neanderthals in Europe" (253). Gradually, over a long period of evolution, this more holistic Hmmmmm language would have become segmented into a compositional language like we use today (259). However, this new referential system of language was not as effective as Hmmmmm at things like expressing emotion or forging group identities (266). Consequently, Mithen suggests, once a compositional language evolved, Hmmmmm language did not completely disappear but rather became specialized in various forms of emotional expression and manipulation. One descendent of Hmmmmm is music, with its holistic nature and its potential to elicit powerful emotional effects, both individual and communal (275). Yet Mithen finds another, perhaps even closer, remnant of this musical language in the ways that people talk to infants, using changing pitch, repetition, and rhythm to engage their attention and modulate their emotions. He weaves together evidence from archaeology, psychology, neuroscience, and musicology to support his theory.

Though Mithen's hypothesis is just one among many possible answers to what has been called "the hardest problem in science," the origins of human language (Christiansen and Kirby), his ideas, based as they are on his treasure trove of research and evidence, offer insight in the field of poetics. His description of a holistic, multimodal, manipulative, mimetic, and musical form of communication reveals some of the mechanisms at work behind experimental sound poems. Across the twentieth century and into the twenty-first, on both page and stage, sound poems have been understood as adopting and engaging various protosemantic elements and energies such as those Mithen explores. These theories, among others, help expand previous understandings of the protosemantic in experimental poetics and its transformational potential for audiences.

The Protosemantic, or Dada versus Mama

Avant-garde sound poetry emerges around the turn of the twentieth century, most significantly in the Modernist movement known as Dada. A response to the senseless slaughter of the Great War, Dada famously called into question and worked to destroy traditional values in art and bourgeois society. The movement arguably originates at the Cabaret Voltaire in Zurich, where in 1916 artists began to experiment with raucous forms of performance such as simultaneous poetry and sound poems. Hugo Ball, the proprietor of the Cabaret Voltaire along with his partner, Emmy Hennings, claims to have invented the sound poem, or *lautgedicht*. His most famous performance occurred one night just before closing; he dressed in a cardboard costume that looked like the Tin Man or a space robot, and performed this nonsense sound poem:

> Gadgi beri bimba
> Glandridi lauli lonni cadori
> gadjama bim beri glassala
> Glandridi glassala tuffm i zimbrabim
> blassa galassasa tuffm i zimbrabim (qtd. in Rasula, *Destruction* 27)

Ball was apparently so overcome by the performance that he had to be carried offstage. He writes in a diary entry, later used in the program notes for a sound poem performance, "In these phonetic poems we totally renounce the language that journalism has abused and corrupted. We must return to the innermost alchemy of the word, we must even give up the word too, to keep for poetry its last and holiest refuge. We must give up writing second-hand: that is, accepting words (to say nothing of sentences) that are not newly invented for our use" (71).

Dada sound poets turned in particular to so-called primitive energies to find "newly invented" words. As Jed Rasula writes, Dada poet Richard Huelsenbeck "longed for the primitive origins of humankind; his poems plunged consciousness into a cauldron of primal forms, bits of raw terrestrial matter out of which anything might emerge in the evolutionary spiral: 'pig's bladder kettle drum cinnabar cru cru cru' begins one of his 'Fantastic Prayers'" (*Destruction* 9). Similarly, Raoul Hausmann "wanted to reach a primal place, where language had yet to evolve and the human animal vocalized without words," pioneering a performance mode in which he produced wild sound effects from "the chaotic oral cavity" (Rasula, *Destruction* 73).[2] Dada sound poets were clearly interested in tapping the potential of protosemantic energies—perhaps like our Neanderthals.

However, Dada sound poets always describe and enact these protosemantic elements in their work as a means of destruction and violence. "The Gorgon's head of a boundless terror smiles out of the fantastic destruction," Ball observed of one of Huelsenbeck's sound performances (qtd. in Rasula, *Destruction* 9). If humankind was bent on destroying itself in the Great War, then Dadaists would take that methodology to an extreme, using destruction as a creative weapon to dismantle the bourgeois values, systems, and bureaucracies that had led to it (Rasula, *Destruction* 301).

Steve McCaffery also theorizes the protosemantic in terms of its destructive potential. The protosemantic forces that "rumble beneath the word" act as Deleuzian "dissipative structures," according to McCaffery, destabilizing the complex, seemingly secure system of language that operates above them, "pressur[ing] the dominant system into disequilibrium and expenditure" (*Prior* xix, xviii). Poems, he argues, can function as one of these dissipative structures, acting as "informational excesses that in part impale and in part escape readers" (xx). McCaffery turns to the role of the protosemantic in experimental sound poetry specifically in a chapter that traces the "Voice in Extremis" of sound poems across the twentieth century. From early Dada and futurist examples, through the Lettristes and Ultralettristes at midcentury, to the "paleotechnic" experiments of the 1970s, he explains, the "extreme mission" of the sound poem was "the killing of speech in its capitalist, propositional embodiments" (186). Like the Dadaists, then, for McCaffery the protosemantic in poetics is predicated on rupture, waste, expenditure, delirium, killing, and loss. Reading experimental poems can certainly feel like one's consciousness has been violated or "impaled" at times, and productively so. But is the force of the protosemantic always a force of destruction and violence?[3]

Ultimately, McCaffery finds that the sound poetry movement ended in a "failure in the 1970s to establish the poem as community" (*Prior* 162). Perhaps part of the reason for this failure arose from a limited understanding of protosemantic processes. McCaffery, at the time a member of Canadian performance group the Four Horsemen, analogizes these performances to "a scream escap[ing] from pain"[4] and acknowledges that "a scream can never be a social contract" (186). Indeed, as the performing bodies on stage enact a "loss of self" and "rupture [of the] signifying system" in their "sonic outlay" (183), what is the potential role, response, or experience of the audience? In an attempt to incorporate the audience into his understanding of the "community" created by the poem, McCaffery considers the model of a Deleuzian "machinic assemblage" (183), but he freely admits the difficulty of reconciling this concept to any more concrete notion of community (184). In the end, he wonders if the sound performance isn't just recovered for audiences as another instance of Debord's society of the spectacle (186).

Extending McCaffery's sound poetry genealogy into the twenty-first century permits exploration of how some contemporary sound poets reveal a different approach to the protosemantic and its relationship to audience and community. These poets certainly rely on the dissipative processes that McCaffery explores, but they also point to another side of the protosemantic—one that is generative rather than destructive, inducing not delirium but human connection and development.[5]

This different angle on the protosemantic is well illuminated by Steven Mithen's theories about language's protosemantic origins in his singing Neanderthals. It is interesting to think about those early hominids Hmmmmming around a horse carcass as proto–sound poets, communicating through their nonsemantic, holistic, tonal utterances.[6] Considering McCaffery's chosen facet of the protosemantic in this context, I imagine that "a scream escap[ing] from pain" would provoke powerful reactions within the group—shock, fear, flight, violence, protectiveness, empathy, or some combination. As Mithen portrays it, however, there is a great deal more nuance to this protosemantic language than primal outbursts alone.

An important selective pressure in the emergence of Hmmmmm language was the interaction between mothers and their infants (Mithen 192). The increasing helplessness of human babies over the course of evolution created the need for enhanced mother–child interactions, and musical sounds were the ideal enhancement (196). According to psychologist Ellen Dissanayake, a form of "rhythmic, temporally patterned, jointly maintained communicative interactions" coevolved in infants and mothers, which "produced and sustained positive affect—psychobiological brain states of interest and joy—by displaying and imitating emotions of affiliation, and thereby sharing, communicating, and reinforcing them" (qtd. in Mithen 197). Remember that Mithen thinks this musical protolanguage lives on today in what is known as infant-directed speech, or IDS, the hyperinflected way of speaking that parents use with babies. Cognitive linguists once thought that IDS was merely a tool for a child's language acquisition, a primer introduction (indoctrination?) into the language system. But Anne Fernald, a researcher at Stanford, has uncovered other uses for IDS that precede semantics and that change as the baby grows, such as engaging and maintaining the child's attention (gently rising pitches create eye opening, while abrupt rising pitches create eye closure and withdrawal), modulating arousal and emotion, and communicating the speaker's feelings or intentions (71). Ultimately, in IDS, the meaning of the words does not matter; "the melody is the message" (72).

This more generative, developmental, and connective element of the protosemantic is at work in the contemporary sound poems of Tracie Morris and Lisa Jarnot. McCaffery remarks on the struggle to find where the chaos of the protosemantic fits in the process of becoming: "Is it the birth of order or its breakdown?" (xvii). The answer, of course, is both. If Dada performances and the sound poems of the 1970s worked to precipitate a breakdown of identity and a killing of speech, more recent sound poems seem to operate at the level of rebirth and reorientation—not into some stable form of presence or meaning, but into other, higher-order, complex systems of identity and community.[7] They also engage their readers/listeners in a different bodily and affective register than the "impaling" gestures of earlier sound poems. Through combinations of rhythm, rhyme, pitch, repetition, and melody, contemporary sound poems capture audiences into a more affiliative relationship, engaging their attention and modulating arousal and emotion to provoke states of interest, even joy. At the same time, however, these poems question the power of that engagement even as they invoke it, working to harness that feeling of jouissance to an active résistance.

Tracie Morris: How to (Re)do Things with Words

When poet Tracie Morris was asked to define poetry, she described it in protosemantic terms as "the first form of communicating."[8] Morris—

a poet who wrote her doctoral dissertation on J. L. Austin—aims for a poetry that makes something happen.[9] Austin famously argues that poetic utterances cannot have the same transformational "force" as the performative utterances he explores in *How to Do Things with Words,* for the words of poetry are merely "parasitic" on their normal uses (104). Morris resists Austin's claim, arguing that poetry cannot be a parasite on everyday speech because poetry actually precedes ordinary language:

> Austin's "dismissal" [of poetry as a performative] only works in a certain order: It presumed that everyday speech was the first thing folks said when humans started speaking and poetry is some sort of "flourish" that came after ordinary language use. However, the roots of the performative utterances for humankind are not utilitarian everyday speech. People originally uttered, and were motivated to frame thoughts through utterances, as attempts to speak of/speak to/speak *as* the extraordinary, the unexplainable, the divine.... Utterances originate in our human need to respond to something beyond our imagining.... I keep coming back to the beginnings.... The beginning of humanity and the beginning of humankind's relationship to language (that is fundamentally poetic). (*Who Do with Words: Rapping* 28, 31)

Morris thus links the force of poetry directly to the protosemantic, primordial energies that Steven Mithen describes. At the origin of human language lies an embodied, musical, rhythmic form of communication that he calls "Hmmmmm language" and she calls "poetry." Because poetry came first, Morris claims, its force is what grounds every speech act (*Who Do with Words: Rapping* 32), and its utterance can have profound cognitive and embodied effects. She describes her sound poems in an interview with Charles Bernstein as being "about the viscera ... [about] getting things out and impacting the body's insides."[10] Morris's definition of poetry is helpfully ambiguous, suggesting that poetry is the "first form of communicating" in an evolutionary sense across deep time, but also in a developmental sense, within a single lifetime. The phenomena of IDS and music seem to encompass both of these time lines, lying at the foundation of human language development and reflecting language's evolutionary origins. Part of the impact of Morris's sound poetics arises from these foundational energies.

Another key component to Morris's visceral sound poetics can be found in Fred Moten's *In the Break*,[11] in which he explores the origins of the "radical materiality and syntax that animates black performances" (7). He begins with the relationship between Frederick Douglass's description of the "heart-rending shrieks" of his Aunt Hester while the master violently assaulted her, and the analysis of slave song and music that follows (6). Douglass's exploration, Moten argues, offers a critique and disruption of Enlightenment linguistic projects that would "reduce phonic matter to verbal meaning or conventional musical form" (6). He quotes a relevant passage from Édouard Glissant's *Caribbean Discourse:* "For Caribbean man, the word is first and foremost sound. Noise is essential to speech. Din is discourse.... Since speech was forbidden, slaves camouflaged the word under the provocative intensity of the scream. It was taken to be nothing but the call of a wild animal. This is how the dispossessed man organized his speech by weaving it into the apparently meaningless texture of extreme noise" (Moten 7). For Saussure, Chomsky, and other linguists, such speech is "degraded" by its material difference or agrammaticality, but Moten finds a revaluation of values in noisy Black performances that disrupt the oppositions of speech and writing, spirit and matter (14). Interestingly, he links the *being material* of Black performance to a *being maternal* that arises from enslavement and the resistance to enslavement (16). Moten deploys a decidedly psychoanalytic, Kristevan sense of the maternal here and its critique of logocentrism and connection to the semiotic.[12] The phenomenon of IDS is less essentialized to a female/maternal body than Kristeva's semiotic, but it offers another way into exploring the creative "ani*mater*iality" of Black performance that Moten theorizes and Morris enacts (18).

Tracie Morris began her poetry career as an award-winning performance poet on the slam circuit, but she eventually went rogue and began performing sound poems in a much more experimental vein. These largely improvised poems unquestionably exemplify Moten's "radical materiality" of Black syntax and performance, involving singing, scatting, scratching, ululating, screaming, heavy breathing, gurgling, and subtly bending repeated words in her "vocalese" until new meanings, as she says, are "almost heard" (Hume 223).

Intriguingly, her embodied poetics often mirrors the characteristics of IDS: "a higher overall pitch, a wider range of pitch, longer 'hyperarticulated' vowels and pauses, shorter phrases, and greater repetition than are found in speech directed to older children and adults" (Mithen 69).[13] The exaggerated prosody of IDS thus takes on a musical character, and babies are much more engaged by it than by normal adult speech. The roles of IDS shift as the child grows, from engaging attention and emotion to communicating the speaker's feelings and intent, and eventually IDS becomes an essential tool in the child's language acquisition. Its pauses and prosody help babies identify individual words within the sound stream, and infant brains are apparently hyperattuned to any new, unusual words that might emerge in that stream. According to researcher Jenny Saffran, infants are "natural-born statisticians" as they learn language (Mithen 76), identifying statistical regularities in the language sounds they hear ("and now it's lunchtime," "and now it's story time," "and now it's bedtime"). They learn to ignore words that they have heard a great deal and show more interest in the nonsense, the "part-words" and "non-words" that show up in that stream (Mithen 76). Though Morris's listeners are no longer infants, her rhythmic and musical performances made of sound flows of ambiguous words that are "almost heard" seem to engage and draw on these early protosemantic processors in the brain.[14]

Morris's performance of the poem "Africa(n)" at the Arizona Poetry Center in May 2008 reveals many of these mechanisms at work.[15] The poem is built on various repetitions of the sentence "It all started when we were brought here as slaves from Africa." It was inspired, Morris explains, by a recording of actor Geoffrey Holder speaking this line with what she describes as his "Afro-Shakespearean voice" ("Africa(n)"). Holder, a native of Trinidad, is an interesting choice because of his co-optation into US popular culture as an ethnic stereotype, playing tribal leader Willie Shakespeare X in the 1967 film *Dr. Dolittle,* a voodoo-practicing Bond villain, and the Caribbean guy on the old 7-Up commercials who extols the virtues of "the Uncola." Morris's performance takes the almost avuncular storytelling voice of Holder's line and, to use Deleuze and Guattari's language, "lays hold of the refrain and deterritorializes it, and deterritorializes the voice,... send[ing] it racing off in a rhythmic sound block" (303). This performance is thus not a "killing of speech," as McCaffery has it, but a reconstitution of speech that works to "extend the territory" of its audience's cognition itself (Deleuze and Guattari 372).[16]

This extension and reconstitution begins at the level of the protosemantic. Her first delivery of the line is slow, clear, rhythmic, and musical, with a huge shift in pitch between "all" (at a high pitch) and "started" (very low pitch), between "slaves" (the highest pitch) and "Africa" (the lowest). The wide range and quick leaps in pitch that occur throughout the performance seem to activate the affective dimension of early language sensation, intensifying listeners' attention and even anxiety as the top pitch she hits moves higher and higher. At one moment in the performance, she scats back and forth between "when" and "we" in a low-to-high pitch that sounds like the chirp and wail of a police siren. At the same time, the statistical processors of the protosemantic brain could be aroused and puzzled by the almost-heard part-words and nonwords that erupt from the flow. When she speaks the sentence a second time, it sounds something like this: "Itallsitallsitallsitallsidarsidarsidarsidartsidallstarted when we were brought here asassass slavslavslavslapslabslafsas slaves from Af. . . ." Before she finishes the final word, before we can determine if we heard "sit," "art," "ass," "slap," "slab," "laugh," maybe even "Siddhartha" in there, she's racing into a new riff on the line.

Clearly, the semantic dimension of the sentence is not lost for listeners, but Morris's performance uses the protosemantic to manipulate their affective response to the content. I have been describing Morris's pitch changes in the poem using the customary terms "high" and "low." However, Mithen cites musicologist Deryck Cooke, who argues that we should also think of the "out-and-in" and "away-and-back" of musical pitch. According to Cooke's theory, rising pitches express an "outgoing" of emotion. Depending on tone and context, the effect can be "active, assertive, aggressive, striving, protesting, or aspiring." Falling pitches, in contrast, convey an "incoming" of emotion, one that is "relaxed, yielding, assenting, welcoming, accepting, or enduring" (Mithen 92). Though Morris's repetitions of the line play with phonetics and rhythm, the pitch modulation of certain words is more consistent. While the general trajectory of pitch throughout the poem moves higher, out and away, toward a more aggressive and aspiring effect, the word "Africa" most often occurs on a falling pitch, caressing and welcoming the continent with an emotional turn inward, a connection and identification also reflected in the title, "Africa(n)." In contrast, the words "all," "slaves," and "we" occur most often on rising pitches, an outgoing of emotion expressing aggressive protest against "all" that "slaves" suffered in the transatlantic slave trade and asserting the voice and power of the "we" who were brought here. Indeed, one of Morris's joyful rhythmic scats on the line sounds like, "when we when, when we when, when we win, we we we win." As if to make a final assertion of this emotion and aspiration, Morris concludes this performance on the word "we" at a rising pitch.

Many of Morris's sound poems cross over from IDS-like musically inflected language to music itself—"where shriek turns speech turns song," as Fred Moten writes (22). Performances such as "Chain Gang" and "The Mrs. Gets Her Ass Kicked" are more sung than spoken, playing with familiar lines from pop music,[17] while others, like "My Great Grand Aunt Speaks to a Bush Supporter" and its "Coda," make use of spiritual tunes and tones. In a reading at the Kelly Writers House in November 2013, Morris performs another poem in this vein, "Mahalia Theremin," which she describes as an "Afro-Futurist piece"—a mash-up of famous gospel singer Mahalia Jackson's name and the theremin, an early electronic instrument named for its Russian inventor, and often associated with science fiction film and television. Morris explains the connection in her introduction to the performance: "They were both looking toward another kind of a future—him the speculative and her the concrete—during the Civil Rights era."[18] The poem begins by closely mimicking Jackson's performance of "Joshua Fit the Battle of Jericho," a spiritual the precise origins of which are unknown. It was likely composed by enslaved people in the first part of the nineteenth century, and as with many of these songs, its message of "the walls came tumblin' down" had a powerful resonance for its singers beyond the biblical story of Joshua (Jones 55–56). Morris sings the chorus three times, gradually gaining in intensity and volume. Then she begins to mix in the theremin sound, imitating it with her voice. Her theremin follows the basic tune of the song at first, but eventually adds some more sci-fi-sounding riffs. Though Morris is certainly singing, she inserts long pauses between each iteration of the chorus, as if to keep listeners from getting caught up in the catchiness of the song. Instead, with the seeming critical distance of a phonologist or a sound mixer, she plays, stops, and replays the musical phrase, inviting a close analysis of its elements and effects.

Morris's imitation of the theremin in the piece supports this invitation. The theremin is unique among musical instruments in that it is played without any physical contact by the performer. Two metal antennae sense the position of the thereminist's hands; one hand controls an oscillator for pitch; the other, volume. Interestingly, because the instrument emits a constant stream of sound, the thereminist must actively play the rests—the silence—in the song as well. The theremin thus breaks sound down to its most protomusical, protosemantic elements, highlighting the interplay of pitch, volume, silence, and gesture. When Morris begins to mix in the theremin voice, she sings the first word of the chorus, "Joshua!" and then ululates as a theremin, following Jackson's unique upward pitch shifts on the repeated word "Jericho." But she returns to vocalizing the final trium-phant lines of the chorus, "the walls came tumblin' down." This choice seems to highlight the power of such protosemantic elements alone to bring about change. Indeed, in the biblical story of the battle of Jericho, the walls are brought down not through physical effort, but after the Israelites marched around the city and blew their shofars. Musical sound itself can unite a community and trigger a revolution.

After this jubilant revolutionary moment, the sound poem begins to project a future with its speculative-feeling sci-fi theremin riffs on the song. In an Afrofuturist mode, the performance thus connects the history of the slave spiritual and Mahalia Jackson's civil rights–era battles to a technological future. Morris's leaps in pitch can bring to mind the ther-emin sound of the original *Star Trek* theme, which was also voiced by a studio soprano rather than by the instrument. The long-running sci-fi franchise imagines a space-age future devoid of racism, but Morris's piece is perhaps not so utopian. Her poetic contributions to the special issue of *Social Text* on Afrofuturism offer a decidedly dystopian vision of what's to come, foreseeing environmental catastrophe and social engineering.[19] As many critics have noted, representations of sci-fi racial utopias such as

Star Trek continue to manifest the problematic racial ideologies of their particular cultural moment (see Bernardi). Indeed, in her shift to the futuristic theremin sound, the powerful lyrics of the spiritual are lost. Eventually the original song's melody becomes unrecognizable.

Underneath all the futuristic metamorphosis of the song, however, the performance stays in the same key and uses many of the same intervals as the original. Perhaps the maintenance of these foundational elements suggests that all is not lost in the transformations of the future. Morris performs the piece in the key of D minor, which Nigel Tufnel of the spoof metal band Spinal Tap claims is "the saddest of all keys" (*This Is Spinal Tap*). Such impressionism about a specific key is obviously a joke, but recent musicology research has demonstrated that people across multiple cultures often attribute the same emotional meanings to a particular musical interval, suggesting this significance might arise from some fundamental features of human physiology or psychology (Mithen 91). Deryck Cooke's research focuses only on Western music, but he too uncovers a potential correlation between certain musical intervals and particular emotions. The major third, he finds, is generally an expression of joy and happiness in both classical and popular music. In contrast, the minor third is used to express painful emotions, such as the "doom-laden" first movement of Beethoven's Fifth Symphony. Cooke claims "the strong contrast between the 'natural' pleasurable major third and the 'unnatural' painful minor third has been exploited throughout musical history" (qtd. in Mithen 91).

In Morris's performance, the upward shifts in pitch at the end of the word "Jericho" are all "painful" minor thirds, as well as the final interval to the word "down." The sound poem ends with Morris's theremin voice climbing from D to B flat, a minor sixth, which is not in the minor triad and so needs to be "resolved," creating "a feeling of acutely painful dissatisfaction … of *anguish*, in fact," according to Cooke (Mithen 69). The anguish resolves in the final rising fifths of A to E, D to A. These concluding fifths leave out the "painful" minor third, so they can sound more like a major chord. But with the "history" of all of those minor thirds still ringing in their ears, listeners are able to hear the final notes as both the hopeful major and the painful minor. "Mahalia Theremin" thus becomes an Afrofuturism embodied in the protosemantic sounds of the voice itself. In the performance's final seconds, Morris pushes her voice to its lowest possible register and then strains it to its highest, reflecting and effecting not only the up and down, in and out, of complex emotions but also the "away and back" motion of Afrofuturism itself, telling a new story about identity, technology, and the future while reaching back into the rich and painful history of African diasporic experience (Nelson 9).

This dual, musical motion lifts Morris's performance beyond the limits of McCaffery's "a scream escapes from pain" definition of sound poetry (*Prior* 186). It is a radical ani*mate*riality "where shriek turns speech to song" (Moten 18). Morris writes, "We know fantastic world-making through words when we see them. We always make new worlds. We refashion them out of the sounds we said at the beginning of human-kind. We make them out of all the atoms of sounds, even those spoken to harm us. This is what we do: Out of all these building blocks we wail a rhythmic world, create joyful noises, the first thing and new things with words" (*Who Do with Words: Rapping* 103). Indeed, her poetics suggests that perhaps the "paleo-technic" sound poems of the 1970s weren't fully or sufficiently "paleo," embracing Neanderthals that "create joyful noises" and that sing as well as scream. Morris's sound poems certainly work to "dissipate" the stability of voice, presence, and meaning in their perfor-mance, as McCaffery describes. Their sound, however, is used not only to impale, shock, or rupture but also to welcome, engage, and arouse.[20] The exaggerated prosody and musical elements of her poetics return listeners to the integrative and connective possibilities of "the first form of commu-nicating." In contrast to McCaffery's description of the sound poem's audience/listener relationship as a "machinic assemblage," Morris writes, "I consider these poems to be living entities that invite a live moment between the listener and the utterer" ("Poetics Statement" 213). The result of this invitation, this living embodied moment, is not a new stable state of being or order; nor is it a descent into chaos. Rather, it is a rebirth and reorientation, launching the development of a self and community in process.

Lisa Jarnot's (Non)canonical Babbling

If Tracie Morris engages the protosemantic devices of music and musically inflected IDS in her performances, then Lisa Jarnot takes her inspiration from the other side of the parent/child interaction: baby chatter, or what experts call canonical babbling. Perhaps poetry is "the first form of communicating" for the infant too. Indeed, if we return to Mithen's singing Neanderthals, it is easy to see and hear how the child's early protosemantic efforts to convey emotions and influence adult behavior are also holistic, multimodal, manipulative, mimetic, and even musical, particularly in their experimental play with the voice's elements of sound, pitch, and rhythm.

Jarnot's 2014 book *A Princess Magic Presto Spell* was begun right after her daughter, Bea, was born.[21] As a new mother with little time for writing, she aimed to compose just three words a day in her notebook ("the right amount of writing to do with a two-year-old in the house"). She compiled these at the end of each year into chunks that became three long poems. The first section of the book was "written in the sleepless state of having a [new] baby, and it's very hallucinatory," as she explains in the Kelly Writers House reading. The second and third sections began to document words, phrases, and sentences as her daughter acquired them, so that these parts, she quips, are "mostly plagiarized from her." The title of the book, which is also its final line, may contain a reference to a popular PBS character, Princess Presto, whose magic wand makes things materialize by spelling out their names. To be sure, the child's brain is attuned to this "magic" power of language: say "milk," and it miraculously appears. However, a great deal of an infant's babble involves not this consumerist exchange of word for thing or action but rather an experimental play with sounds that the voice and mouth can make: the art of vociferation. "This ba ba ba (first instance of)" (8), Jarnot records in section 1 of the book. It is this protosemantic joie de vivre,[22] this childlike *joie de langue,* that Jarnot adopts as a poetics in much of her work and attempts to reactivate in her audience—not impaling or rupturing (a la McCaffery) but catching them up in the infectiousness of her poems' rhythms and sounds. Yet the poems' performance of a "toddler mentality" is just as transformative in the thinking as in the feeling it inspires.

Language is clearly a beneficial adaptation within human evolution; however, some researchers have found it useful to think of language itself as a nonconscious life-form evolving independently of the creatures infected by it (Christiansen and Kirby; Deacon). In order to survive, language must be particularly infectious within its host environment: language learners. The virus of language has thus "adapted to the quirks and traits of the child's mind" (Kenneally 236). One interesting quirk is that before the age of two, infants function to some extent like a split-brain adult—that is, like an adult with a severed corpus callosum (the broad band of nerve fibers connecting the right and left hemispheres of the brain; Annett). Over the course of early development, the child's corpus callosum will become myelinated, wherein the nerves are coated with a fatty insulating substance (myelin) that allows signals to be transmitted more quickly and efficiently between the two hemispheres. With their nonmyelinated corpus callosum, infants and toddlers start out learning and processing language in both hemispheres. As they develop, however, much of this work is eventually "lateralized" to the left hemisphere, a shift that begins around the end of the third year of life (Kane 41). In most fully developed adult brains, the two hemispheres end up with different job descriptions; the left hemisphere processes speech and operates the analytical, mathematical, and linguistic aspects of consciousness, while the right hemisphere deals with spatial perception and social and emotional functioning, including the emotional aspects of sound and voice—melody, prosody, intonation, singing, cursing, and praying (Joseph). To infect, develop, and thrive in a nonlateralized environment, then, the virus of language must appeal to the infant mind's need to analyze, name, and categorize the world around it. It must also appeal to the infant's desire for sound, cadence, and music, along with the emotions they convey and conjure.

Jarnot's poetics, inspired by the infected/infectious language of the child, is born out of this nonlateralized foundational relationship to words—from the right brain's "first k sound" to the left brain's naming of things "milk, apple, cracker … bird, rock, ring … dance, art, owls" (*Princess* 16). For the more split-brain infant, however, the names for things and actions are also apparently quite fun to say, whether they "make

sense" or not: "dance, art cow!   eat and dance!" "owl ice   owl"
"nice   shirt   moon" (17, 18). The infant's canonical babbling
reminds us that words "make sensation" as well as sense. The adult reader's brain is already lopsided with language lateralized to the logical left,
however. It's no fun to say "apple" anymore for someone who's said it for
decades. To reengage the vestigial linguistic joie de vivre for readers, Jarnot
has to up the ante; she has to give us, like new language learners, something to say we've possibly never said before. "Say quercus borealis," she
requests, the Latin name for the red oak tree; then the mysterious "peabok
sea quay" (16). Or the catchy dactylic opening line of the book, "Into the
eve of a picnic of trees of the strawberry rugulet rabbit tyrone" (5). Some
of these unusual lines seem to come from Bea's childlike "mistakes" with
sound, as in "an octurnal nowl / in a kite of neige" (18), with rebracketed
words, switched consonants, or misheard vowels, as in the title of the
second poem, "A Boa Constructor" (15). Jarnot peppers the poems in this
book with such neologisms, likely coined by her daughter: "peabok" and
"rugulet," or, later, "a massalinging hoco" (29). Remember that infants are
natural-born statisticians as they listen to adult speech directed at them,
paying more attention to the "part-words" and "non-words" that they hear
(Mithen 76). Jarnot's book reverses this dynamic, revealing how infant
speech directed at adults generates more interest in the nonsense—or,
better, what has become "non-sensed" in the adult brain: the sound sensations of words. "This debauched kinesthesia" (18), Jarnot writes, in another
novel phrase for readers but one that also nicely describes her infantile (in
the best sense of the word) poetics, giving in to the sensual pleasures of
the kinesthetics of language.[23]

Some scholars have noted poetry's unique ability to unite and ignite
both hemispheres of the brain. Following researchers at Haskins Laboratory, cognitive linguist Reuven Tsur describes the brain's dual forms of
sound perception as nonspeech mode and speech mode. He argues for
a third "poetic" mode of sound perception, however, in which some of
the rich sensory detail of nonspeech sound is still "vaguely" perceived, as
when we attribute particular emotional overtones to "dark" vowel sounds
($/o/$, $/u/$) or "bright" vowels ($/i/$, $/e/$) (viii, 9), or particular values to firm,
clear-cut dental stops versus slipperier palatal consonants. For example,

he finds that the famous quote from Hamlet—"O, that this too too solid flesh would melt / Thaw and resolve itself into a dew!"—is subliminally reinforced by the sound patterns of the line, with the more clearly differentiated sounds dissolving into less differentiated ones (61). Sound echoes sense; right and left hemispheres are working together.

In a similar vein, researcher Julie Kane brings together a wealth of research in "Poetry as Right-Hemispheric Language." She covers each of the traditional elements of poetry (imagery, metaphor, personification, metonymy, paradox, connotation, sound, rhyme, and prosody) and shows that it is "either dependent upon the right hemisphere for comprehension/production, or capable of being processed by the right hemisphere as well as the left" (22). Kane's research suggests that "the degree of right-hemispheric involvement in language is what differentiates 'poetic' or 'literary' from 'referential' or 'technical' speech and texts" (22). Kane uses John Frederick Nims's *Western Wind: An Introduction to Poetry* for her definitions of poetic elements and for many of her examples, so, like Tsur, she focuses her claims and research on traditional lyric poetry. Even if poetry is to varying degrees a "right-hemispheric language" in her examples, it is still a language that means something semantically to the left hemisphere too.

These two theorists suggest that reading a lyric poem can productively stimulate both hemispheres of the brain as the poetic language crosses and recrosses the corpus callosum, exciting the right brain with its musical, figurative, and emotional content, and the left with its semantic and denotative elements (see Luck). This harmonious intertwining doesn't happen so easily when reading/hearing experimental poems, however. In fact, such poems often work to confound it. "Into the eve of a picnic of trees of the strawberry rugulet rabbit tyrone" is delightful to hear, but it certainly doesn't mean anything in any logical way. Kane mentions studies showing that preschoolers produce more spontaneous figures of speech and use less abstract language and more imagery than eight- to ten-year-olds (43, 45) (e.g., "can you believe that the sun has eyes" and "I like tripping so rainbows come out of my mouth," as Jarnot transcribes [*Princess* 26, 30]). However, Kane's research doesn't extend into the earlier stages of language development in which the child can produce seemingly exclusively right-brain language, playing with sound and cadence but with little attention to semantics. Watch the delightful shift from left to right hemisphere language processing in Jarnot's lines: "have a big house, a yellow telephone, a blue car, / have *mango turkey boobie*" (21). That's a laugh-out-loud line, and part of the fun is how it makes your mouth move. "Write silly gilly gumball," Bea later demands (29). Jarnot complies, following her daughter's coercive poetics of right-brain vociferation with her own cheerful efforts: "a chamomile bluejay," "a wilkinson wallachia that causes all the meows" (29, 30).

Jarnot's poetics harnesses the power of the child's infectious, whole-brain relationship to language, stimulating the adult's atrophied language processors of the right hemisphere and confounding the left hemisphere's easy translation of sound to sense. In addition to being the site of language, analysis, and logic, the left brain is also, paradoxically, the great confabulator, indulging in minor denials and rationalizations to maintain preestablished belief systems and a coherent sense of self (Ramachandran 266–67). Indeed, according to neuroscientist V. S. Ramachandran, "if left unchecked, the left hemisphere would likely render a person delusional or maniac" (267). The left brain's "egocentric," unifying, and thus confabulatory nature needs to be tempered by the right brain's more "allocentric," detached, and objective view of the world and the self (267). One of the left brain's confabulations is to hear and use language as a transparent system that straightforwardly and coherently links names to things and actions in the world. To be sure, this fiction is beneficial for everyday use; experiencing a Derridean crisis of slippery signification every time we attempt to communicate certainly would not be advantageous for survival. Occasionally, however, it seems important that the left hemisphere be "jolted" into an awareness, and even revision, of its narratives by the right hemisphere (Ramachandran 267).

Interestingly, research suggests that children learn language inductively, as a signifying system, first, rather than deductively, memorizing word–object relationships. That is, they intuit the Saussurean *langue* behind all the *parole*. This is what makes them so good at learning language. One of the paradoxes that has fascinated scientists and parents alike is why young children, whose immature brains are inept at so many cognitive tasks, are much better than adults at acquiring a new language. Children are actually slow to map words to objects, even ones that occur in the same context, and they can remember only the most global structure–function relationships, finding it difficult to hold more than a few words in short-term memory at a time (Deacon 135). Neural net research by Jeffrey Elman and Elissa Newport, however, suggests that these seeming handicaps are actually great advantages for language acquisition. As Terrence Deacon explains it, "Precisely because of children's learning constraints, the relevant large-scale logic of language 'pops out' of a background of other details too variable for them to follow, and paradoxically gives them a biased head start. Children cannot tell the trees apart at first, but they can see the forest and eventually the patterns of growth within it emerge" (135).

If this ability to unearth relevant large-scale logics from confusing and variable systems does, in fact, lie latent in the adult brain, it would be a powerful skill to resuscitate for navigating a postmodern environment.[24] Frederic Jameson famously describes the schizophrenic subject of post-modernism who is unable to fashion a coherent representation of her current experience, resulting in an art, such as Jarnot's, made up of "heaps of fragments" (25). Jameson finds that these "heaps" of language exem-plify all that is wrong with postmodernism, both as an aesthetic and as a cultural dominant: the weakening of historicity, the waning of negative affect, the loss of coherence. Sianne Ngai in *Ugly Feelings* analyzes Jame-son's use of this metaphor, however, noting that the provocative image of the heap quickly disappears from the essay, replaced by the more abstract concept of "fragmentation" (287–88). This shift suggests a "desire to emphasize the process in which wholes break down into parts, rather than the way parts might be made to cohere" (288), for, as she points out, "a heap *does* seem to be a coherence of some sort" (288), even if its coher-ence is not an external aesthetic or formal ideal but instead something that must be created by the one who encounters it (289). Here is where the child brain's unique abilities come into play: language first comes to her in seeming "heaps of fragments," filled with gaps, inconsistencies, and seeming nonsense. Facing this heap, the child, rather than falling into the depthless high of Jameson's postmodern "euphoria" (28) or even the para-doxical stimulation/fatigue of Ngai's "stuplimity" (271), instead wields an energy to seek the patterns in the heap and an agency to make something of its contents.

Inspired by her toddler's language play, Jarnot's fragments thus represent the heap not as a privative formless form but as a productive form of thinking—a form for thinking. This protosemantic heap works to realert readers to the large-scale logic of language as a system, reengaging an inductive relationship to words that is less worried about smoothing over inconsistencies and gaps. Instead, stimulated by the mechanisms of the child's mind, her readers focus on those gaps, on the nonsense, and work to find coherence, a way for meaningful frameworks to "pop out" of the noise; they also seek to create coherence themselves, to find a way through.[25] Here's one "heap" from part 2 of the poem:

I see you, camels, I see you copernicus triangle food odyssey,

that seventy-nine commandos
and a dog were involved

that they blew some people up and down

catch it!
stop it!
go there!
I want to do that (20)

The opening line seems like nonsense at first glance—four random nouns seemingly drawn out of a hat. Yet its placement next to her daughter's simple statement of fact suggests further investigation. Breaking it down into its parts reveals that "Copernicus Triangle" is a park in Maspeth, New York, where Jarnot and her daughter could have certainly begun a "food odyssey." A more open, playful relationship to words allows these larger logics of the system to emerge—or even its il-logics, as with the lines that follow, referencing the mission to kill Osama Bin Laden by a Navy SEAL team (and a dog) on May 2, 2011.[26] How does her daughter (and how do we) make sense of this incident, or the events of September 11, 2001, that precipitated it, even at the level of language itself? What does it mean to "blow some people up"? And don't up and down always go together?

Blowing something up and down sounds relatively innocuous, like sheets billowing on a clothesline. This distance from violence is furthered by saying that it just happened to "some people." Her daughter's simple commands of action listed afterward become a call to personal arms and action in the face of the illogical language and events of our time. They also reflect on the daughter's earlier statement, "I see you, camels," which itself graduates from mere statement of fact to Austinian speech act. Seeing the camels and stating that one sees them seems to acknowledge the I/thou relationship that the act of seeing creates, thus becoming a kind of ethical act in itself, a way of seeing/being in the world with others that emerges in the structure and logic of the sentence itself—a sentence that only a child would utter.

Rather than conjuring the paralyzing shock, anxiety, emptiness, or fatigue of the grown-up avant-garde, Jarnot's protosemantic fragments reflect and invoke feelings of energy, agency, and attention experienced by the new language learner. Moreover, these affects are inextricably bound up with the intuitive and skeptical forms of whole-brain linguistic thinking that her child-inspired fragments enable. Though no cognitive scientist has yet mapped the transformative potential of experimental sound poetry in the brain specifically, physiological evidence exists that the right brain's latent language ability can work to stimulate new linguistic capacities. For example, stroke patients with aphasia caused by damage to the left hemisphere have been highly successful in relearning how to speak by singing or chanting their sentences (Thaut et al.). Their language brain, and thus much of thinking itself, is rebuilt and restored on the more open, allocentric foundations of the right hemisphere. Though listening to and reading experimental sound poetry for the unimpaired brain certainly cannot elicit the recovering aphasic person's remarkable expansion of agency and expressiveness; as we have seen, it may prove effective for a more modest cognitive "recuperation" process for navigating and creating among the fragments and incoherence of a postmodern world.[27]

The sound poetry of Lisa Jarnot and Tracie Morris is built on the idea that poetry is "the first form of communicating," whether for early humans in the caves of ancient Europe or for early humans in the crib down the hall. By exploiting these foundational energies, their poems reveal that the protosemantic in experimental sound poetics is not always the boa constrictor that kills speech and ruptures readers but perhaps Bea's "Boa Constructor," causing a much-need jolt to old systems and structures— a jolt that is constructive rather than destructive, launching new forms of thinking and possibilities for resistance. Furthermore, this alternative source for the protosemantic—in the ancient forging of group identities through rhythm, pitch, and music, in the communication between parent and child—projects an affective space more conducive to human affil-iation and connection. If the sound poetry projects of the 1970s ended in a "failure to establish the poem as community," as McCaffery claims (*Prior* 162), then perhaps the sound poems of the twenty-first century will have better success beginning with the poem as community, a site where new forms of thinking are born, develop, and thrive.

Teaching through Experimental Poems

> Isn't the avant-garde always pedagogical, she said,
> I mean altruistically bugbearish
>
> —LYN HEJINIAN, *MY LIFE*

I'd like to begin this final chapter with an experimental "deformance" of a literary text, reversing Lyn Hejinian's terms in the epigraph to ask, "Isn't the pedagogical always avant-garde?" Posing this question is not meant to imply that all pedagogy is inherently innovative; as Joan Retallack and Juliana Spahr note, "contemporary literary pedagogy is chronically behind contemporary literature by about half a century" (xii). A more literal interpretation of the term "avant-garde" is needed here—an interpretation that deploys pedagogy to the front lines, a vanguard in which experimentalism meets its most resistant—and most significant—audience. Certainly experimental poetry has an important audience in poetry readings, conferences, journals, and publishers where avant-gardists share their work with one another, but these venues are generally frequented by the already converted. For experimentalism to have its viral, micropolitical effects on the culture, there is no more fertile site than the trenches of the classroom.

This assertion brings up the question of the thorny relationship between experimental poetries and the academy more generally. Alan Golding outlines the debate between Ron Silliman and Bob Perelman on this point. While Perelman "still believes that effective teaching of, and from the position of, experimental poetics can be accomplished in the university setting," Silliman does not, as he finds the academy utterly resistant to change (Golding 22). Golding stresses the need for more anecdotal evidence and narratives of experimental pedagogies to ground this debate (23). I offer the experiences outlined in this epilogue as evidence of the potential effectiveness of such pedagogies. As Silliman implies, the avant-garde necessarily seeks to avoid the permanent, sealed-off spaces of the art museum, the gallery, or the ivory tower of academia. The classroom, however, in my experience and practice, is not located inside that ivory tower. It is a permeable, shifting, social space that can certainly be used to embody, teach, and uphold the hierarchies of the academy and the values of other dominant cultural institutions—but it can also subvert them.[1] The classroom's borderland status is particularly acute at a university like Cal State San Bernardino, where around 80 percent of our students are the first in their families to attend college. They likely come to the university hoping not to subvert the power of the cultural elite but to gain some of that power for themselves. What group could be more in need of Foucault's "tiny … device permitting the introduction, into the very roots of thought, of notions of *chance, discontinuity* and *materiality*" (qtd. in Golding 24)? To use Hejinian's terms, I want to practice an "altruistically bugbearish" pedagogy—one that benevolently introduces students to an object of dread, annoyance, a thorn in the flesh, for their own well-being and empowerment in the world. The classroom would become a space in which the bugbearish virus of experimentalism could infect students' thinking, producing skeptical creative readers, both within the discipline of English and in their lives outside the classroom.

With these goals in mind, I have created and taught multiple sections of an upper-division course in Experimental Poetry and Poetics. I imagined the classroom might serve as a laboratory for me to test the claims of this book. How do students think through experimental poems? How can I best prepare them to do so? However, a hierarchical model of detached experimenter inserting tiny devices and observing helpless subjects contradicted the values of my course topic, not to mention my own values as a teacher. Experimental poetry breaks down hierarchies, subverts author-ity, and empowers readers, inviting them to collaborate in the making of meaning. To deliver a definitive lecture on the meaning and purpose of Ron Silliman's *Ketjak* would no doubt have the poet spinning in his office chair somewhere. No, my pedagogical experiments in the classroom needed to be modeled on the experiments of innovative poetries themselves. For each of the experimental modes we studied, I worked to uncover and implement the forms of teaching within the forms of thinking that each poetics engendered.[2] The resulting class was filled with experiments in collective reading and performance, with varying rates of success. But perhaps most gratifying is the way that the constant focus on process that experimental poetry invites, even demands, produced a course dominated by metacognition, which educational psychologists tell us is essential to student learning and success in any discipline. Thus, a class that might have been perceived as one of those eccentric, teacher's-pet-project, outlier-topic courses managed to generate students much more knowledgeable, savvy, and excited about the process and discipline of literary criticism.

Collective Reading and Performance

On the thirteenth day of my Experimental Poetry and Poetics course, the students arrived with their toys. There were Dinos and Elmos, Batmen and He-Men, Gokus and Homies. We had all read excerpts from Bob Perelman and Francie Shaw's experimental collaboration *Playing Bodies,* in which Perelman writes poetic responses to Shaw's drawings of two toys, a human and a dinosaur, locked in some sort of possibly violent, possibly erotic struggle. We began the class by examining our own experiences with toys and games and with the collaborative dynamics of play. This context established, we dove into Perelman and Shaw's text, which is both a meditation on play and an enactment of it, as the artists' texts on facing pages also seem to interact in their own sometimes violent, sometimes erotic wrestling match. Then it was time for our own playful collaboration. Students joined a partner and experimented with different configurations of toys until they found the most interesting playful tableau. In the next step, they moved to a different group's toy sculpture and collaborated on some Perelman-esque poetic lines in response to the image, which they placed next to the toys. We concluded the activity by wandering our gallery of Playing Bodies and discussing new insights into play that the configurations raised. The sculptures and poems the students created helpfully maintained the ambiguity of the original text. In one tableau, Spyro the dragon was trapped (or was he taking refuge?) inside a novelty Dodgers helmet. *Toy Story*'s three-eyed alien lay with an ear pressed against a giant toy telephone, inspiring the poem "Watch the Planet of the Aliens / Call ET home / Playtime is over." My personal favorite was a Batman action figure holding onto the long, extended legs of a wind-up frog launching into the air, accompanied by this poetic meditation on collaboration and play: "Live and let live / I can fly / Hold you back / lift you up."

As we have seen throughout this book, experimental poetry often functions more as an event to be experienced than an object to be studied. The words "experiment" and "experience" both come from the same Latin root, *experiri,* which means to try, to test, to attempt, to find out, to experience. The active nature of this verb undercuts the passiveness of the term "pedagogy," which implies the child *(paedo)* is guided or shaped/modeled *(agogic)* by the teacher. How to shape a lesson into an active experience or event that is also pedagogical? As my Playing Bodies event reveals, performance was the key.[3]

To be sure, all teaching involves performance. My colleagues and I joke about doing our "dancing bear" routines to keep students engaged and awake. But this pedagogical model, despite its energy, still creates the active author–passive audience dynamic that my course topic rejected. Teaching experimental poetics meant having the students join the circus too. I began with a bit of the dancing bear, though, to ease them into the performative climate of the class and perhaps make myself a bit vulnerable, if I were going to ask them to do the same later. On the first day of class, before giving out the syllabus, I performed an over-the-top, line-by-line backward reading of the course description, which began (at the end):

Take *in* the classroom and *in* your written assignments.

Open and play! Full attitude about the texts. We *read,* and "the playful"
   approaches. We *will*

quite different than any methods you've encountered before. The point is
   to *keep* an[y]

modes of reading, writing, and teaching that we practice in this course.
   May end-up!

None of the students could guess what I had done to generate this
nonsense, even with the text projected on the screen. I will say, though,
that when I read it "correctly" from bottom to top, it generated a collective
gasp of recognition and pleasure that I have never heard before when
reading a course description on the first day.

Making the classroom a stage for such performative events not only
engages students but also empowers them by helpfully decentering the
authority of the teacher and the author. Early on, we explored the roots of
experimentalism in the avant-garde movements of the twentieth century,
including Fluxus. Merely showing them Fluxus images and asking for
interpretations would likely make students feel what Lynn Keller calls the
"shadow authority" of indeterminate texts (33): there must be a "correct"
interpretation of this bizarre text that I'm just not smart enough to get. I
hoped a performative mode would subvert this shadow authority. I told
students about György Ligeti's Fluxus composition "Symphonic Poem,"
which consists of detailed instructions on the windings for one hundred
metronomes.[4] Inspired by this piece, we performed a "Cellphonic Poem."
Half the room set their phone alarm to 2:43 PM, the other half to 2:44 PM,
and we continued on with our regular classroom activities. When the electronic burblings and rock music and bird sounds and heaven knows what
else interrupted class later on in a two-minute wave of sound, this was a
completely unique event that all of us, students and teacher, were experiencing for the first time.

Though I had given the instructions, the event clearly had no essential
intent or meaning behind it that students were meant to guess or uncover.
Consequently, they dove into discussing it with creativity and enthusiasm, my voice just another among them. They noted how many people

apparently woke up to simulated "natural" sounds; a student brought up Baudrillard and the hyperreal. Other students were surprised that all the phones didn't go off at precisely the same time. Weren't they all synched to the "real" time via satellite? From philosophical discussions of the arbitrary nature of time, we moved to the affective experience of cellphone interruptions in class, and how our event was launched by that initial burst of annoyance or fear but was followed by a new kind of listening. Someone noted that the individual alarms all came in waves—no continuous ringing of the mechanical windup clock—which made our cellphonic poem into a fluctuating sonic landscape, with sounds swelling and fading, even seeming to call and respond to one another. This early in-class performance became a touchstone during the quarter when the specter of an experimental text's shadow authority appeared, reminding students that the experimental artist offers a constraint or a score, but it is up to us the audience to perform it, experience it, and make something of it.

The idea of performance also inspired me to use the space of the classroom to physically stage the kinds of reading that experimental poetry encourages. Though an in-class discussion of a text is technically an exercise in collective reading, the traditional classroom configuration—students in rows, seated at desks, facing a standing teacher—spatially undermines this value.[5] I was inspired by Lynn Keller's essay on the "centrifugal classroom," where she explains that experimental poetries require a different model of reading and classroom dynamics. While lyric poetry invites a "centripetal" motion, plunging students into the depths of their/the poet's inner worlds (30), experimental poetry is centrifugal, moving outward into the world through "a dispersion of consciousness and of significance" (31). What if I staged the classroom so that this centrifugal motion and dispersion of consciousness happened physically as well as intellectually in our reading of the text?

Our discussion of Lyn Hejinian's *My Life* provided a perfect opportunity to perform a centrifugal classroom discussion. My objectives were for students to trace the shifting meanings of the book's tag lines and to collaboratively experience and experiment with the generative rather than directive nature of her open text. To facilitate the centrifugal motion, I taped nine posters around the perimeter of the classroom that contained a repetition of the tag line "a name trimmed with colored ribbons," along with the different sentences surrounding it. Students wandered around the room and wrote onto the poster their particular take on the meaning of the tag line in each new context. As Keller writes, the collective reading process that experimental poetry enables tends to build through a kind of "yes, and" or "yet at the same time" mode rather than the correction and contradiction of class discussions of traditional poetry (32). I thus encouraged students to try out this additive model in their responses, interacting not only with Hejinian's text but also with their peers' notes, trying to add something new to the conversation. (I joined in the collaborative effort as an equal voice.) The activity turned out to be highly successful. Certainly the novelty of wandering around the classroom and writing on the walls was part of it, but there was no circus atmosphere; it felt more like an interactive museum gallery. Students walked quietly from poster to poster, engaging with the voices there with much more seriousness than I anticipated. The resulting posters of notes were an excellent visual representation of the productive centrifugal splatter of a dispersed interpretive consciousness—piles of sentences, questions, circled words, and arrows responding, extending, and exploding into multiple interpretations.

Skeptical readers may be thinking this theatrical business is all well and good for entertaining today's jaded students and maybe expanding their critical thinking skills, but what about the important stuff? What about their essays? These in-class performances correlated to a stronger performance in more traditional forms of writing and criticism. At the end of our study of *My Life,* students wrote a thesis-driven analytical essay in which they traced a tag line of their choosing in the book, making a claim about the ideas, themes, and issues that seem to emerge around it.[6] I know two samples does not a sufficient empirical study make, but for the record, I had given the same assignment in a different upper-division course a couple of years earlier, and the essays from this class, where we performed so much experimental reading, were far richer in their interpretation of Hejinian's text. Continually staging and performing the generative multiplicity of experimental texts ended the habitual game of "guess the author's intent" by author-izing the students into a creative, performative analysis of their own. The results were so striking that a case may be made for the value of students adding more experimental forms of criticism to their repertoire as English majors.

Deformance and the Process of Creative Criticism

Extracting forms of teaching from innovative poetries means experimentation not only in classroom performance but also in assignment design. What might an experimental criticism look like? There are many possibilities, but experimental poetry's emphasis on process and poiesis, on its own making or doing, is one inspiration. These poems materialize not so much the content as the activity of cognition, as this book argues. Thus, when designing the central writing project for the course, I wanted an experimental assignment that would materialize the activity—the moves—of literary criticism itself.

Part of this assignment would definitely involve defamiliarizing these critical moves. I took my inspiration from Lisa Samuels and Jerome McGann's notion of deformative criticism, as well as Charles Bernstein's idea of "creative wreading." Following Samuels and McGann's lead, as an alternative to traditional papers and tests, Bernstein asks students to alter works they read through reordering, rewriting, translating, imitating, and performing, emphasizing "ways of reading poetry that do not produce 'understanding' but rather response, questions, disorientation, interaction, more poems" (*Attack* 10). Whereas Bernstein sees deformance as a kind of alternative to traditional criticism, however, I wanted the assignment to highlight the ways that performance, and indeed deformance, is actually a part of the process of literary criticism.

My assignment sheets for literary analysis essays in every class ask for students to "make a clear, provocative, and nonobvious claim about the text." It is this quality—call it interestingness—that is so difficult to teach. How to get students beyond rehearsing the plot or the theme to say something interesting, surprising—something that needs to be argued? My English department, like many around the nation, divides faculty and students into creative writing or literature people (among other subdisciplines), unhelpfully implying that the imagination is involved in the genres of student poetry and fiction, but not in reading literature, and certainly not in writing analytical essays. Bernstein counteracts this divide by teaching what he calls a "creative wreading" workshop, in which he explores "ways to intensify the experience of poetry, of the poetic" for students; ultimately, though, he is "less concerned with analysis or explanation of individual poems" (*Attack* 18). Yet these two processes do not have to be mutually exclusive. The process of analyzing and explaining poems can itself intensify students' experience of poetry—and can be, dare I say it, creative writing.

It would be much easier to trade this rusty genre for some jazzy new experimental forms rather than trying to jump-start a mode that has been drained of its spark and coolness by the generations of tweedy English teachers who assigned it before me. However, I still find significant cognitive, even civic, value in the analysis essay, which requires and engenders in students deep attention and complex thinking, particularly at a time when discourse seems to favor sound bites and gut feelings over careful, in-depth argument. Deformance thus became a way for me to intensify students' experience of poetry, as well as to reenergize their experience of literary analysis. Samuels and McGann, in "Deformance and Interpretation," find that poems can "lose their vital force when they succumb to familiarization" (154); the same thing can be said for the ubiquitous literary analysis essay. To combat this dulling effect, the authors borrow Emily Dickinson's suggestion from a scribbled note on an undated piece of stationery: "Did you ever read one of her Poems backward, because the plunge from the front overturned you? I sometimes (often have, many times) have—a Something overtakes the Mind—" (152). Deforming a poem, reading a poem backward in this way, shifts the interpretive question from "what does the poem mean?" to "how do we release or expose the poem's possibilities of meaning?" (154). We as readers become "dwellers in possibility," as Dickinson wrote, rather than, as students often perceive their role, passive receivers of some transmitted meaning. Deformance thus highlights the way that literary interpretation is something that we do to a text, and that the analytical essay is a performative, creative event in its own right.

To launch the process of estrangement, I started with the familiar. Students began by choosing a traditional lyric poem as their focus for the project, for which I asked them to write a close reading. In class discussion about this first step, we went meta by describing the moves we make to generate literary analyses and where we understand the "meaning" we ascribe to the text to come from. For the next step, I wanted to go beyond the foundational moves of close reading to consider the larger theoretical moves we make within the discipline of literary criticism. I sent students to research their poem and/or poet by querying the MLA database. They had to choose and read two critical essays and complete a "says/does" analysis of them, summarizing the article's content in one paragraph, then describing the interpretive moves that the critic made in another para- graph. I asked, "Where and how does the 'meaning' of this poem seem to emerge for each critic?" Unsurprisingly, the students struggled the most with the "does" question, often just rehashing what the essay said about the text. The next time I try this assignment, I will spend more time discussing the kinds of moves that we make in the discipline, perhaps even giving students a list of methods they might look for. To me, this difficulty highlights not only that pedagogy is behind contemporary literature by about fifty years, but also that it is behind contemporary literary criticism by about the same amount. Students do not recognize the moves that contemporary literary critics make because we do not necessarily ask them to make those moves, or we fail to do a good job of making these moves transparent to our students when we make them in lecture or discussion.

Focusing so much on the poiesis of literary criticism in this assignment resulted in another damning revelation: students hated reading literary criticism, finding it dry, boring, and pretentious. Certainly students often resist reading material that they perceive as complex, difficult, and "long," but we would be too quick to dismiss such a critique as merely the whining of the naive or lazy. I (and my students seem to) agree with Charles Bernstein that "academic prose … tends to avoid animation in favor of caution and to defer exuberance in favor of interminable self-justification and self-glossing" (*Attack* 17). Bernstein blames the tyranny of blind peer review, which encourages "blandness and conformity" in presentation and style (*Attack* 17), but the roots of the problem may go even deeper: into undergraduate curricula in English, where we tone down exuberance and creativity in favor of a conventional, staid academic voice and style. My assignment was making literary analysis "strange" for my students, but not in a good way so far.

I hoped that the critical deformance would provide an opportunity to inject style and exuberance back into the process of criticism. We read and discussed Samuels and McGann's essay and tried out some deformances of

William Carlos Williams's "The Red Wheelbarrow" together in class. For part three of the project, they were to try out at least two of the deformative modes that Samuels and McGann suggest on their chosen poem:

1. reordering (e.g., reading backward)
2. isolating (e.g., reading only verbs or other parts of speech)
3. altering (e.g., changing the spatial organization, typography, spelling, or punctuation of a work)
4. adding (e.g., inserting your own new language into the text) (162)

In an analytical essay, they explored the possibilities for meaning that were exposed by their deformances, then concluded by reflecting on the process of deformance itself in relation to the first two parts of the assignment.[7] Their performance on this final section was successful across the board.

Though the specter of the author still haunted some students, who admitted to a little "queasiness" about mucking around with a famous text, all of them performed the analysis of their deformances with the creativity and exuberance I was hoping for. They often described the process in jubilantly violent terms: "I feel like I am holding Wallace Stevens' poem hostage with a creativity gun. I have to pull the trigger and see what new creation it forms"; "deforming a poem allows the reader/critic not to find the key to unlock the meaning, nor even to pick the lock, but to smash it with a hammer to see what is inside." Several students used the language of "empowerment" when describing the assignment. One concluded:

> I am rather fond of Wordsworth's poetry and I was a little worried that I would somehow ruin it or its effect if I altered it. How could I possibly do anything to improve upon or add interest to a poem written by one of the most famous poets of the Romantic period? Now the act of deforming a poem, especially one by an author whose work I immensely enjoy, allows me to feel an even greater connection to their work. It is rather empowering to feel like I can weave my own threads of meaning and thought into a poem and then step into the landscape right alongside of the poet.

Many students "step[ped] into the landscape" of the poem by choosing the fourth option of adding their own language. Samuels and McGann describe this as the "most subjective" of the deformance poetics, and it is the only one they do not model within the essay. One student wrote that it "lets you live out what you think the poem was about." Of course, we try to break students of the habit of fixating on one small detail or line in a poem to anchor their tangential idea of what the poem is about while ignoring all the many details that seem to complicate it. However, I found that within the context of the deformance, this seemingly reductive, hypersubjective mode had a more salubrious centrifugal effect. One student focusing on Emily Dickinson's "Wild Nights!" added her "own urban flavor to it" by connecting it to "the newly popular slogan YOLO" (you only live once), merging Dickinson's language with rap lyrics from Drake's "YOLO" and Wiz Khalifa's "Young, Wild, and Free." I was particularly gratified that some students who seemed to struggle with writing in other papers and classes with me came alive as creative interpreters in this assignment. One student conducted what she described as an "erotic translation" of Dickinson's poem—and got so into it that she felt the need to apologize at the end of the essay.

In the end, though, I think that another student had it right when she found that "the process of deformance is more valuable than the deformances themselves." The act of deforming the poem seemed to help students understand the original poem better. One writer was confused by the speaker and verb tenses, generating an incoherent traditional analysis of "Wild Nights!" in part one of the assignment. In part three, though, she did a reordering deformance in which she read every other line of the poem and generated a hilarious "pirate" reading of it (including the helpful homonym of "ourrrrrrrrrrr luxury"). By just playing with the poem's separate lines, she was able to untangle what confounded her in her initial reading. As another student described her experience with e. e. cummings, "I now feel as though I know the poem from the inside out, because this time, I found myself on the inside rather than on the outside looking in." To further explore this effect, I may add a fourth step to the assignment in which students return to the original poem to write another traditional close reading, this time with their new insider knowledge of the poem.

At the end of the quarter, I asked students in an anonymous evaluation to describe which of the many experimental activities or assignments we did in the class was their favorite, and eight of seventeen chose the deformance. One student wrote, "My favorite experimental activity/assign-ment was the deformance. I had believed it would be stupid, difficult, and un-scholarly. HOWEVER, I found myself yelling at my brain to dig deeper, offer some 'new' insight to work with a poem analyzed 20+ times before. To read the finished product made me extraordinarily impressed and happy." This was certainly the first time that students chose their final paper as their favorite activity in a class, but what most pleased me about comments like this is the sense of renewed enthusiasm about the process and product of analysis that it conveys. I hope that all of my students leave my classes yelling at their brains to dig deeper and offer new insight—not only into poems but also into the complex texts and problems within the culture around them. Other student comments suggested that the bugbear of experimental poetry had indeed infected their thinking and approach to more than just poems: "It changes the way you see prevalent, taken-for-granted uses of language and spaces like Facebook newsfeeds and billboard signs"; "It's funny because I often read signs or sayings in fragments and consider the meaning that may reside there, regardless of whether or not it was intentional."

Such comments suggest that the avant-garde is in fact pedagogical, as Lyn Hejinian writes. It becomes particularly potent when the pedagogy is avant-garde—when we allow experimental poetics to reshape not only how we think but also how we teach on the front lines of the classroom. The virus of experimental poetry paradoxically enables rather than disables, engaging and empowering students (and teachers) to be finders, exper-imenters, asserters, and makers of meaning. Let me conclude with one more piece of evidence for this virus's virulence; it's also another first for me. Along with the anonymous evaluation that I asked students to write, they also filled out the official "Student Opinion of Teaching Effective-ness" (SOTE) surveys, which go into my tenure file and thus become subject to the panoptic gaze of the university's bureaucracy. Happily, the course earned one of the highest average ratings from students that I have received in my thirteen years of teaching here. But what at first baffled and then pleased me more than any score was that one of the students chose a response to the form in the spirit of the avant-garde, turning its discourse of observation and control back on the system itself. The comment section, rather than discussing my teaching, offered a screed against tuition hikes and wasteful spending on administrative salaries in the Cal State system, concluding: "Top execs waste our money instead of paying those who deserve it: teachers & in-need students. Use your $$ on us! The students & teachers." Experimental poetry had done its work.

Notes

Introduction

1. Unfortunately, YouTube has now disabled the comments on this video, so these playful interpretations are no longer accessible.

2. Brian Reed has no illusions about writing's ability to compel readers to do or feel anything: "What if, for example, Shakespeare really did have the power to compel people to rethink patriarchal, racist, and heteronormative assumptions? I'd spam politicians around the world with extracts from *As You Like It*" (xxv). Chapter 4, which addresses the response of US congressmen to Aram Saroyan's poem "lighght," offers an example of how this might work.

3. I am grateful to Nicholas Dames's excellent book *The Physiology of the Novel* for making me aware of this quote from Williams.

4. Others, including Barsalou, prefer the language of "grounded cognition" to "embodied cognition" because they worry that the latter "produces the mistaken assumption that all researchers in this community believe that bodily states are necessary for cognition and that these researchers focus exclusively on bodily states in their investigations," when clearly some cognition can happen more independently from embodied concepts or experience (619).

5. Wang notes that when Asian American avant-garde writing is discussed, race is not treated, emphasizing how the avant-garde is so often coded as white (44). Cecire argues that "while there are certainly aspects of experimentalism to value, including politically, there is a fundamentally racist strain

to experimentalism ... understood as a historical discourse rather than a set of formal traits" (33). Cecire does important work in pointing out the ways that the Language movement of the 1970s and 1980s and its critical advocates defaulted to "centering whiteness" (35), with their use of performative language serving "as a *proxy for* radical politics" without confronting racism directly (34). However, many contemporary poets of color have been drawn to the radical politics of experimental forms and techniques. In this book, I explore those "aspects of experimentalism to value" that have inspired white and minority writers and readers alike.

6. In Renee Gladman's contribution to the special issue of *Tripwire* on innovative Black writing, she wonders, "Why is there a resistance in literary criticism to consider a writer's experience in the world as having a direct effect on the form of the work, as well as content? How can we begin to see formal experimentation as an extension of a writer's experience in the world, as a kind of negotiation of that experience?" ("Catch a Fire" 5).

7. See Gregg and Seigworth's *Affect Theory Reader* for a broad and helpful introduction and sampling; and see Papoulias and Callard for an "interrogation" of the affective turn.

8. Affect theory approaches to experimentalism have tended to focus mostly on the modernist avant-garde rather than contemporary experimental poems.

9. Hayles worries that this Deleuzian paradigm at times "veers toward the ideological" and risks becoming a "self-enclosed discourse" that fails to connect to actual material processes in the real world (670)—a problem I hope my engagement with cognitive theory will correct for.

10. Other critics have also drawn various useful distinctions between the modernist and postmodernist avant-gardes. Ming-Qian Ma describes a "fetishism of method" in modernism but a "critical inquiry into method itself" in the postmodern (6). Brian McHale argues that the dominant of modernist writing is epistemological while the dominant of postmodernism is ontological (58, 60). Sarah Dowling notes an interesting divide "between modernist break, rupture, or resistance, and the postmodernist depression and resignation that derive from the suffocating exhaustion brought on by the neoliberal reconfiguration of work" (146).

11. Nikki Skillman persuasively argues that post-1950 poets are also more aware of biological systems than poets of any other era, and that poems in this age thus become refined instruments for tracing the scope of cognitive potential. However, the focus on lyric and how the mind sciences have transformed the ways that American poets conceive of the writing self behind the lyric "I" (30) leaves open the question of how these refined instruments of cognitive potential affect the reader.

12. Cecire rightly points out the irony that postwar Language writers interested in the "politics of form" would turn to writers of the modernist avant-garde "whose politics range from muddled to terrible" (ix).

13. Cognitive linguist Joanna Gavins's 2020 book *Poetry in the Mind* provides a nuanced example of this approach and its payoffs, with its exploration of the role of world building, conceptual integration, embodiment, and extended cognition in reading poems. Although the contemporary British poems that Gavins chooses for her case studies illustrate instability and play with the boundaries of cognition, they are all still operating in a lyric mode and do not cross over to the experimental techniques I examine here.

14. Erin Manning and Brian Massumi make this point about phenomenology in *Thought in the Act*.

15. In addition to Zunshine, *Why;* Vermeule; and Scarry, see also *The Oxford Handbook of Cognitive Literary Studies,* edited by Lisa Zunshine, which contains only one article about poetry—specifically, on temporal experience in Wordsworth's *The Prelude*.

16. Several critics have pointed out this problem with cognitive literary studies and neuroaesthetics; see Massumi; Clune; Beaulieu; and Jackson.

17. In *Cognitive Ecopoetics,* Sharon Lattig uses theories of embodied and embedded cognition to offer a new theory of lyric poetry. Rather than just recording a mimesis of the world, lyric, she argues, "recapitulates the perceptual activity" of the writer and "thus the basic dynamics of cognitive functioning" (18, 19). Experimental poetry is similar, except I think that its experiments are not just recapitulations of perception but actual attempts to transform perception and cognition itself. Hume and Osborne provide an important introduction to *Ecopoetics*.

18. Sometimes I found answers there and sometimes I didn't. When I contacted cognitive neuroscientist and experimental poet Jan Lauwereyns with a research question for the chapter on the New Sentence about how the brain responds to ambiguity between sentences, he pointed out that researchers are not yet there: "The habits of research in cognitive neuroscience lead to an extremely skewed focus on within-sentence processing" (email, 22 Nov. 2019).

Chapter 1

1. See Harryman (120); and McCaffery and McHale's interview with Hejinian (127).

2. *My Life* was originally published in 1978, when the author was thirty-seven years old, and contained thirty-seven sections composed of thirty-seven sentences each. The book was republished eight years later in 1986, with eight

new added sections at the end of the book, as well as eight new sentences incorporated seamlessly into the original sections, giving it an expanded 45 × 45 structure. *My Life in the Nineties* did not revise the original forty-five sections, but added ten sections of around sixty sentences each. There is evidence in interviews and the archive that Hejinian worked on expanding the original book into a 60 × 60 structure but abandoned the project. "I may be ruining it," she said in an interview with Alison Georgeson. "I seem to be rupturing seams by inserting more material" (290).

3. Paisley Livingston provides a fine-grained philosophical exploration of the role of intention in the production and appreciation of the work of art. He makes a strong case for the role that intentions play in producing and interpreting a work of art while also acknowledging that authors' intentions can be unconscious or spontaneously realized. Ultimately, however, Livingston's theory of a "partial or moderate" intentionalism focuses on more conventional fiction, film, and visual art and does not consider the added complexities that experimental modalities bring to a theory of intention (173).

4. Hejinian explains in the Georgeson interview, "poetry is making a real contribution at the moment by offering new styles and new forms of thinking. New processes of thought" (288).

5. Carla Harryman describes Hejinian's *Writing as an Aid to Memory* as "an example of a Jamesian consciousness." Like Gertrude Stein, she argues, "Hejinian transports James's ideas about the psychological dimension of language to the question of aesthetic practice: why ought poetry to draw from consciousness only that which is easy to objectify, clear, and discernable, when the 'subjective stream' offers so many instances of unclarity? Isn't unclarity— even impossibility and unrepresentability relevant to thought?" (120).

6. For readings of *My Life* in the context of its engagement with the genre of autobiography, see H. Clark; Johnston; and Spahr, "Resignifying."

7. Sianne Ngai, in *Ugly Feelings,* makes a similar critique of Jameson's argument. She notes that the image of the heap disappears from his essay, replaced by the more abstract concept of fragmentation, which allows him to focus on the breakdown of wholes into parts rather than on how those parts might cohere: "a heap *does* seem to be a coherence of some sort" (288). I explore this question more fully in chapter 5. Silliman also pushes back on Jameson's characterization: "What endows [the New Sentence] with precisely the intensity or power that makes it worthy of our consideration are the many ways in which individual sentences are *not* 'in free-standing isolation,'" as Jameson claims (*New Sentence* 92).

8. Hejinian questions James's famous metaphor for consciousness in one of her Stein talks: "I myself don't always experience consciousness as a 'stream.' Instead it often does appear broken up, discontinuous, sometimes radically, abruptly, and disconcertingly so" (*Language of Inquiry* 103). Her stream of ambiguously connected sentences clearly reflects this more postmodern take on James's stream.

9. Hejinian contrasts James's view of intentionality as a kind of volitional will power with his student Gertrude Stein's less optimistic view (*Language of Inquiry* 281). While James sought "truth," Stein sought "understanding," "a shift of emphasis, from perceived to perceiving, and thus to writing, in which acts of observation, as complex perception, take place" Hejinian writes (*Language of Inquiry* 93). Hejinian takes on a similar phenomenological project in her collaborative poem *Sight,* written with Leslie Scalapino: "It seems as if our emphasis was not on the thing seen but on the coming to see. As I see it, this book argues that the moment of coming to see is active and dialogic" (vi).

10. Silliman ends *The New Sentence* with a chapter called "Zyxt," the last word in English in the *OED,* which is an obsolete Kentish form, the second person indicative present of the verb "see." "Language even ends in the eye," Silliman writes (191).

11. Megan Simpson reads Hejinian's definition of description as "the process of perception in language" (25). Ming-Qian Ma explores how this poetics of description has a counterpart in Maurice Merleau-Ponty's "phenomenology understood as direct description" or as "a phenomenology of phenomenology" (166). John E. Drabinski's essay considers how both James and Merleau-Ponty critique dualist notions of self/world, mind/body, representation/thing-itself in the modern reflective tradition in philosophy (138), arguing instead for "a *radically pre-reflective tissue* of experience," the "stuff" that comprises all these abstractions (148). Drabinski argues that James's concerns are more epistemic and Merleau-Ponty's more ontological (152). It is interesting to think about how Hejinian's poetics of description engages with both the epistemic and ontological questions surrounding phenomenological experience.

12. Here Lauwereyns avoids the "mereological fallacy," or ascribing psychological attributes or experiences to particular parts of the brain rather than the whole person. For a meticulous philosophical critique of some of the conceptual underpinnings of contemporary neuroscience, including the mereological fallacy, see Maxwell Bennett and Peter Hacker, along with responses from Daniel Dennett and John Searle, in Bennett et al.

13. Hejinian explains that these repeated tag lines were meant to "emphasize the ways in which structures of thinking echo structures of language and then

reconstruct them ... [and] the ways in which language echoes and constructs thinking" (*Language of Inquiry* 166). Quoting Gertrude Stein, she seeks "repetition but not sameness" (167). Hilary Clark reads the tag lines in relation to the vicissitudes of memory and identity construction: "As early tags become associated with the beginnings of both the life and the *Life,* their repetition pulls childhood into adulthood, the written past into the present time of writing a life" (326).

14. "The rejection of interruption" line is also perhaps a reference to James's stream of consciousness, which he explains is never fragmented or "interrupted" by a new object, image, or thought, but always a continuous flow (239).

15. "Everything begins as an error of vision," Hejinian once wrote to Arkady Dragomoshchenko (qtd. in Edmond 556).

16. Cognitive research has studied jazz musicians' brains during improvisation and found that areas of the brain associated with inhibition are stifled while activity increases in areas associated with self-expression (Limb and Braun). The study also notes the similarities between the brains of improvisers and the brains of people in REM sleep. Coauthor Allen Braun explains, "It's tantalising to think some connection exists between improvisation and dreaming, which are both spontaneous events. These musicians may in fact be in a waking dream" (qtd. in Loria). Hejinian too seems to link the work of dreams to the work of description and improvisational writing. Dreams are one of the "strange terrains" for description that she cites in "Strangeness." The word dream appears nineteen times in *My Life,* many of them relating the content of her own dreams. She writes in *My Life in the Nineties,* "I think that to write is to refigure, though refiguration is likewise the work of dreams. The night is never neutral to us. The obvious analogy is with music" (136).

17. Myopia is a significant line of inquiry in Hejinian's *The Cell;* it also opens her piece "The Green" from *The Cold of Poetry:* "I am nearsighted and therefore cannot tell, though I would, whether the shapes in a field across the road are rocks, or shrubs, or cows" (127).

18. One of Hejinian's journals confirms this intuition: "My first memory is of something yellow—a dandelion flower or a bee in the grass" (Lyn Hejinian Papers, 1973–94, Box 46, Folder 2, Journal, 2 Apr. 1981–21 Dec. 1981, Geisel Special Collections, University of California–San Diego [hereafter Hejinian Papers]).

19. Hejinian concludes her poem "Ponderable" by celebrating her myopic vision: "Invincible is my myopia, great is my waist, choral are my ideas, / wingéd are my eyebrows, deep is my obscurity—who am I?"

20. In "The Rejection of Closure," Hejinian defines the "open text" as "open to the world and particularly to the reader. It invites participation, rejects the authority of the writer over the reader and thus, by analogy, the authority implicit in other (social, economic, cultural) hierarchies. It speaks for writing that is generative rather than directive. The writer relinquishes total control and challenges authority as a principle and control as a motive" (*Language of Inquiry* 43).

21. In "An Exchange of Letters," Hejinian writes to Tyrus Miller, "I mean my lines to be read as if hyphenated—one cognition" (36).

22. "Sentence meaning reason" also appears as a sentence in the essay/long poem "Happily" at the end of Hejinian's *Language of Inquiry* (388).

23. Amusingly, James also offers the example of "the obscurer passages in Hegel," whose rationality seems to come only from "the fact that the words all belong to a common vocabulary, and are strung together on a scheme of predication and relation" (254–55). "Yet there seems no reason to doubt that the subjective feeling of the rationality of these sentences was strong in the writer as he penned them, or even that some readers by straining may have reproduced it in themselves" (255).

24. There is evidence in the archive at UCSD that Hejinian considered titling *My Life* with just such an ambiguous phrase. The original title of one manuscript is *One Side, Around,* and in a journal entry, Hejinian plays with various permutations of it: "303. One Side A Way A Side / A Way Always A Way / Around Around Around / Variations before A Way, One Side Around" (Hejinian Papers, Box 45, Folder 7, 1978–80).

25. Silliman notes, "The new sentence is a decidedly contextual object. Its effects occur as much between, as within, sentences. Thus it reveals that the blank space, between words or sentences, is much more than the 27th letter of the alphabet. It is beginning to explore and articulate just what those hidden capacities might be" (*New Sentence* 92).

26. In Hejinian's analysis of Stein's "Stanzas in Meditation" in "A Common Sense—," she argues that it is "not simply a response to meaning; rather it is the articulation of being in meaning—in the stream of meaning" (*Language of Inquiry* 365).

27. Gerrig and Wenzel study reader responses to mystery novels and note that people differ in their ability to engage in the divergent, novel forms of thinking that more complex texts require; their motivation to try it may be influenced by their "self-efficacy for creativity"—that is, their belief that they can perform well on a creative task (382). Oren Izenberg argues that Language poets "tend to treat the objects of their art—or poems—as epiphenomenal evidence of

a constitutively human capacity for free and creative agency that is the real object of their interest" (136). This does raise some important questions in relation to teaching these poems. The possible salubrious effects of reading them may depend to some extent on readers' "self-efficacy for creativity," their willingness to try to make meaning of the text at all. I share some strategies for generating students' self-efficacy for creativity in the epilogue.

28. In metonymy, the whole may represent a part ("The White House introduced its new policy") or a part may stand in for the whole (aka synecdoche, as in "Lands belonging to the crown"). Causes may take the place of their effects ("The pen is mightier than the sword"), and places or dates may represent events (the Alamo, 9/11).

29. John Shoptaw explains that Hejinian's style is not disjunctive but discontinuous: "The gaps in Hejinian's poems are meant to present readers not with walls but with projects" (58).

30. Olson was interested in Mayan hieroglyphs and the ways that they functioned as more than just an abstract lexicon; they also had force as carved, three-dimensional objects ("Project" 96). I explore this experimental dimension further in chapter 3.

31. Hejinian writes in a set of "Notes for a Talk on *My Life*" from the 1970s, "The simple sentence rendered complex by overloading the word. Condensation: in the briefest possible space one wants to convey the maximum connotative complexity. To make each sentence as loaded and complex as a dream. To internalize the pressure" (Hejinian Papers, Box 40, Folder 12).

32. Graesser et al. make a distinction between the inferential bridges that readers make between sentences next to each other and the "distal bridges" that occur between sentences located earlier in the text (306). Hejinian builds a lot of distal bridges across the text with her tag lines.

33. Hejinian Papers, Box 45, Folder 4, Journal, 21 Aug. 1974.

34. This also seems to be the overarching thesis of Joan Retallack's book *The Poethical Wager*. Ron Silliman, Carla Harryman, Lyn Hejinian, Steven Benson, Bob Perelman, and Barrett Watten write in their Language poetry manifesto on "Aesthetic Tendency and the Politics of Poetry," "This is often what the use of the *I* in our work has involved—to propose, in the inherent terms of the work, that sense of a connection between discrete conceptions which has been habitually effaced from the processes of thought and language and to recharge this neurological scar tissue with some new synapses" (Silliman et al. 266).

35. In a journal entry from the late 1990s, Hejinian writes: "The difference between classical music (e.g.) and improvised or avant-garde music is that classical music invites its audience to be knowers whereas avant-garde music

invites its audience to be learners. To accept the invitation to become a learner requires humility & imagination (learning requires imagination)" (Hejinian Papers, Box 112, Folder 27, Notebook, Mar. 1997–Aug. 2000, p. 79).

Chapter 2

1. Mullen's elision of *U* from her dictionary suggests that the reader's own essential notion of self will be compromised by the book. The final question in "Why You and I" suggests that this erasure of "I," the writer, and "U"/You, the reader, is itself a kind of resistance to the tyranny of language, a way to "strike the orderly alphabet." Yet puns on the word "strike" here evoke a much more complicated relationship to language for Mullen. It can mean to go "on strike" (as the word "union" implies), to attack, or to delete, but also to begin a journey, to ring like a bell, to discover like gold, or to take on or assume, like a pose. Amy Moorman Robbins reads this poem as a performance of overt disempowerment in relation to Bruce Andrews's similar poem *I Don't Have Any Paper* (357).

2. I discuss this issue more fully in the introduction. Robbins points out this problematic tendency of critics associating, or even demanding of, minority writers a unified authentic "voice," while white writers, even those with an accessible voice, are treated as innovative and aesthetically complex (352). She delves into landmark critical studies, author interviews, and literary histories of Language writing to explore the problematic erasures and contradictions arising from the movement's "deep disinterest in poetics of identity," as Bob Perelman writes (qtd. in Robbins 341). Robbins argues that *Sleeping with the Dictionary* "both solicits and frustrates reader demand" for a display of an African American female subject by creating a speaker, like that of Language writing, that is "conspicuously absent," but she also "re-races the absent subject … as implicitly African American, pointing to the political and historical differences between concealing or refusing a white identity and concealing or refusing a black one" (356).

3. Benjamin Lempert explores Mullen's "contemporary jazz voice" in *Sleeping with the Dictionary*—one that does not privilege the revelation of an individual voice, as traditional jazz performance might, but rather privileges a voice "unmistakably figured as African American, yet one achieving this figuration by setting its version of corporeality within a space and time saturated with the indeterminate temporality of jazz improvisation. Refusing either the ossification of sound into text or the reduction of text to sound, Mullen's poetry thereby offers a provocative reading of blackness as experienced in its multiple guises: sonic, temporal, visual" (1060). In a similar vein, Lisa Mansell argues

that Mullen's work "directly addresses the untruthful dichotomy between formal practice and the 'feel' of the line—its lyricism" (127).

4. Courtney Thorsson writes an interesting essay on "foodways" in Mullen's work that destabilizes this binary, asserting that the early poetry is just as formally innovative as the later, and that the later poems are just as much a storehouse of African American vernacular forms as the earlier, more voice-based poems (189).

5. Mullen explains, "I write beyond the range of my voice and the social boundaries of identity, yet within the limits imposed on my work and my imagination by language and its cultural significance. The idea of identity informs my poetry, insofar as identity acts upon language, and language acts upon identity. It would be accurate to say that my poetry explores the reciprocity of language and culture" ("Imagining" 198). Mullen critics such as Kathleen Crown ("Choice Voice Noise"), Elisabeth Frost, Mitchum Huehls, Deborah Mix, and Juliana Spahr ("Resignifying") have answered her call for a more inclusive view of her work, analyzing it both for its formal innovation and its African American themes and aesthetics. They explore the ways that her formal experimentation, particularly her use of puns, manifests the experiences of a uniquely Black subjectivity (Huehls), or that her "signifying" on Gertrude Stein adds racial color to a white experimental foremother (Frost and Mix).

6. Derek Attridge similarly describes the act of creation as "both an act and an event, both something that is done intentionally by an effort of the will and something that happens without warning to a passive, though alert, consciousness" (26), though he is ultimately most interested in the act and event of reading a literary text.

7. Emily P. Beall applies Peter Stockwell's methodologies from *Cognitive Poetics,* such as defamiliarization, prototypicality and actualization, sequential and summary scanning, and mapping of cognitive metaphors to analyze what she calls Mullen's "cognitive similes" in *Sleeping with the Dictionary,* but she ends by rightly noting the limitations of his theory "to address a text as radically open to readerly work as Mullen's" (136).

8. According to Riley's research, schizophrenia occurs when "the hearer's own capacity to recognise that these are still self-generated voices, even where they're experienced as peremptory invasions," breaks down (64).

9. Riley writes, "For inner speech is no limpid stream of consciousness, crystalline from its uncontaminated source in Mind, but a sludgy thing, thickened with reiterated quotation, choked with the rubble of the overheard,[...] then crammed with slogans and jingles, with mutterings of remembered accusa-

tions, irrepressible puns, insistent spirits of ancient exchanges, monotonous citation, the embarrassing detritus of advertising, archaic injunctions from hymns, and the pastel snatchings of old song lyrics" (73).

10. In an insightful reading of Mullen's *Muse & Drudge*, Evie Shockley argues that the book "pushes black vernacular to such extremes that it ceases to function as the authentication of a coherent, singular black identity. Rather than 'a black voice,' *Muse & Drudge* presents a parade, a crowd, a chorus of black (women's) voices" (87). If *Muse & Drudge* turns outward to sound the polyvocality of the Black community, then *Sleeping with the Dictionary* turns inward, exploring the polyvocality that exists within one Black woman.

11. Massumi borrows this notion of a "confound" from a vision researcher who describes "the brightness confound" as the difficulty of objectively describing the color of an object because of the variations caused by illumination (162). What you are seeing is always a combination of color and brightness and the color's relation with colors around it. It is impossible to separate out these individual pieces because "color is a field, a nondecomposable relational whole" (163).

12. Oulipeans prefer newly invented constraints or revivified traditional constraints such as Raymond Queneau's *Cent Mille Milliards de poèmes* (One hundred trillion poems). At first glance, the book appears to be a collection of ten sonnets, but a closer look reveals that each line of each poem may replace or be replaced by its corresponding line in the nine other poems. The result is the possibility of ten to the fourteenth power, or one hundred trillion, sonnets (Motte 3).

13. Georges Perec famously wrote the novel *La Disparition* in this mode, excluding the letter *e* throughout. See Marjorie Perloff's helpful discussion of the Oulipo group in *Radical Artifice* (139–45), as well as the anthology *Oulipo*, edited and translated by Warren F. Motte Jr., which Mullen, in her interview with Barbara Henning, says she was reading (41). Mullen explains that Oulipo's "idea of 'potential literature' liberates the writer to concentrate on the process, rather than the product, of writing. Far from being elitist, they make the creative process more accessible as they deflate the divine afflatus of artistic inspiration" (26).

14. Mullen acknowledges her modifications of Oulipean constraints in her interview with Daniel Kane (136). In her interview with Barbara Henning, she notes, "I think that Oulipo is interesting because it has rules for how to break rules. That's what its constraints are, I think—rules for how to break rules. I'm less interested in randomly breaking rules, but often I'm breaking rules in a way that points to the paradoxical effects of language" (42).

15. In her interview with Henning, Mullen explains that her use of anaphora in the book was inspired by Walt Whitman and Aimé Césaire (86).

16. These parodies reveal Mullen's poetics of both/and, as they can be read both as the Oulipean game of Literary Prosthesis, or "improving on" already existing texts, and in terms of the African American tradition of "signifying" on canonical texts of Western literature. Mullen also makes up her own games and constraints to generate poems. The poem "Between," for example, is composed solely of words that we use with the word "between" (Scylla and Charybdis, shit and shinola, a rock and a hard place, thighs, sheets, ears, jobs, the lines, etc.), generating lines such as "Rock the lines me / Scylla her breasts shinola" (9).

17. Mullen explains to Barbara Henning, "Substituting 'Mickey Mouse' for 'mistress' gave the poem a little more coherence and direction than a random [N] + 7" (63).

18. Mullen tells Barbara Henning that "Swift Tommy" also "comments on the role of knowledge workers or gatekeepers of information … mocking the authoritative tone that we assume as academics trained in our particular disciplines" (95).

19. Mullen's book *Trimmings* explores women's clothing and its reflection of cultural values of white and Black femininity. Another potential pun here is on Lewis Carroll's "Mock Turtle."

20. Amy Moorman Robbins's excellent reading points out that displacing an assumed "I" onto a "metonymically slant 'my' also exemplifies Mullen's pointed avoidance throughout *Sleeping with the Dictionary* of the frequently too visible, too 'accessible' embodied speaking subject" (365).

21. Another fun homophonic poem in the book is the prose poem "Kirsten-ography," a life story that begins, "K was burn at the bend of the ear in the mouth of Remember. She was the fecund chill burn in her famish" (46). The meaning is translatable if read aloud, but the meanings of the homophonic words also resonate in interesting ways. The "mouth of Remember" is a beautiful metaphor for thinking about storytelling and passing down memories. Nadia Nurhussein, in a reading of "Kirstenography," notes, "It returns the reader to a virtual state of early literacy, forcing a reading experience similar to the beginning reader's experience of 'sounding out.' It forces articulation, vocalizing what would be silent reading" (43).

22. Intriguingly, doubled words beginning with the letters *E, Q, U*, and *X* are excluded from the list.

23. My sister, an actor in Boston, has taken to reciting this poem as a warm-up before performances.

24. Mullen says in her interview with Henning, "'Blah-Blah' is like a baby learning to talk, and [its companion poem] 'Jinglejangle' is that basic melodic impulse of chiming and rhyming, which we hear a lot in advertising and political slogans. Together they represent the DNA or building blocks of poetry" (55). Henning sees a relationship between these sound poems and Aimé Césaire's African sound poems (55). I explore this connection between sound poetry and baby talk more fully in chapter 5.

25. The word "gaga," mentioned earlier as baby talk, is prominent in a song by rock group Queen about the babble of the information age: "Radio Ga Ga." It also evokes the name of pop diva Lady Gaga.

26. Daniel Heller-Roazen writes, "It is always possible to perceive in one form of speech the echo of another. Depending on the idiom and the sensitivity of the ear turned toward it, however, the nature and significance of the resonance may vary considerably" (99). Certainly different readers of Mullen's "Blah-Blah" will hear different echoes within the litany.

27. Mullen also includes the word *dada*. Dada practitioners appreciated that the word means "hobbyhorse" and "nursemaid" in French, the tail of a sacred cow for an African tribe, a cube or a mother in some regions of Italy, and "yes, yes" in Romanian (Rasula, *Destruction* x). Hugo Ball notes in his Dada manifesto that it also referenced a German soap brand (Rasula, *Destruction* 23).

28. In 1997, many refugees at Tingi Tingi died of malnourishment or were used as human shields against the rebel Tutsis by the Zaire government. This process of Googling the words "blah blah" and searching for global cross-references and patterns made for a helpful assignment and a fun discussion when I taught this book.

29. Jayne Cortez created a 2007 documentary about the subsequent 2004 conference entitled *Yari Yari Pamberi: Black Women Writers Dissecting Globalization.*

30. The character of Echo has been taken up by many philosophers, poets, and critics as a representation of the poet and even an originary figure of deconstruction. See Berger and Gabara's helpful summary of these many treatments of Echo by writers such as John Hollander, John Brenkman, Claire Nouvet, Maurice Blanchot, and Jacques Derrida.

31. Mullen says during her interview with Henning, "Once I focused on the dictionary as a writer's companion, collaborator, and partner, I had a more coherent framework for the book as a whole. I understood more clearly that all along I had been writing about the potential of language for power and play, and I could imagine the dictionary as a speaker or character in the work" (91).

32. Though my association of her language here with bodice rippers might suggest a kind of heteronormative coupling of poet and dictionary (note the

possible puns on the male anatomy in "dicker" and "dictionary"), Mullen's language throughout the poem seems to avoid that normative move. Her partner never gets a gendering pronoun; the opening lines involve a lot more tongues and licking than penetration; indeed, later in the poem it is *she* who "penetrates" the dictionary.

33. Mullen explains in her interview with Henning, "The idea of sleeping with the dictionary suggests not only being intimate with language but also a relationship with dreams and altered states of consciousness. Our use of language is not only rational, but also irrational, unconscious, and intuitive" (40).

Chapter 3

1. Though phenomenologists and cognitive scientists use disabled subjects all the time in their work, surprisingly little scholarship has been done using phenomenology as a lens in disability studies. Miho Iwakuma notes the rich possibilities of the pairing.

2. Grenier and Faville include a copy of Eigner's typescript of this poem in their appendix; it appears that Eigner had a fresh ribbon in his 1940 Royal manual typewriter, such that the *e*'s in the word "eye" are almost completely filled-in black circles, intensifying this visual effect (1719).

3. As Hillary Gravendyk writes, "Eigner calls upon this shared sense of embodiment in his poetry as he asks us not to register *his* physical situation, but to pay attention to our own" (5).

4. Grenier writes of his first meeting with Eigner, "I couldn't understand *At All* what he was saying—in his barrage of palsied speech—he had not had 'opportunity to converse' for so long!" (vii).

5. Nathan Brown highlights the tensions between understanding Olson as prioritizing organicism, the biological body, or objectism, "the 'body' of us as object" (60). Peter Middleton, in *Physics Envy*, offers a rich exploration of the influence of nuclear physics on Olson's thinking in "Projective Verse."

6. There is more evidence that Eigner may be thinking about Olson in this poem. Eight months later, Eigner wrote a poem with the parascript "A letter on Olson" that includes "poetry, writing might be no more / difficult than / plumbing the senses / ... I was always curious // visible how does it work" (*Collected Poems* 942).

7. Eigner does not write "the eyes are more than the *ears*." His poems are filled with sound play. Seth Forrest provides an interesting article on Eigner's aural and visual poetics in relation to the radio—an early and constant companion for Eigner, and the medium that introduced him to contemporary poetry when he heard Cid Corman's radio program in 1949.

8. In a letter to his sister-in-law, Janet Eigner, who was writing a paper on his poetry for a university course, Eigner calls this "my rightward bent" (Bartlett and Hart 231).

9. Michael Davidson does an excellent reading in this vein in "Missing Larry." Additionally, George Hart's essay takes an ecocritical approach informed by disability studies, using Eigner's unique spatial orientation to uncover the ableist biases in the upright human bodies of ecocriticism and of projectivist poetics.

10. "Lacuna sometimes felt as tension, yes," he writes in his letter to Janet Eigner (Bartlett and Hart 230). In the Stony Hills interview, Eigner describes this tension in relation to prose: "to say what I want to when I think of it, before I forget it or how to say it." However, he seems to find poetry much more relaxing: "While with a poem, there's no or relatively little need to attain length" (*areas* 149).

11. McCaffery and Nichol similarly point out that the conventional book "organizes content along three modules: the lateral flow of the line [and] the vertical or columnar build-up of the lines on the page," with depth occurring only through such a buildup of pages on pages (qtd. in Perloff, "Concrete Prose"). Though Eigner's lines curve, like the lines of non-Euclidean geometry, I begin in a more rigid Euclidean space in order to discuss the effects of his form.

12. This reading suggests a connection to concrete poetry, a form particularly popular in Europe and Brazil, if not the United States, in the twentieth century. Mary Ellen Solt, in her comprehensive *Concrete Poetry*, compares the form to projective verse, speculating that US poets were more interested at the time in learning to speak an American language. She writes: "The concrete poet sees a need for moving farther away from grammar and syntax to a constellation of words with spatial syntax, or to the ideogram than does Olson, who stays with the line. Also the concrete poet has discovered greater possibilities in the space presented by the page and in the typewriter than Olson suggests" (48). Eigner's poetics seems to push further along the continuum, away from the grammatical line to this spatial syntax of word constellations.

13. Barrett Watten writes, "I see Eigner's work as a continuous moment of decision—a series of cruxes between alternative meanings—that connects the making of the work with its open horizon of interpretation" (in Bartlett and Hart 88).

14. Up until the early 1970s, Eigner typed his name, address, and the date at the top of each poem, thus situating the poetic "event" in both space and time. (Later typescripts still include his name and the date.) Stephanie Anderson argues that the date is "a key axis" in Eigner's poems, "marking the movement

between the past-as-past and past-as-present, creating temporal motion" (in Bartlett and Hart 147).

15. As Nathan Brown writes, "For Olson the significance of non-Euclidean geometry is a theory of 'disposition of matter in space,' which implies that the formation of matter is involved with the formation of space, rather than merely occupying space" (68). Peter Middleton traces the genealogy of Olson's interest in non-Euclidean geometry to his reading of H. M. S. Coxeter and Kurt Lewin (121).

16. In Olson's proposed Mayan glyph project, he was interested not only in the individual glyph but also its arrangement in the "glyph-block," which creates a "passage" of glyphs that is "the clue ... of the other important element of this art, time, as the Maya, great masters of time elsewhere, managed it here in their language" (96).

17. This poem might also be understood as an example of what Linda Russo calls Eigner's "sympoetic ecopoetics." Eigner's "poems are not about space, or place, but about biophilia, the awareness and knowledge that arises from attending to spatial relations as ecological relations" (in Bartlett and Hart 195).

18. Steven Fama catalogs only thirty poems with overt historical references among Eigner's more than three thousand poems.

19. This poem illustrates that Larry Eigner can be considered among other New American poets such as Olson, Muriel Rukeyser, and Robert Duncan, whom Peter Middleton describes as manifesting *Physics Envy* in their midcentury poetics.

20. Hillary Gravendyk's phenomenological reading of Eigner's poetics describes this embeddedness: "It might be more useful to think of the body as a hall of mirrors in which the body itself is always at least partially glimpsed within the scene of what it touches, avoids, notices, hears, smells, or tastes" (10).

21. Peter Middleton notes that this famous Olson line is actually an unattributed quote from Alfred North Whitehead: "the human body is indubitably a complex of occasions which are part of spatial nature" (146).

22. Eigner seems to make a similar critique of Olson in his unpublished essay "Religion in the Big World," included in Rippeon's *Letters to Jargon*. Peter Middleton also notes that Olson "never questions the trustworthiness of his own poetic voice" (192).

23. Hart makes a similar argument regarding Eigner's ecopoetics: "The fact of Eigner's disability turns the proprioceptive stance of Olson's upright poetics to the *chora* rather than the *topos*. His disability ecopoetics produces environment poems, emphasizing the environing surround in relation to the subject rather than the subject's conversion of the surround into place" (167).

24. Felski cites Bernstein on the artifice of absorption, but in her chapter on "enchantment."

25. Olson describes a similar form of reading in *The Special View of History*, connecting Keats's notion of negative capability to the Heisenberg uncertainty principle. Only Keats's man, who "is capable of being in uncertainties, mysteries, doubts," can grasp "*both* mass and momentum, or substance & motion" (39). Historians, like particle physicists, must never stop, or they will get only part of the story.

26. Another connection to concrete poetry emerges here. Eugen Gomringer, considered the founder of concrete poetry, also uses the term "constellation" to describe his poetics: "The constellation is the simplest possible kind of configuration in poetry which has for its basic unit the word, it encloses a group of words as if it were drawing stars together to form a cluster" (in Solt 67). The Brazilian Noigandres poets expand Gomringer's hypervisual concretism into the "verbicovisual," which could easily describe the interplay of voice and vision in Eigner's work. They also define concrete poetry as embodying "tension of things-words in space-time" (in Solt 72).

27. Eigner's poems often play with the word *still*, perhaps inspired by William Carlos Williams's ambiguous use of it in "Spring and All." Eigner has an early poem "for w c w" that ends "the word still" (534).

28. Stephanie Anderson finds that "in Eigner's work from this period, we can begin to think of walls as planes, flat surfaces through which a subject tries to see" (in Bartlett and Hart 159).

29. Mayan glyph blocks are also read in "paired columns" rather than in single rows or single columns, which creates a zigzagging reading pattern (Montgomery). It is unclear whether Olson knew about this reading practice, although he is fascinated by the "motion on stone in time" that the glyph blocks invoke ("Project" 96).

30. Hillary Gravendyk does a similar reading of Eigner's multiple-columned long poem "there's / a season," following different pathways through the poem and exploring the multiple simultaneous perceptions they enable (4).

31. These subtle shifts in the grid line of the poem were important to Eigner. Barrett Watten, who published Eigner's poems in the journal *This*, writes, "Eigner was exceptionally diligent in copying the exact typographic relation of words, indentations, line spacings, and marginal notes in each version of his poems, and he worked assiduously … to translate spatial relations into typography, as well as to preserve all idiosyncrasies of spelling and punctuation" (Bartlett and Hart 109). You can also see this precision in some of his letters to Jonathan Williams: "22x spaces shoved over to the right/so that <u>outsid</u> [*sic*]

comes under <u>moment</u>, above.... Also change moved over to begin under <u>t</u> in wi<u>th</u>" (Rippeon 40).

Chapter 4

1. In an email to me (1 Feb. 2022), Saroyan pointed out an error in Ian Daly's Poetry Foundation article about the controversy, noting that George Plimpton supervised the NEA anthology but did not choose the poem for the award, as Daly suggests. Robert Duncan was actually the judge chosen for the poetry category. Saroyan's email to me noted that Duncan told Saroyan several years later that "he had weighed several poems by me that had appeared that year, among them more traditional pieces, but had chosen 'lighght' because an angel told him to do it."

2. Ronald Reagan was still making critical references to the poem in the 1980s, and Dinesh D'Souza attempted to use the poem to revive the debate again in the 1990s (Saroyan, "Most Expensive").

3. More recent research by Dehaene and others has revealed another route he calls "reading by hand," which will become relevant later when we turn to vispo (Nakamura et al. 20766).

4. For helpful introductions to the aesthetics of concrete and visual poetry, see Waldrop, Higgins, and Bohn. For an excellent history of the international movement, see the introduction to Mary Ellen Solt's *Concrete Poetry*.

5. Marjorie Perloff names concretism what Deleuze and Guattari call a "minor literature," born on the peripheries in places like Brazil, Scotland, Switzerland, and Sweden, rather than Paris, London, or New York ("Constraint" 697).

6. Gomringer would eventually go full capitalist, becoming the chief design consultant for Rosenthal, a famous china and glass manufacturer (Perloff, *Unoriginal* 64).

7. Indeed, Concrete poetry and vispo are crucial predecessors of new media poetics and digital poetry, which are built on the synergy of writers, readers, and machines. Morris and Swiss provide an essential introduction. As the essays in this collection emphasize, new media poetics involves more than just a migration of words from page to screen; "it is, in important aspects, a different order of writing" (9). It thus requires a different form of reading than the print-based work I examine in this chapter.

8. Excited at discovering a pictographic source for the Chinese ideogram for "to be," Fenollosa observes, "Here the baldest symbol of prosaic analysis is transformed by magic into a splendid flash of concrete poetry" (qtd. in Bayard 18).

9. Johanna Drucker writes, "The compelling aspect of this work is that it refuses either pictoriality or literary form, sitting precisely between the two, requiring that one shift between the activities of reading for sense and looking for sensation" (*Visible Word* 135).

10. Craig Dworkin, in *Reading the Illegible,* cites Jed Rasula and Bruce Andrews on this distinction.

11. Webster makes a compelling case for the ascendency of authorial intent in the work of three other modernist visual poets: Guillaume Apollinaire, Kurt Schwitters, and e. e. cummings.

12. Fortuitously, Dworkin writes, "As a 'pataphysical' investigation of minute particulars, radical formalisms hew to the concrete. Where 'concrete' is what the street is made of" (*Reading the Illegible* 5). But also poems!

13. As evidence that this clean aesthetic fails to map perfectly onto all manifestations of concrete poetry in the 1960s, see Craig Dworkin's analysis in *Radium of the Word* of visual poetry by Russell Atkins, D. A. Levy, Don Thomas, and T. L. Kryss, which often deploys a more disfluent aesthetic.

14. This poem is also inscribed on the side of a building in the Netherlands. Concrete poetry obviously dances on the borders between verbal and visual art, private reading and public viewing.

15. The Greek word for "alphabet" is *stoicheia,* which also means "elements." To the Greeks, letters, like the elements of the material world, were atomistic, indecomposable (Drucker, *Alphabetic Labyrinth* 56).

16. Bob Grumman nicely interprets the poem as "the center of an alphabet just starting to form, between its m and n." He also notes that this poem was cited in the *Guinness Book of World Records* as the world's shortest poem.

17. This poem is a good example of Kenneth Goldsmith's claim that Concrete poetry is a protodigital genre whose true medium is the web. The poem would work well as a Flash animation.

18. Williams's *Anthology* even includes a critic describing the poem as an "inverted-delta" (n.p.).

19. A resurgence of concrete methodologies has appeared in the work of some contemporary poets, including giovanni singleton's *American Letters: Works on Paper* and Douglas Kearney's *The Black Automaton,* as well as more recent work published on the Futurefeed blog (future-feed.net). In addition to concrete aesthetics, this work draws on alternative traditions of the visual in African American poetry and letters—what Aldon Lynn Nielsen calls "the calligraphy of black chant" (37), as well as the visual forms of comics, in the case of Kearney.

20. In the very first concrete manifesto written in 1953, Öyvind Fahlström writes, "SQUEEZE the language material: that is what can be titled concrete. Do not squeeze the whole structure only: as soon as possible begin with the smallest elements, letters and words" (in Solt 78).

21. *On the Just Shaping of Letters* is a famous constructed alphabet by artist Albrecht Dürer (Drucker *Alphabetic Labyrinth* 163).

22. Bök acknowledges the complexity and potentially problematic nature of the gender politics of these pieces in *Jacket2*: "for me, the *Odalisques* also suggest the extreme degrees to which a poet might begin to fetishize the sensual, optical appeals of language itself, admiring the contours of letterforms in a manner reminiscent of obsessive, libidinal fixations" (qtd. in Barwin).

23. See Dworkin's *Reading the Illegible* for some deft readings of the formal politics of many postmodern illegible poems.

24. These benefits also translate into the classroom. In one experiment, students in an AP high school classroom were assigned fluent and disfluent versions of the same worksheets. The students who learned from the disfluent materials had significantly higher exam scores (Alter 439).

25. Gareth Jenkins, email to Jessica Luck, 15 Nov. 2016.

26. Gary Barwin notes that "surprisingly little visual poetry uses 'cursive' fonts." Derek Beaulieu calls vispo "machine-based poetry" (in Vassilakis and Hill 76). Furthermore, all of the poems in Dworkin's *Reading the Illegible* work with typewritten and (over)printed works.

27. Grenier's drawing poems were apparently influenced by Larry Eigner's palsied handwriting. Eigner lived with Grenier and Kathleen Frumkin in Berkeley for ten years (Bartlett and Hart 5).

28. Interestingly, a 2008 handbook for calligraphy and hand lettering offers "Shout/Speak/Whisper" as a helpful heuristic for creating good page design in multimedia pieces. One element on the page should "shout" as the eye-catcher and focal point, another should "speak," and the third, such as illegible "words scribbled in the background," should "whisper" (Engelbrecht 144).

29. Jesse Glass, email to Jessica Luck, 19 Jan. 2017.

30. As I worked to decipher this poem, following the curving gestures of the cursive and rotating the book to follow the curving lines, I was reminded that "verse," that old name for poetry, comes from the Latin *vertere*, "to turn."

31. Psychologist Nico Frijda writes that "frowning when meeting an obstacle in thinking is not in any way a means of expressing concentration but a means of maintaining it" (21).

32. In a personal email (19 Jan. 2017), Glass mentioned that he is "fascinated by the connection between visual poetry and sound poetry … esp. the connection between the hand-written vispo and the human voice." Handwriting bears, indeed *is*, the mark of the unique body that produced it, much like the voice.

33. The *OED* cites several examples of this metonymic use of "shell," including Dryden, Thomas Gray, and Byron, who refers to fellow poets as "My brethren of the shell."

Chapter 5

1. Mithen pushes back specifically on Steven Pinker's claim that the evolution of language is primarily tied to the need for logical reasoning rather than anything related to musical cognition. For Pinker, music is mere "auditory cheesecake" (534).

2. Dada sound poetry at times made a problematic connection between such "primitive" energies and the racial other, particularly an African other. Ball wrote of Huelsenbeck in his diary, "He pleads for stronger rhythm (negro rhythm)," and Huelsenbeck and Tristan Tzara wrote poems in faux African lingo (Rasula, *Destruction* 8, 9)—although Tzara later used excerpts of authentic African songs he found in anthropology journals that he read in Zurich (McCaffery, "Cacophony" 119). As Barry Schwabsky writes, Dada artists longed for a kind of "racial transformation" ("We want a new skin color," Huelsenbeck wrote), but it was one based entirely on racial stereotypes.

3. Irene Gammel and Suzanne Zelazo have explored women's contributions to sound poetry. They note that Dada poet Baroness Elsa von Freytag-Loring-hoven's sound poems "hinge on the generative, the slippage into perpetual possibility," rather than the destructive (263), which might suggest a gendered understanding of this destruction/construction binary in Dada performance.

4. One of the Four Horsemen's performances, from the 1982 documentary *Poetry in Motion,* is available on YouTube. It begins with a five-second primal scream from all four men. See "'The Four Horsemen's' Emotional Poetry," YouTube, uploaded by barambia, 21 Nov. 2009, youtu.be/843OobTVKHQ.

5. Jed Rasula argues that Dada's influence culminated in the 1966 Destruction in Art symposium, organized in London. There, Yoko Ono gave a talk in which she affirmed, "The only kind of intentional destruction that I'm interested in at this point is a kind of destruction that brings about larger construction" (qtd. in Rasula, *Destruction* 307).

6. McCaffery himself defines the "first phase" of sound poetry as the "paleo-technic era," "the vast, intractable territory of archaic and primitive poetries, the many instances of chant structures and incantation, of syllabic mouthings

and deliberate lexical distortions still evident among many North American, African, Asian, and Oceanic peoples" (*Prior* 163).

7. McCaffery is clearly aware of the order-birthing possibilities of the protosemantic in his Deleuzian model, explaining that "a bifurcation can precipitate a dissipative structure into either a higher order of complexity or complete disarray" (*Prior* xviii). Yet his approach to the protosemantic spends most of its time on the disarray, rather than the rebirth of higher orders. For example, in his chapter on Karen MacCormack's *Quirks & Quillets,* he seems to embrace the dual effects, destructive and reconstitutive, of the protosemantic: "What the work demands for a minimum encounter is a double reading: both as an experience of delirium … and as a construction from or recuperation of underdetermined significations" (155). However, he never goes on to show us what such a construction or recuperation might look like and what role it might play in the work of experimental texts.

8. Tracie Morris, interview, "Tracie Morris Poetry Videos," *East Los Angeles Dirigible Air Transport Lines* (blog), 30 Apr. 2011, atomikaztex.wordpress.com/2011/04/30/tracie-morris-poetry-videos/.

9. Expanding on the work of her dissertation, Morris is planning a trilogy of books approaching J. L. Austin's theory from an Afrocentric perspective. The first, *Who Do with Words: A Blerd Love Tone Manifesto,* came out in 2018 and was revised and reissued in 2019.

10. Tracie Morris, interview by Charles Berstein, PennSound, 22 May 2005, writing.upenn.edu/pennsound/x/Morris.php (accessed 3 Sep. 2021). Morris writes, "For my sound poetry, the answer lies *in viscera.* In my poetic imagination the sound poems' meanings are clearly generated 'inside out': Vibrate the organs, touch the ones in you too, the others resonating in the cavity of the corpus, the hidden parts of ourselves…. Reverberation as utterance manifests as the body's agency in speaking for itself" (*Who Do with Words: Blerd* 16). "On the inside I'm always trying to get at that 'thing.' Some call it 'that music.' Whatever it is, it's poetic" (17).

11. Morris took a graduate seminar with Moten at New York University in which he also first introduced her to J. L. Austin (*Who Do with Words: Blerd* 31).

12. Parisa Vaziri takes a deep dive into the poststructuralist strain in Moten's work, specifically its engagement with Kristeva and Derrida.

13. These characteristics of IDS have been found to be similar across many different cultures (Mithen 72).

14. The experience of hearing someone speak baby talk when you are not an infant is, of course, deeply annoying, even insulting, if it's directed at you. I

don't think listeners to Morris's performances would say that they sound just like IDS. She manages to engage some of the "poetics" of IDS without actually speaking IDS.

15. Tracie Morris, "Africa(n)," performance at Poetry Center, University of Arizona, 29–31 May 2008, writing.upenn.edu/pennsound/x/Morris-Tucson .php (accessed 3 Sep. 2021). Although Morris performs the same sound poems at various events, each performance is different; her poems are improvised and do not have written scripts. She is happy to have the sound files archived, along with statements about her work, on sites such as PennSound. However, she does not want them to become "a dead recording that is understood as object" ("Poetics" 213). As Fred Moten admonishes, "Say something whose phonic substance will be impossible to reduce, whose cuts and augmenta- tions have to be recorded. Speak and break speech like a madrig, like a matrix (material, maternal)" (211).

16. Kathleen Crown, in a feminist reading of Morris's performance poetry, wonders "whether and how poetic 'voice' might be detached from its baggage of transparency, presence, authenticity, and identitarian claims to represen- tativeness *without* losing its ability to invoke communal participation and meaningful political response." "We need both/and, not either/or" ("Sonic Revolutionaries" 217). Chapter 2 addresses Harryette Mullen's similar decon- struction of the idea of voice.

17. Kathleen Crown and Christine Hume both address these poems in their essays on Morris. Crown's claim that Morris's sound poems draw on the auto- nomic capacity of language and Hume's sense that they are "showing us a CAT scan of how language gets generated" dovetail with my understanding of the role of the protosemantic ("Sonic Revolutionaries" 217).

18. Tracie Morris, "Mahalia Theremin," performance at Kelly Writers House, University of Pennsylvania, 14 Nov. 2013, writing.upenn.edu/pennsound/x /Morris.php (accessed 9 Sep. 2021).

19. Her poem "AfroFuture—Dystopic Unity" imagines this scenario: "In a covert bell curve moment, the lower than average intelligence quotient of bleached D.C. allocated 20 mill, a buck a pop & mom, to equalize Negroes with psychic self-correcting breakfast which would allow their leaders to auto-repair the rest of us. / Above grounded, it was called the Contemporary Ancestral Pacifier, guaranteed to have all in your business. Coming out open folks called it getting a 'cap through yo' ass'" (93–94).

20. Kathleen Crown argues similarly that "disarticulation in Morris's work is an ethical poetic method capable of rearticulating lost connections and building a collective sensibility" ("Sonic Revolutionaries" 222).

21. Jarnot explains the origins of this book in a reading in Philadelphia at the Kelly Writers House on 22 Apr. 2014, which I quote here; see "Lisa Jarnot," PennSound, writing.upenn.edu/pennsound/x/Jarnot.php (accessed 9 Sep. 2021).

22. Jarnot's *Selected Poems, 1992–2012* is titled *Joie de Vivre*. It contains parts 1 and 2 of *A Princess Magic Presto Spell*, which are marked as "For Bea" (90).

23. Roman Jakobson has famously theorized that babies can make the phonetic sounds of all human languages during the developmental period he calls the "apex of babble." However, as babies acquire their first language, they lose the ability to produce those phonemes, including many of the phonemes required for their native language. Contemporary research into infant language acquisition confirms his early thesis; see, for example, research by Patricia K. Kuhl at the University of Washington and Janet F. Werker at the University of British Columbia. As Daniel Heller-Roazen writes in his book on *Echolalias*, "It is as if the acquisition of language were possible only through an act of oblivion, a kind of linguistic infantile amnesia" (11). Interestingly, however, children can still reproduce those lost phonemes when they are imitating inhuman noises such as animal or mechanical sounds (13), which suggests that the right and left hemispheres play different roles in producing these sounds.

24. Proulx and Heine have found that when adult brains are confronted with nonsense or "meaning threats," their brains are primed to sense patterns that other brains miss (1125).

25. *A Princess Magic Presto Spell* also includes artwork from Emilie Clark, the heaps of fragments of which sometimes appear like piles of garbage or masses of organic matter, and other times seem to cohere into one entity with many parts.

26. Jarnot mixes other oblique references to current events into her heaps of language, including "trapped chilean miners" (16) and Italian President Berlusconi's scandal with an "under-aged / Moroccan pole-dancer" (17).

27. Interestingly, several cases have documented a sudden onset of poetry writing in patients with left-brain damage who had never written it before (J. Kane 46).

Epilogue

I extend thanks to editors Joan Retallack and Juliana Spahr and the writers collected in *Poetry and Pedagogy: The Challenge of the Contemporary*, whose ideas inspired much of the experimentation in the class I describe here.

1. Witness all the anxieties manifesting themselves in legal cases, state laws, and textbook revisions around the United States that attempt to discipline

this potentially anarchic space of the classroom, such as legislation banning discussions related to critical race theory.

2. After a brief review of roots in the modernist avant-garde, the bulk of the class focuses on experimental modes from the 1970s to the present: Language poetry, conceptualism, Oulipo, collaboration, concrete poetry and vispo, sound poetry, post-Language modes, Avant-Latinx, Poet's Theater, and Twitter Poetics.

3. We did more performances in the class as well, including Khadijah Queen's performance poem "The Dream Act," following her cues for sound and projection as well.

4. A great performance is available online; see "György Ligeti—Poème Symphonique for 100 Metronomes," YouTube, uploaded by GBM Channel TV, 18 Apr. 2007, youtu.be/-mUv705xj3U.

5. During our discussion of conceptual poetry, one student suggested a conceptual classroom spatial reversal in which the teacher sat in the little desks while all the students stood at the front and fired questions at her about the readings. Though we never got a chance to try it, I'm intrigued by the idea, particularly if students have to work as hard to generate their discussion questions as the teacher does. The person in the hot seat could rotate after the teacher answered the initial barrage.

6. As Keller writes, "Innovative poems may be 'around' or 'out from' identifiable subjects, while not 'about' them" (34). I tried throughout the course to use more centrifugal prepositions to describe the work of experimental poems and our interpretation of them, rather than the directive and limiting language of what the poem is "about."

7. In keeping with the class's emphasis on collective reading, I staged another centrifugal performance in which students wandered a gallery of their peers' deformed poems on the walls of the classroom and wrote their own ideas for interpreting them, as in the Hejinian activity I describe.

Works Cited

Ackerman, Ondrea E. "Wandering Lines: Robert Grenier's Drawing Poems." *Journal of Modern Literature*, vol. 36, no. 4, 2013, pp. 133–53. doi:10.2979 /jmodelite.36.4.133.

Alter, Adam L. "The Benefits of Cognitive Disfluency." *Current Directions in Psychological Science*, vol. 22, no. 6, 2013, pp. 437–42. doi:10.1177/0963721413498894.

Andrews, Bruce, and Charles Bernstein, eds. *The L=A=N=G=U=A=G=E Book*. Southern Illinois UP, 1984.

Annett, Marian. *Left, Right, Hand, and Brain: The Right Shift Theory*. Lawrence Erlbaum, 1985.

Ashton, Jennifer. *From Modernism to Postmodernism: American Poetry and Theory in the Twentieth Century*. Cambridge UP, 2005.

Ashton, Jennifer. "Two Problems with a Neuroaesthetic Theory of Interpretation." *NONsite.org*, 12 Jun. 2011, nonsite.org/two-problems-with-a-neuroaesthetic -theory-of-interpretation/.

Attridge, Derek. *The Singularity of Literature*. Routledge, 2004.

Austin, J. L. *How to Do Things with Words*. Clarendon, 1975.

Ball, Hugo. *Flight Out of Time: A Dada Diary*. Edited by John Elderfield. Translated by Ann Raimes. Viking, 1974.

Bara, Florence, et al. "The Visuo-haptic and Haptic Exploration of Letters Increases the Kindergarten-Children's Understanding of the Alphabetic Principle." *Cognitive Development*, vol. 19, no. 3, 2004, pp. 433–49. doi:10.1016/j.cogdev .2004.05.003.

Bargh, John A., and Idit Shalev. "The Substitutability of Physical and Social Warmth in Daily Life." *Emotion,* vol. 12, no. 1, 2012, pp. 154–62. doi:10.1037/a0023527.

Barry, Peter. "Concrete Canticles: A New Taxonomy of Iconicity in Poetry." *American, British, and Canadian Studies,* vol. 18, 2012, pp. 73–86.

Barsalou, Lawrence W. "Grounded Cognition." *Annual Review of Psychology,* vol. 59, 2008, pp. 617–45. doi:10.1146/annurev.psych.59.103006.093639.

Bartlett, Jennifer, and George Hart, eds. *Momentous Inconclusions: The Life and Work of Larry Eigner.* U of New Mexico P, 2020.

Barwin, Gary. "Not Sultans of Poetry but Thralls to Its Charms: Christian Bök's 'Odalisques.'" *Jacket2,* 2 Jun. 2013, jacket2.org/commentary/not-sultans-poetry -thralls-its-charms-christian-b%C3%B6k%E2%80%99s-odalisques.

Bayard, Caroline. *The New Poetics in Canada and Quebec: From Concretism to Post-modernism.* U of Toronto P, 1989.

Beall, Emily P. "'as Reading as if': Harryette Mullen's 'Cognitive Similes.'" *Journal of Literary Semantics,* vol. 34, no. 2, 2005, pp. 125–37.

Beaulieu, Anne. "Fast-Moving Objects and Their Consequences: A Response to the Neuroscientific Turn in Practice." *The Neuroscientific Turn: Transdisciplinarity in the Age of the Brain,* edited by Melissa M. Littlefield and Jenell M. Johnson, U of Michigan P, 2012, pp. 152–62.

Bennett, Maxwell, et al. *Neuroscience and Philosophy: Brain, Mind, and Language.* Columbia UP, 2003.

Berger, Anne-Emmanuelle, and Rachel Gabara. "The Latest Word from Echo." *New Literary History,* vol. 27, no. 4, 1996, pp. 621–40. doi:10.1353/nlh.1996.0043.

Bernardi, Daniel Leonard. *"Star Trek" and History: Race-ing toward a White Future.* Rutgers UP, 1998.

Bernstein, Charles. *Attack of the Difficult Poems: Essays and Inventions.* U of Chicago P, 2011.

Bernstein, Charles. *A Poetics.* Harvard UP, 1992.

Bernstein, Charles, ed. *Close Listening: Poetry and the Performed Word.* Oxford UP, 1998.

Bishop, Elizabeth. "In the Waiting Room." *The Complete Poems: 1927–1979.* Noonday, 1983, pp. 159–61.

Blake, Randolph. "A Primer on Binocular Rivalry, Including Current Controversies." *Brain and Mind,* vol. 2, 2001, pp. 5–38. doi:10.1023/A:1017925416289.

Boden, Margaret A. *The Creative Mind: Myths and Mechanisms.* 2nd ed., Routledge, 2004.

Bohn, Willard. *Modern Visual Poetry.* U of Delaware P, 2001.

Brown, Nathan. *The Limits of Fabrication: Materials Science, Materialist Poetics.* Fordham UP, 2017.

Carey, Benedict. "How Nonsense Sharpens the Intellect." *New York Times,* 5 Oct. 2009, www.nytimes.com/2009/10/06/health/06mind.html.

CBS. "Serene Branson—CBS Reporter Serene Branson Has Stroke on Air?," *YouTube,* uploaded by Shamrokk, 17 Feb. 2011, www.youtube.com/watch?v= AVKDm4PhEwI.

Cecire, Natalia. *Experimental: American Literature and the Aesthetics of Knowledge.* Johns Hopkins UP, 2019.

Christiansen, Morten H., and Simon Kirby. "Language Evolution: The Hardest Problem in Science?" *Language Evolution,* edited by Morten H. Christiansen and Simon Kirby, Oxford UP, 2003, pp. 1– 15.

Clark, Andy. *Supersizing the Mind: Embodiment, Action, and Cognitive Extension.* Oxford UP, 2010.

Clark, Hilary. "The Mnemonics of Autobiography: Lyn Hejinian's *My Life.*" *Biography,* vol. 14, no. 4, 1991, pp. 315–35. *JSTOR,* www.jstor.org/stable /23539602.

Clay, Jon. *Sensation, Contemporary Poetry and Deleuze: Transformative Intensities.* Continuum, 2010.

Clune, Michael W. *Writing Against Time.* Stanford UP, 2013.

Connolly, William E. *Neuropolitics: Thinking, Culture, Speed.* U of Minnesota P, 2002.

Conte, Joseph M. *Unending Design: The Forms of Postmodern Poetry.* Cornell UP, 1991.

Coolidge, Clark. "Calypso." *Space.* Harper & Row, 1970, p. 36.

Coolidge, Clark. "Larry Eigner Notes." *The L=A=N=G=U=A=G=E Book,* edited by Bruce Andrews and Charles Bernstein, Southern Illinois UP, 1984, pp. 224–27.

Cortez, Jayne, dir. *Yari Yari Pamberi: Black Women Writers Dissecting Globalization.* Third World Newsreel, 2007.

Crown, Kathleen. "'Choice Voice Noise': Soundings in Innovative African-American Poetry." *Assembling Alternatives: Reading Postmodern Poetries Transnationally,* edited by Romana Huk, Wesleyan UP, 2003, pp. 219–45.

Crown, Kathleen. "'Sonic Revolutionaries': Voice and Experiment in the Spoken-Word Poetry of Tracie Morris." *We Who Love to Be Astonished: Experimental Women's Writing and Performance Poetics,* edited by Laura Hinton and Cynthia Hogue, U of Alabama P, 2002, pp. 213–26.

Daly, Ian. "You Call That Poetry?!" *Poetry Foundation,* 25 Aug. 2007, www.poetryfoundation.org/articles/68913/you-call-that-poetry.

Damasio, Antonio. *The Feeling of What Happens: Body and Emotion in the Making of Consciousness.* Harcourt Brace, 1999.

Dames, Nicholas. *The Physiology of the Novel: Reading, Neural Science, and the Form of Victorian Fiction.* Oxford UP, 2007.

Davidson, Michael. *Ghostlier Demarcations: Modern Poetry and the Material Word.* U of California P, 1997.

Davidson, Michael. "Missing Larry: The Poetics of Disability in the Work of Larry Eigner." *Sagetrieb,* vol. 18, no. 1, 1999, pp. 5–27.

Deacon, Terrence. *The Symbolic Species: The Co-evolution of Language and the Brain.* Norton, 1998.

Dehaene, Stanislas. *Reading in the Brain: The New Science of How We Read.* Penguin, 2010.

Deleuze, Gilles, and Félix Guattari. *A Thousand Plateaus: Capitalism and Schizophrenia.* Translated by Brian Massumi. Continuum, 2004.

Dowling, Sarah. "Supine, Prone, Precarious." *Poetics and Precarity,* edited by Myung Mi Kim and Cristanne Miller, SUNY P, 2018, pp. 145–60.

Drabinksi, John E. "From Experience to Flesh: On James and Merleau-Ponty." *Phenomenological Inquiry,* vol. 21, 1997, pp. 137–55.

Drucker, Johanna. *The Alphabetic Labyrinth: The Letters in History and Imagination.* Thames & Hudson, 1995.

Drucker, Johanna. *The Visible Word: Experimental Typography and Modern Art, 1909–1923.* U of Chicago P, 1997.

Dworkin, Craig. *Radium of the Word: A Poetics of Materiality.* U of Chicago P, 2020.

Dworkin, Craig. *Reading the Illegible.* Evanston: Northwestern UP, 2003.

Edie, James M. *William James and Phenomenology.* Indiana UP, 1987.

Edmond, Jacob. "'A Meaning Alliance': Arkady Dragomoshchenko and Lyn Hejinian's Poetics of Translation." *Slavic and East European Journal,* vol. 46, no. 3, 2002, pp. 551–64.

Eigner, Larry. *areas / lights / heights: Writings, 1954–1989.* Edited by Benjamin Friedlander. Roof Books, 1989.

Eigner, Larry. *The Collected Poems of Larry Eigner.* 4 vols. Edited by Curtis Faville and Robert Grenier. Stanford UP, 2010.

Eigner, Larry. *earth / birds.* Circle P, 1981.

Emerson, Lori. "Materiality, Intentionality, and the Computer-Generated Poem: Reading Walter Benn Michaels with Erin Mouré's Pillage Laud." *English Studies in Canada,* vol. 34, no. 4, 2008, pp. 45–69. doi:10.1353/esc.0.0158.

Engelbrecht, Lisa. *Hand Lettering and Contemporary Calligraphy.* Crestline Books, 2017.

Fama, Steven. "Reading *The Collected Poems of Larry Eigner* (Part 1)." *Glade of Theoric Ornithic Hermetica* (blog), 28 Mar. 2010, stevenfama.blogspot.com/2010/03/reading-collected-poems-of-larry-eigner.html.

Felski, Rita. *Uses of Literature.* Blackwell, 2008.

Forrest, Seth. "The Body of the Text: Cerebral Palsy, Projective Verse, and Prosthetics in Larry Eigner's Poetry." *Jacket,* vol. 36, 2008, jacketmagazine.com/36/forrest-eigner.shtml.

Foster, P. J., and Y. Jiang. "Epidemiology of Myopia" *Eye (London)*, vol. 28, no. 2, 2014, pp. 202–8. doi:10.1038/eye.2013.280.

Frijda, Nico. *The Emotions.* Cambridge UP, 1987.

Frost, Elisabeth A. "Signifyin(g) on Stein: The Revisionist Poetics of Harryette Mullen and Leslie Scalapino." *Postmodern Culture*, vol. 5, no. 3, 1995. doi:10.1353/pmc.1995.0023.

Gammel, Irene, and Suzanne Zelazo. "'Harpsichords Metallic Howl—': The Baroness Elsa von Freytag-Loringhoven's Sound Poetry." *Modernism/modernity*, vol. 18, no. 2, 2011, pp. 255–71. doi:10.1353/mod.2011.0033.

Gavins, Joanna. *Poetry in the Mind: The Cognition of Contemporary Poetic Style.* Edinburgh UP, 2020.

Gerrig, Richard, and William G. Wenzel. "The Role of Inferences in Narrative Experiences." *Inferences during Reading,* edited by Edward J. O'Brien et al., Cambridge UP, 2015, pp. 362–85.

Gilbert, Alan. *Another Future: Poetry and Art in a Postmodern Twilight.* Wesleyan UP, 2006.

Gladman, Renee. "'Catch a Fire': The Role of Innovation in Contemporary Writing." *Tripwire*, vol. 5, 2001, pp. 5–6.

Gladman, Renee, and giovanni singleton, eds. "Expanding the Repertoire: Continuity and Change in African-American Writing," special issue, *Tripwire*, vol. 5, 2001.

Golding, Alan. "'Isn't the Avant-garde Always Pedagogical?' Experimental Poetics and/as Pedagogy." *Poetry and Pedagogy: The Challenge of the Contemporary,* edited by Joan Retallack and Juliana Spahr, Palgrave Macmillan, 2006, pp. 13–29.

Goldsmith, Kenneth. "From (Command) Line to (Iconic) Constellation." *Ubuweb Papers,* www.ubu.com/papers/goldsmith_command.html. Accessed 19 Oct. 2021.

González, Julio, et al. "Reading Cinnamon Activates Olfactory Brain Regions." *Neuroimage,* vol. 32, 2006, pp. 906–12. doi:10.1016/j.neuroimage.2006.03.037.

Graesser, Arthur, et al. "Constructing Inferences in Naturalistic Reading Contexts." *Inferences during Reading,* edited by Edward J. O'Brien et al., Cambridge UP, 2015, pp. 290–320.

Gravendyk, Hillary. "Chronic Poetics." *Journal of Modern Literature,* vol. 38, no. 1, 2014, pp. 1–19. doi:10.2979/jmodelite.38.1.1.

Gregg, Melissa, and Gregory J. Seigworth, eds. *The Affect Theory Reader.* Duke UP, 2010.

Grenier, Robert. Introduction to *The Collected Poems of Larry Eigner,* edited by Curtis Faville and Robert Grenier, Stanford UP, 2010, pp. vii–xiii.

Grieve-Carlson, Gary. "Charles Olson and the Poetics of Postmodern History." *Olson's Prose,* edited by Gary Grieve-Carlson, Cambridge Scholars, 2007, pp. 89–120.

Grumman, Bob. "MNMLST POETRY: Unacclaimed but Flourishing." *Thing.net*, 1997, www.thing.net/~grist/l&d/grumman/egrumn.htm. Accessed 19 Oct. 2021.

Harryman, Carla. "Rules and Restraints in Women's Experimental Writing." *We Who Love to Be Astonished: Experimental Women's Writing and Performance Poetics*, U of Alabama P, 2002, pp. 116–24.

Hart, George. "'Enough Defined': Disability, Ecopoetics, and Larry Eigner." *Contemporary Literature*, vol. 51, no. 1, 2010, pp. 152–79.

Hasson, Uri, et al. "Grounding the Neurobiology of Language in First Principles: The Necessity of Non-Language-Centric Explanations for Language Comprehension." *Cognition*, vol. 180, 2018, pp. 135–57. doi:10.1016/j.cognition.2018.06.018.

Hauk, Olaf, et al. "Somatotopic Representation of Action Words in Human Motor and Premotor Cortex." *Neuron*, vol. 41, 2004, pp. 301–7. doi:10.1016/S0896-6273(03)00838-9.

Hayles, N. Katherine. *Unthought: The Power of the Cognitive Nonconscious*. U of Chicago P, 2017.

Hejinian, Lyn. *The Cell*. Sun & Moon, 1992.

Hejinian, Lyn. *The Cold of Poetry*. Sun & Moon, 1994.

Hejinian, Lyn. *The Language of Inquiry*. U of California P, 2000.

Hejinian, Lyn. "Language Poetry: An Interview with Lyn Hejinian." Conducted by Alison Georgeson. *Southern Review*, vol. 27, no. 3, 1994, pp. 285–94.

Hejinian, Lyn. "A Local Strangeness: An Interview with Lyn Hejinian." Conducted by Larry McCaffery and Brian McHale. *Some Other Fluency: Interviews with Innovative American Authors*, U of Pennsylvania P, 1996, pp. 121–45.

Hejinian, Lyn. *"My Life" and "My Life in the Nineties."* Wesleyan UP, 2013.

Hejinian, Lyn. "Ponderable." *Academy of American Poets, Poem-a-Day*, 31 Mar. 2015, www.poets.org/poetsorg/poem/ponderable.

Hejinian, Lyn. "Roughly Stapled: An Interview with Lyn Hejinian by Craig Dworkin." *Electronic Poetry Center*. State U of New York, Buffalo, 1995, writing.upenn.edu/epc/authors/hejinian/roughly.html. Accessed 19 Oct. 2021.

Hejinian, Lyn, and Tyrus Miller. "An Exchange of Letters." *Paper Air*, vol. 4, no. 2, 1989, pp. 33–40.

Hejinian, Lyn, and Leslie Scalapino. *Sight*. Edge Books, 1999.

Heller-Roazen, Daniel. *Echolalias: On the Forgetting of Language*. Zone Books, 2005.

Henning, Barbara. *Looking Up Harryette Mullen: Interviews on "Sleeping with the Dictionary" and Other Works*. Belladonna, 2011.

Hernandez, Ivan, and Jesse Lee Preston. "Disfluency Disrupts the Confirmation Bias." *Journal of Experimental Social Psychology*, vol. 49, no. 1, 2013, pp. 178–82. doi:10.1016/j.jesp.2012.08.010.

Higgins, Dick. "The Strategy of Visual Poetry: Three Aspects." *Visual Literature Criticism: A New Collection*, edited by Richard Kostelanetz, Southern Illinois UP, 1979, pp. 41–49.

Hopkins, Gerard Manley. "I wake and feel the fell of dark, not day." *The Works of Gerard Manley Hopkins,* Wordsworth Editions, 1994, p. 65.

Huehls, Mitchum. "Spun Puns (and Anagrams): Exchange Economies, Subjectivity, and History in Harryette Mullen's *Muse & Drudge.*" *Contemporary Literature,* vol. 44, 2003, pp. 19–46.

Hume, Angela, and Gillian Osborne, eds. *Ecopoetics: Essays in the Field.* U of Iowa P, 2018.

Hume, Christine. "Improvisational Insurrection: The Sound Poetry of Tracie Morris." *Contemporary Literature,* vol. 47, no. 3, 2006, pp. 415–39.

Iwakuma, Miho. "The Body as Embodiment: An Investigation of the Body by Merleau-Ponty." *Disability/Postmodernity: Embodying Disability Theory,* edited by Mairian Corker and Tom Shakespeare, Continuum, 2002, pp. 76–87.

Izenberg, Oren. "Language Poetry and Collective Life." *Critical Inquiry,* vol. 30, no. 1, 2003, pp. 132–59. doi:10.1086/380808.

Jackson, Tony E. "Issues and Problems in the Blending of Cognitive Science, Evolutionary Psychology, and Literary Study." *Poetics Today,* vol. 23, no. 1, 2002, pp. 159–79.

Jakobson, Roman. *Child Language, Aphasia, and Phonological Universals.* Translated by Allan R. Keiler. De Gruyter Mouton, 1968.

James, William. *The Principles of Psychology.* 1890. Vol. 1. 2 vols. Henry Holt, 1918.

Jameson, Frederic. *Postmodernism, or The Cultural Logic of Late Capitalism.* Duke UP, 1991.

Jarnot, Lisa. *Joie de Vivre: Selected Poems, 1992–2012.* City Lights, 2013.

Jarnot, Lisa. *Night Scenes.* Flood Editions, 2008.

Jarnot, Lisa. *A Princess Magic Presto Spell.* Solid Objects, 2014.

Johnston, Georgia. "Lyn Hejinian's Repetition: Reading a Narratology of Autobiography." *Sagetrieb,* vol. 18, no. 1, 1999, pp. 41–57.

Jones, Arthur C. *Wade in the Water: The Wisdom of the Spirituals.* Leave a Little Room, 2005.

Jonik, Michael. "Congruence and Projective Space in Melville and Olson." *Olson's Prose,* edited by Gary Grieve-Carlson. Cambridge Scholars, 2007, pp. 132–50.

Joseph, Rhawn. "The Split Brain: Two Brains–Two Minds." *Journal of Cosmology,* vol. 14, 2011, cosmology.com/Cosmology11.html.

Kahneman, Daniel. *Thinking Fast and Slow.* Farrar, Straus and Giroux, 2011.

Kane, Julie. "Poetry as Right-Hemispheric Language." *Journal of Consciousness Studies,* vol. 11, no. 5–6, 2004, pp. 21–59.

Kearney, Douglas. *The Black Automaton.* Fence Books, 2009.

Keller, Lynn. "FFFFFalling with Poetry: The Centrifugal Classroom." *Poetry and Pedagogy: The Challenge of the Contemporary,* edited by Joan Retallack and Juliana Spahr, Palgrave Macmillan, 2006, pp. 30–38.

Kellner, Douglas, and Stephen Best. *Postmodern Theory*. Guilford, 1991.

Kenneally, Christine. *The First Word: The Search for the Origins of Language*. Viking, 2007.

King, Rosamond S. "Word Plays Well with Others." *Callaloo*, vol. 26, no. 2, 2003, pp. 536–38. doi:10.1353/cal.2003.0050.

Lakoff, George, and Mark Johnson. *Philosophy in the Flesh: The Cognitive Unconscious and the Embodied Mind: How the Embodied Mind Creates Philosophy*. Basic Books, 1999.

Lattig, Sharon. *Cognitive Ecopoetics: A New Theory of Lyric*. Bloomsbury, 2020.

Lauwereyns, Jan. *Brain and the Gaze: On the Active Boundaries of Vision*. MIT P, 2012.

Ledoux, Joseph. *The Emotional Brain: The Mysterious Underpinnings of Emotional Life*. Simon & Schuster, 1998.

Lehrer, Jonah. *Proust Was a Neuroscientist*. Houghton Mifflin, 2007.

Lempert, Benjamin R. "Harryette Mullen and the Contemporary Jazz Voice." *Callaloo*, vol. 33, no. 4, 2010, pp. 1059–78. doi:10.1353/cal.2010.0080.

Leopold, David A., and Nikos K. Logothetis. "Multistable Phenomena: Changing Views in Perception." *Trends in Cognitive Sciences*, vol. 3, no. 7, 1999, pp. 254–64. doi:10.1016/S1364-6613(99)01332-7.

Limb, Charles J., and Allen R. Braun. "Neural Substrates of Spontaneous Musical Performance: An FMRI Study of Jazz Improvisation." *PLoS One*, vol. 3, no. 2, 2008, p. e1679. doi:10.1371/journal.pone.0001679.

Livingston, Paisley. *Art and Intention: A Philosophical Study*. Oxford UP, 2005.

Loria, Kevin. "Something Weird Happens to Your Brain When You Start Improvising." *ScienceAlert*, 11 May 2016, www.sciencealert.com/something-weird-happens-to-your-brain-when-you-start-improvising.

Luck, Jessica Lewis. "Crossing the Corpus Callosum: The Musical Phenomenology of Lisa Jarnot." *Reading the Difficulties: Dialogues with Contemporary American Innovative Poetry*, edited by Thomas Fink and Judith Halden-Sullivan, U of Alabama P, 2014, pp. 188–200.

Ma, Ming-Qian. *Poetry as Re-reading: American Avant-garde Poetry and the Poetics of Counter-method*. Northwestern UP, 2008.

Macedonia, Manuela. "Embodied Learning: Why at School the Mind Needs the Body." *Frontiers in Psychology*, vol. 10, no. 2098, 2019. doi:10.3389/fpsyg.2019.02098.

Mackey, Nathaniel. *Paracritical Hinge: Essays, Talks, Notes, Interviews*. U of Wisconsin P, 2005.

Manning, Erin, and Brian Massumi. *Thought in the Act: Passages in the Ecology of Experience*. U of Minnesota P, 2014.

Mansell, Lisa. "Hearing a New Musical Instrument: Harryette Mullen's Critical

Lyricism." *Black Music, Black Poetry: Blues and Jazz's Impact on African American Versification*, edited by Gordon E. Thompson, Ashgate, 2014, pp. 127–48.

Martin, Taylor, and Daniel L. Schwartz. "Physically Distributed Learning: Adapting and Reinterpreting Physical Environments in the Development of Fraction Concepts." *Cognitive Science*, vol. 29, no. 4, 2005, pp. 587–625. doi:10.1207/s15516709cog0000_15.

Massumi, Brian. *Parables for the Virtual: Movement, Affect, Sensation.* Duke UP, 2002.

McCaffery, Steve. "Cacophony, Abstraction, and Potentiality: The Fate of the Dada Sound Poem." *The Sound of Poetry/The Poetry of Sound*, edited by Marjorie Perloff and Craig Dworkin, U of Chicago P, 2009, pp. 118–28.

McCaffery, Steve. *Prior to Meaning: The Protosemantic and Poetics.* Northwestern UP, 2001.

McHale, Brian. "Change of Dominant from Modernist to Postmodernist Writing." *Approaching Postmodernism*, edited Douwe Fokkema and Hans Bertens, John Benjamins, 1986, pp. 53–79.

Merleau-Ponty, Maurice. *The Merleau-Ponty Aesthetics Reader: Philosophy and Painting.* Edited by Galen A. Johnson. Northwestern UP, 1993.

Middleton, Peter. *Physics Envy: American Poetry and Science in the Cold War and After.* U Chicago P, 2015.

Mithen, Steven. *The Singing Neanderthals: The Origins of Music, Language, Mind, and Body.* Harvard UP, 2007.

Mix, Deborah. "Tender Revisions: Harryette Mullen's *Trimmings* and *S*PeRM**KT." American Literature*, vol. 77, 2005, pp. 65–92. doi:10.1215/00029831-77-1-65.

Monroe, Jonathan. "Index and Symptom: 'Connective' Reading, (Post) Language Writing, and Cultural Critique." *Contemporary Literature*, vol. 44, no. 4, 2003, pp. 748–70. doi:10.2307/3250595.

Montgomery, John. *How to Read Maya Hieroglyphs.* Hippocrene Books, 2002.

Morris, Adelaide, and Thomas Swiss, eds. *New Media Poetics: Contexts, Technotexts, and Theories.* MIT P, 2006.

Morris, Tracie. "AfroFuture—Dystopic Unity, Vertical, Mother Earth." *Social Text*, vol. 20, no. 2, 2002, pp. 93–96. *Project MUSE*, muse.jhu.edu/article/31930.

Morris, Tracie. "Poetics Statement: Sound Making Notes." *American Poets in the 21st Century: The New Poetics*, edited by Claudia Rankine and Lisa Sewell, Wesleyan UP, 2007, pp. 210–15.

Morris, Tracie. *Who Do with Words: A Blerd Love Tone Manifesto.* Chax, 2019.

Morris, Tracie. *Who Do with Words: Rapping a Black Tongue around J. L. Austin (Selected Hits from 1979–1989).* ProQuest Dissertations and Thesis, 2006.

Moten, Fred. *In the Break: The Aesthetics of the Black Radical Tradition.* U of Minnesota P, 2003.

Motte, Warren F., ed. *Oulipo: A Primer of Potential Literature*. 1986. Dalkey Archive P, 1998.

Mullen, Harryette. "Interview." Conducted by Daniel Kane. *What Is Poetry: Conversations with the American Avant-garde*. Teachers & Writers Collaborative, 2003, pp. 126–37.

Mullen, Harryette. "An Interview with Harryette Mullen." Conducted by Elisabeth A. Frost. *Contemporary Literature*, vol. 41, 2000, pp. 397–421. doi:10.2307/1208891.

Mullen, Harryette. "Interview with Harryette Mullen." Conducted by Cynthia Hogue. *Postmodern Culture*, vol. 9, no. 2, 1999. doi:10.1353/pmc.1999.0002.

Mullen, Harryette. "Imagining the Unimagined Reader: Writing to the Unborn and Including the Excluded." *boundary 2*, vol. 26, no. 1, 1999, pp. 198–203. *JSTOR*, www.jstor.org/stable/303900.

Mullen, Harryette. *Muse & Drudge*. Singing Horse, 1995.

Mullen, Harryette. "Poetry and Identity." *West Coast Line*, vol. 30, no. 1, 1996, pp. 85–89.

Mullen, Harryette. *Sleeping with the Dictionary*. U of California P, 2002.

Mullen, Harryette. *S*PeRM**K*T*. Singing Horse, 1992.

Mullen, Harryette. *Tree Tall Woman: Poems*. Energy Earth Communications, 1981.

Mullen, Harryette. *Trimmings*. Tender Buttons, 1991.

Mullen, Harryette. "Untitled." "Expanding the Repertoire: Continuity and Change in African-American Writing," edited by Renee Gladman and giovanni singleton, special issue, *Tripwire*, vol. 5, 2001, pp. 11–14.

Nakamura, Kimihiro, et al. "Universal Brain Systems for Recognizing Word Shapes and Handwriting Gestures during Reading." *Proceedings of the National Academy of Sciences of the United States of America*, vol. 109, no. 50, 2012, pp. 20762–67. doi:10.1073/pnas.1217749109.

Nelson, Alondra. "Introduction: Future Texts." *Social Text*, vol. 20, no. 2, 2002, pp. 1–15. *Project MUSE*, muse.jhu.edu/article/31931.

Ngai, Sianne. *Ugly Feelings*. Harvard UP, 2005.

Niedenthal, Paula M., et al. "Embodiment in Attitudes, Social Perception, and Emotion." *Personality and Social Psychology Review*, vol. 9, no. 3, 2005, pp. 184–211. doi:10.1207/s15327957pspr0903_1.

Nielsen, Aldon Lynn. *Black Chant: Language of African-American Postmodernism*. Cambridge UP, 1997.

Nurhussein, Nadia. "The Puzzle of Dialect in Harryette Mullen's *Sleeping with the Dictionary*." *Modern Language Studies*, vol. 42, no. 2, 2013, pp. 34–51. *JSTOR*, www.jstor.org/stable/24616697.

O'Brien, Edward J., et al, eds. *Inferences during Reading*. Cambridge UP, 2015.

Olson, Charles. *Collected Prose*. Edited by Donald Allen and Benjamin Friedlander. U of California P, 1997.

Olson, Charles. *The Maximus Poems.* U of California P, 1987.

Olson, Charles. "Mayan Letters." *Selected Writings of Charles Olson.* New Directions, 1966, pp. 69–130.

Olson, Charles. "Project (1951): 'The Art of the Language of Mayan Glyphs.'" *Alcheringa,* vol. 5, 1973, pp. 94–100.

Olson, Charles. *The Special View of History.* Oyez, 1970.

Ovid. *The Metamorphoses.* Translated by Allen Mandelbaum. Harcourt Brace, 1993.

Papoulias, Constantina, and Felicity Callard. "Biology's Gift: Interrogating the Turn to Affect." *Body and Society,* vol. 16, no. 1, 2010, pp. 29–56. doi:10.1177/1357034X09355231.

Perelman, Bob. "Parataxis and Narrative: The New Sentence in Theory and Practice." *Artifice and Indeterminacy: An Anthology of New Poetics,* edited by Christopher Beach, Tuscaloosa: U of Alabama P, 1998, pp. 24–48.

Perelman, Bob, and Francie Shaw. *Playing Bodies.* Granary Books, 2004.

Perloff, Marjorie. "'Concrete Prose' in the Nineties: Haroldo De Campos's *Galáxias* and After." *Contemporary Literature,* vol. 42, no. 2, 2001, pp. 270–93. *JSTOR,* www.jstor.org/stable/1209123.

Perloff, Marjorie. "Constraint, Concrete, Citation: Refiguring History in Charles Bernstein's *Shadowtime.*" *Poetics Today,* vol. 30, no. 4, 2009, pp. 693–717. doi:10.1215/03335372-2009-010.

Perloff, Marjorie. "Language Poetry and the Lyric Subject: Ron Silliman's Albany, Susan Howe's Buffalo." *Critical Inquiry,* vol. 25, no. 3, 1999, pp. 405–34. doi:10.1086/448929.

Perloff, Marjorie. *Radical Artifice: Writing Poetry in the Age of Media.* U of Chicago P, 1991.

Perloff, Marjorie. *21st Century Modernisms: The "New" Poetics.* Blackwell, 2002.

Perloff, Marjorie. *Unoriginal Genius: Poetry by Other Means in the New Century.* U of Chicago P, 2010.

Pinker, Steven. *How the Mind Works.* Norton, 1997.

Proulx, Travis, and Steven J. Heine. "Connections from Kafka: Exposure to Meaning Threats Improves Implicit Learning of an Artificial Grammar." *Psychological Science,* vol. 20, no. 9, 2009, pp. 1125–31. doi:10.1111/j.1467-9280.2009.02414.x.

Quartermain, Peter. "Syllable as Music: Lyn Hejinian's *Writing Is an Aid to Memory.*" *Sagetrieb,* vol. 11, no. 3, 1992, pp. 17–31.

Queen, Khadijah. "The Dream Act." *Letters to the Future: Black Women/Radical Writing,* edited by Erica Hunt and Dawn Lundy Martin, Kore, 2018, pp. 158–65.

Ramachandran, V. S. *The Tell-Tale Brain: A Neuroscientist's Quest for What Makes Us Human.* Norton, 2012.

Rancière, Jacques. *The Politics of Aesthetics.* Translated by Gabriel Rockhill. Continuum, 2006.

Rasula, Jed. *Destruction Was My Beatrice: Dada and the Unmaking of the Twentieth Century.* Basic Books, 2015.

Rasula, Jed. "Poetry's Voice-over." *Sound States: Innovative Poetics and Acoustical Technologies,* edited Adelaide Morris, U of North Carolina P, 1997, pp. 274–316.

Reed, Brian. *Phenomenal Reading: Essays on Modern and Contemporary Poetics.* U of Alabama P, 2012.

Retallack, Joan. *The Poethical Wager.* U of California P, 2004.

Retallack, Joan, and Juliana Spahr, eds. *Poetry and Pedagogy: The Challenge of the Contemporary.* Palgrave Macmillan, 2006.

Riley, Denise. "'A Voice without a Mouth': Inner Speech." *Qui Parle,* vol. 14, no. 2, 2004, pp. 57–104. *JSTOR,* www.jstor.org/stable/20686176.

Rippeon, Andrew, ed. *Letters to Jargon: The Correspondence between Larry Eigner and Jonathan Williams.* U of Alabama P, 2019.

Robbins, Amy Moorman. "Harryette Mullen's *Sleeping with the Dictionary* and Race in Language/Writing." *Contemporary Literature,* vol. 51, no. 2, 2010, pp. 341–70. *Project MUSE,* muse.jhu.edu/article/403358.

Ronda, Margaret. *Remainders: American Poetry at Nature's End.* Stanford UP, 2018.

Samuels, Lisa, and Jerome McGann. "Deformance and Interpretation." *Poetry and Pedagogy: The Challenge of the Contemporary,* edited Joan Retallack and Juliana Spahr, Palgrave Macmillan, 2006, pp. 141–80.

Saroyan, Aram. "The Most Expensive Word in History." *Mother Jones Magazine,* Aug. 1981, pp. 36–38.

Scarry, Elaine. *Dreaming by the Book.* Princeton UP, 2001.

Schwabsky, Barry. "'We Need a New Skin Color': The Racial Imagination of Dada." *Hyperallergic,* 4 Jul. 2015, hyperallergic.com/219063/we-need-a-new-skin-color-the-racial-imagination-of-dada/.

Shockley, Evie. *Renegade Poetics: Black Aesthetics and Formal Innovation in African American Poetry.* U of Iowa P, 2011.

Shoptaw, John. "Hejinian Meditations: Lives of the Cell." *Journal X,* vol. 1, no. 1, 1996, pp. 57–83.

Silliman, Ron. *The New Sentence.* Roof Books, 1987.

Silliman, Ron. "Who Speaks: Ventriloquism and the Self in the Poetry Reading." *Close Listening: Poetry and the Performed Word,* edited Charles Bernstein, Oxford UP, 1998, pp. 360–78.

Silliman, Ron, et al. "Aesthetic Tendency and the Politics of Poetry: A Manifesto." *Social Text,* vol. 19/20, 1988, pp. 261–75. doi.org/10.2307/466189.

Simpson, Megan. *Poetic Epistemologies: Gender and Knowing in Women's Language-Oriented Writing.* State U of New York P, 2000.

singleton, giovanni. *American Letters: Works on Paper.* Canarium Books, 2018.

Skillman, Nikki. *The Lyric in the Age of the Brain.* Harvard UP, 2016.

Sloan, Mary Margaret, ed. *Moving Borders: Three Decades of Innovative Writing by Women*. Talisman House, 1998.

Solt, Mary Ellen. *Concrete Poetry: A World View*. Indiana UP, 1968.

Spahr, Juliana. *Everybody's Autonomy: Connective Reading and Collective Identity*. U of Alabama P, 2001.

Spahr, Juliana. "Resignifying Autobiography: Lyn Hejinian's *My Life*." *American Literature*, vol. 68, no. 1, 1996, pp. 139–59. doi:10.2307/2927544.

Starr, G. Gabrielle. *Feeling Beauty: The Neuroscience of Aesthetic Experience*. MIT P, 2013.

Stein, Gertrude. *Tender Buttons: Selected Writings of Gertrude Stein*. Edited by Carl Van Vechten. Vintage, 1990.

Stephens, Paul. "What Do We Mean by 'Literary Experimentalism'? Notes toward a History of the Term." *Arizona Quarterly* vol. 68, no. 1, 2012, pp. 143–73. doi:10.1353/arq.2012.0003.

Stockwell, Peter. *Cognitive Poetics: An Introduction*. 2nd ed., Routledge, 2019.

Thaut, Michael H., et al. "Melodic Intonation Therapy (MIT)." *Handbook of Neurologic Music Therapy*, Oxford UP, 2016, pp. 140–45.

This Is Spinal Tap. Directed by Rob Reiner, Embassy Pictures, 1984.

Thorsson, Courtney. "Foodways in Contemporary African American Poetry: Harryette Mullen and Evie Shockley." *Contemporary Literature*, vol. 57, no. 2, 2016, pp. 184–215. *Project MUSE*, muse.jhu.edu/article/630330.

Tsur, Reuven. *What Makes Sound Patterns Expressive? The Poetic Mode of Speech Perception*. Duke UP, 1992.

Turner, Mark. *The Literary Mind: The Origins of Thought and Language*. Oxford UP, 1998.

Tzara, Tristan. *Seven Dada Manifestoes and Lampisteries*. Translated by Barbara Wright. Alma Classics, 2013.

US Congress, House of Representatives. Floor debate on HR 16065. *Congressional Record*, vol. 116, part 16, 30 Jun. 1970, Government Printing Office, 91st Congress, 2nd Session, pp. 22118–52.

Varela, Francisco J., et al. *The Embodied Mind: Cognitive Science and Human Experience*. MIT P, 1991.

Vassilakis, Nico, and Crag Hill, eds. *The Last Vispo Anthology: Visual Poetry, 1998–2008*. Fantagraphics, 2012.

Vaziri, Parisa. "Blackness and the Metaethics of the Object." *Rhizomes*, vol. 29, 2017. doi:10.20415/rhiz/029.e16.

Vermeule, Blakey. *Why Do We Care about Literary Characters?* Johns Hopkins UP, 2011.

Vydrin, Eugene. "Open Field Scholarship: Charles Olson's *Proprioception*." *Olson's Prose*, edited by Gary Grieve-Carlson, Cambridge Scholars, 2007, pp. 177–85.

Waldrop, Rosmarie. "A Basis of Concrete Poetry." *Bucknell Review*, vol. 22, no. 2, 1976, pp. 141–51.

Waldrop, Rosmarie. "Thinking of Follows." 24 Apr. 2000, writing.upenn.edu/epc /authors/waldropr/thinking.html.

Wang, Dorothy J. *Thinking Its Presence: Form, Race, and Subjectivity in Contemporary Asian American Poetry*. Stanford UP, 2014.

Watten, Barrett. "Missing 'X': Formal Meaning in Crane and Eigner." *Total Syntax*. Southern Illinois UP, 1985.

Webster, Michael. *Reading Visual Poetry after Futurism: Marinetti, Apollinaire, Schwitters, Cummings*. Peter Lang, 1995.

Wildgen, Wolfgang. "Ambiguity in Linguistic Meaning in Relation to Perceptual Multistability." *Ambiguity in Mind and Nature: Multistable Cognitive Phenomena*, edited by Peter Kruse and Michael Stalder, Springer, 1995, pp. 221–40. doi:10.1007/978-3-642-78411-8_12.

Williams, Emmett. *An Anthology of Concrete Poetry*. Something Else, 1967.

Williams, Raymond. *Politics and Letters: Interviews with "The New Left Review."* Verso, 2015.

Williams, William Carlos. *The Collected Poems of William Carlos Williams, Vol. 1: 1909–1939*. New Directions, 1991.

"Yari Yari Pamberi: Black Women Writers Dissect Globalization." *Black Scholar*, vol. 38, no. 2/3, 2008. *JSTOR*, www.jstor.org/stable/41069940.

Yeats, W. B. "The Second Coming." *The Collected Poems of W. B. Yeats*, 2nd ed., Edited by Richard J. Finneran, Scribner, 1996, p. 187.

Yu, Timothy. *Race and the Avant-garde: Experimental and Asian American Poetry since 1965*. Stanford UP, 2009.

Zunshine, Lisa, ed. *The Oxford Handbook of Cognitive Literary Studies*. Oxford UP, 2015.

Zunshine, Lisa. *Why We Read Fiction: Theory of Mind and the Novel*. Ohio State UP, 2006.

Index

Glass, Jesse, 125, 126–28, 187n32
Glissant, Édouard, 136
globalization, 61–62
glyphs and hieroglyphs, 41, 76, 78, 80, 84, 174n30, 182n16
Golding, Alan, 19, 154
Goldsmith, Kenneth, 101
Gomringer, Eugen, 98–99, 101, 104, 107, 183n26, 184n6
González, Julio, et al., 7
Graesser, Arthur, et al., 40, 174n32
Gravendyk, Hillary, 180n3, 182n20
Greenberg, Clement, 12
Grenier, Robert, 83, 123–25
Grieve-Carlson, Gary, 82–83
Grumman, Bob, 185n16
Grünewald, José Lino, 112

Hall, Durward Gorham, 96, 97
Harryman, Carla, 170n5
Hart, George, 181n9, 182n23
Hausmann, Raoul, 131
Hayles, Katherine, 9–10, 168n9
Heine, Steven J., 5, 14
Hejinian, Lyn, 8, 17, 21–47, 50, 153, 154, 165; on description, 28–29; improvisation in, 32–33, 34, 47, 174n35; metonymy in, 40–41, 43–45; on music analogy, 31–32, 35, 45; myopia/nearsightedness and, 8, 33–35, 72, 172nn17–19; on "open text," 173n20; tag lines in, 24, 29, 31–32, 33, 38–39, 43, 158–59, 171n13. See also "I"; James, William; New Sentence; perception
Heller-Roazen, Daniel, 179n26
Hennings, Emmy, 131
Holder, Geoffrey, 137
Hopkins, Gerald Manley, 45
Huelsenbeck, Richard, 131, 132, 187n2
Hume, Christine, 189n17

"I": in Hejinian, 43–44; in Language poetry, 174n34; in Mullen, 49–50, 51, 54, 64, 175n1; in traditional lyric, 4, 168n13. See also voice and identity
ideograms, 101, 104–5, 112, 184n8

implicit learning, 5
improvisation, cognitive studies of, 172n16
indeterminacy, 8
infant-directed speech (IDS), 19, 134, 135, 136–37, 139, 145, 188nn13–14
inner voice. See under Mullen, Harryette
intentionality, 17, 21–39, 46–48, 159, 170n3, 171n9, 185n11
isomorphism, 101, 104
Izenberg, Oren, 173n27

Jackson, Mahalia, 139, 140
Jakobson, Roman, 190n23
James, William, 23–29, 37–38, 47, 52, 171n11; on attention, 17, 26; on Hegel, 173n23; Hejinian and, 21–22, 24, 38, 170n5, 171nn8–9. See also stream of consciousness
Jameson, Frederic, 22, 24–26, 39, 45, 46, 148, 170n7
Jarnot, Lisa, 3–4, 19, 134, 143, 144–45, 147, 149–50
jazz performance, 172n16, 175n3
Jenkins, Gareth, 122–23
Johnson, Mark, 6
Jonik, Michael, 86

Kafka, Franz, 5
Kahneman, Daniel, 125–26
Kane, Julie, 146
Kekulé, Friedrich von, 55
Keller, Lynn, 157, 158–59
King, Ronald, 93
Kristeva, Julia, 136

Lakoff, George, 6, 15
language, origins of. See protosemantic language
Language poetry, 12, 17, 22, 28, 47, 50, 51, 59, 68, 168n5, 169n12, 173n27, 174n34, 175n2. See also Eigner, Larry; Hejinian, Lyn; Mullen, Harryette
Lattig, Sharon, 169n17
Lauwereyns, Jan, 16, 26–27, 29, 30–31, 34, 36–37, 41–42, 169n18
Lehrer, Jonah, 73

CONTEMPORARY NORTH AMERICAN POETRY SERIES

The Collaborative Artist's Book: Evolving Ideas in Contemporary Poetry and Art
by Alexandra J. Gold

Gary Snyder and the Pacific Rim: Creating Countercultural Community
by Timothy Gray

Urban Pastoral: Natural Currents in the New York School
by Timothy Gray

Nathaniel Mackey, Destination Out: Essays on His Work
edited by Jeanne Heuving

Poetry FM: American Poetry and Radio Counterculture
by Lisa Hollenbach

Poetics and Praxis "After" Objectivism
edited by W. Scott Howard and Broc Rossell

Ecopoetics: Essays in the Field
edited by Angela Hume and Gillian Osborne

Racial Things, Racial Forms: Objecthood in Avant-Garde Asian American Poetry
by Joseph Jonghyun Jeon

We Saw the Light: Conversations between the New American Cinema and Poetry
by Daniel Kane

Ghostly Figures: Memory and Belatedness in Postwar American Poetry
by Ann Keniston

Poetics of Emergence: Affect and History in Postwar Experimental Poetry
by Benjamin Lee

Contested Records: The Turn to Documents in Contemporary North American Poetry
by Michael Leong

History, Memory, and the Literary Left: Modern American Poetry, 1935–1968
by John Lowney

Poetics of Cognition: Thinking through Experimental Poems
by Jessica Lewis Luck

Paracritical Hinge: Essays, Talks, Notes, Interviews
by Nathaniel Mackey

Behind the Lines: War Resistance Poetry on the American Homefront since 1941
by Philip Metres

Poetry Matters: Neoliberalism, Affect, and the Posthuman in Twenty-First Century North American Feminist Poetics
by Heather Milne

Hold-Outs: The Los Angeles Poetry Renaissance, 1948–1992
by Bill Mohr

In Visible Movement: Nuyorican Poetry from the Sixties to Slam
by Urayoán Noel

Reading Project: *A Collaborative Analysis of William Poundstone's* Project for Tachistoscope [Bottomless Pit]
by Jessica Pressman, Mark C. Marino, and Jeremy Douglass

Frank O'Hara: The Poetics of Coterie
by Lytle Shaw

Renegade Poetics: Black Aesthetics and Formal Innovation in African American Poetry
by Evie Shockley

Questions of Poetics: Language Writing and Consequences
by Barrett Watten

Radical Vernacular: Lorine Niedecker and the Poetics of Place
edited by Elizabeth Willis